ALONZO T. JONES

General Conference Bulletins

1895

The Third Angel's Message

General Conference Bulletins 1895

by

Alonzo T. Jones

This book is a collection of sermons presented by Alonzo T. Jones at the 1895 General Conference session of Seventh-day Adventists.

© **2020**

ISBN: 978-0-9945585-7-2

Contents

Sermon 1 7
Sermon 2 18
Sermon 3 30
Sermon 4 40
Sermon 5 47
Sermon 6 55
Sermon 7 63
Sermon 8 73
Sermon 9 82
Sermon 10 93
Sermon 11 101
Sermon 12 110
Sermon 13 119
Sermon 14 127
Sermon 15 136
Sermon 16 147
Sermon 17 154
Sermon 18 166
Sermon 19 176
Sermon 20 186
Sermon 21 197
Sermon 22 206
Sermon 23 215
Sermon 24 224
Sermon 25 235
Sermon 26 250

Sermon 1

February 4, 1895

We all understand very well, no doubt, that every lesson that will be given will be on the Third Angel's Message – it matters not by whom it may be given. But there has been assigned to me that particular phase of the Third Angel's Message that relates especially to the prophecies of the beast and his image and the work that they are to do. We shall begin with that tonight and follow it up as the lessons may come. All that I shall attempt to do in this lesson will be merely to state the case, to present the evidence; the arguments will come afterward, upon the evidence of the case as stated. In the time we shall have this evening the case cannot be stated fully, only the case as relates to the side occupied by the image of the beast. The next lesson we will have to consider the case as developed in respect to the papacy – the beast – itself.

I need not undertake to give a definition in detail of what the image of the beast is; we all know well that it is the church power using the government, the civil power, for church purposes. That is definite enough to recall to the minds of all, the general subject. The case to be presented this evening will be simply the outline of what the professed Protestants of the country are doing; and the evidence that they are doing it in such a way that all may see the situation as it now stands before the country, and not only stands temporarily but stands before the country in such a way that it is intended by those who are conducting the measures to be permanent.

The year 1894 alone we will touch. About the middle of the year there was the Cedarquist case which arose in the regular army at Omaha. Cedarquist had refused to fire at targets on Sunday. He was court-martialed for disobedience of orders and sentenced to a term of six months' imprisonment, I believe. We are not to touch upon the merits of the case as it arose in the army. We are to notice the use that was made of it at the time. With this, no doubt, a good many are familiar; but I simply call attention to it now as one of the points in the general array of evidence that is before us. As soon as that was done and the proceedings had been published, the Secretary and General Manager of the Sunday League of America, Rev. Edward Thompson of Columbus, O., sent a communication to the President of the United States, a part of which – the material portion – I will read. This is from *The Sunday Reform Leaflets*, Vol. 1, No. 8, Sept. 1894:

Office of the Sunday League of America, Columbus, O., July 21 1894

To His Excellency, Grover Cleveland, President of the United States and Commander in Chief of the United States Army:

Distinguished Sir: Please permit me, in the name of over one hundred thousand voters of the United States, whom I have the honor to represent officially, to petition your excellency for the pardon of Private Charles O Cedarquist, of Co. C, Second Infantry, United States Army, who is now, we learn, imprisoned at hard labor, in Omaha, under sentence of two months and with a requirement attached to the penalty of "imprisonment at hard labor," that he "pay a forfeiture of $10 per month out of his monthly pay."

The reason that we ask for this pardon is that Cedarquist was punished because he refused to engage in "target practice" on Sunday and that he refused on the grounds that the said target practice was in violation of the laws of Nebraska, where he was; in violation of his personal religious convictions; in violation of the principles of Christian civilization and of the laws of nearly every state in the Union. Since the Supreme Court of the United States decided in the "Holy Trinity" case on the 29th of February 1892, that "this is a Christian nation," and said Private Cedarquist had the right to expect that no regulations or requirements would be made in the army of this nation out of harmony with the general laws and customs of that type of Christianity which our history has illustrated.

Then he refers to the Constitution and exemption of Sunday from the time which the President has to sign a bill. The result was, that the man was pardoned and the officer who ordered Cedarquist to do the shooting on Sunday was ordered to be court-martialed, but his fellow officers acquitted him.

That shows that the combination as represented in that particular form of organization has used the government for its purposes and proposes to do it upon the strength of "over one hundred thousand voters of the United States," whom the General Manager has "the honor to represent officially."

Not far from that same time the postmaster of Chicago, who is a United States officer, proposed to hold an inspection of mail carriers of the city of Chicago, on Sunday, and the directions were given that whosoever among them had any conscientious convictions against such work or service on Sunday were at liberty not to appear. But the parade was not allowed to be held at all, because the churches of Chicago combined and sent such a protest to Washington, the President and his cabinet that the postmaster was forbidden to hold his parade on Sunday.

Likewise, there has been before the country for two or three years the campaign headed by Dr. Parkhurst of New York City against the municipal management. It culminated in the election last November, in which this political "reform" element triumphed, and that triumph spread the fame and the influence of the leader of that movement through the nation and other cities that had formerly followed the same course which he was conducting in New York City have since invited him to come to their cities to give instruction on how best to carry on their campaign in the same line of things. Chicago is the first one that has done this since election. About two years ago the city of Washington, with some of the United States Senators, invited him down there, and he went and made several speeches, to teach them how to conduct government.

The other day he was in Chicago at the invitation of a certain club of that city. And I have his speech here. I will make a few quotations from it, merely to illustrate the actuating spirit of that movement that you may see precisely what it is – that it is not intended to be political only, but *religio*-political. It is intended to be the church interfering – no, not simply interfering, but *managing, controlling* and *guiding* the government by her dictation, and according to her interpretation of morality, of the Scriptures, and as it is said, of the ten commandments.

And one thing that you will notice too as I shall read these evidences, not only from this speech, but from others that I shall bring, is the prominence that is being given to the ten commandments. Now our work from the beginning has been to set forth the integrity of the ten commandments, and to insist upon them, and we have expected that the issue upon the ten commandments would become national sometime, and one of the points in the evidence that I am to set before you now, is that the time is very nearly, if not entirely here, when the ten commandments are to be made a general question, a question for general discussion, and that they are to have a place in national affairs.

It is true that on the part of these politico-religionists, the ten commandments are put before the nation in a false light, and a false use is made of them all the time, but that matters not.

When the enemy sets up the ten commandments and makes a false use of them and perverts them, it simply gives the Lord's truth and His cause that much more leverage to insist on them as God gave them and as they mean. And that simply opens the way for the Third Angel's Message to have a larger place and to do more work than otherwise. So that in all these things we need not look at that side as really opposed to the Third Angel's Message. They intended it so of course, but as I remarked once before in your presence, I think all that is merely the *other side* of the message, but it is all working together to help forward the message.

I will first read three or four statements that were made by Dr. Parkhurst in his speech in Chicago that you may see the character of the procedure, as he is the grand representative of it, that you may see what kind of sentiments are made prominent and what are the representative sentiments of the movement.

Here is one of his expressions: "Damnable pack of administrative bloodhounds." Another is, "A lying perjured, rum-soaked, and libidinous lot." Another is, "Purgatory to politicians and chronic crucifixion to bosses."

Another, "'Thou shalt not kill'; 'Thou shalt not commit adultery'; 'Thou shalt not steal' – these are ethical 'chestnuts,' but they laid out Tammany." And all this, not in the heat of an earnest, spontaneous discussion, but in a cold, deliberate essay written out in the study and there read from manuscript.

Another series of expressions will help to illustrate this thing. I read these from his speech as published in the Chicago *Inter Ocean* of January 24, 1895:

> It is not well to discourage people, but it is always wholesome to face the entire situation. To use an illustration that I have used a great many times at home, in order to accomplish anything that is really worth the pains it takes to accomplish it, you will have to "regenerate" your city. The word is a quotation from Presbyterian theology, but answers the purpose well even if it is.
>
> And since all this course has been endorsed by the Presbytery of New York as a presbytery, and as that means the endorsing of him and approving of his course as a presbytery, it is all Presbyterian theology, according to the phase of it as held by the Presbytery of New York. So it is with a double emphasis that he can quote from Presbyterian theology – as held by the Presbytery of New York, at least.
>
> It means more than reformation. Reformation denotes a change [illegible] only. Regeneration denotes a change of heart – the inauguration of a new quality of municipal motives and impulses. If you say this is dealing with the ideal, of course it is dealing with the ideal. What do you propose to deal with? You are not going to win except by the pressure of a splendid enthusiasm, and you will start no popular enthusiasm by any effort that you make to achieve half measures.

Another series of expressions:

> I wonder how many there are in this great city that are willing to take their coats off and keep them off until they die or Chicago is *redeemed*. That is what will do it and it is the only thing that will do it. You will have to take your life in your hands and your comfort and your ease in your hands and conquer victory step by step. There is no call for the *dilettante* or dude in this work. Reform clubs are numerous and they have large enrollments, but somehow they do not succeed in saving their city. There is no short cut to municipal *salvation*. You cannot win it by the prestige or the wealth of the reform organizations, municipal leagues, civic clubs or by whatever other name the institution may be distinguished. You will avail nothing except to the degree that you fling your personality and all that it stands for directly against the oncoming tide of evil, even at the risk of being inundated and swamped by it. If this language is more strenuous than fits into your predilections, you have only yourselves to blame for it, for I came here at your bidding, not my own. If you have any object in life that means more to you than *the redemption of Chicago,* I would counsel you to keep out of the municipal regeneration business.

Jesus Christ said, "Seek ye first *the kingdom of God.*" This system says, "Seek first of all, have most important of all, the government of cities and kingdoms of this world."

However, I am simply reading these items now; we will sum them up presently. Again:

> There is no Republican and no Democrat in the ten commandments... Our movement, then, has had no partisanship in it and no sectarianism in it. An all-around man is bigger than either party, and the Decalogue is as broad as Protestantism, Catholicism, and Judaism all placed alongside of each other...
>
> Responsibility need not be taken from the shoulders of the laity but the relations proper to be occupied by the clergy is a crisis like yours here and ours in New York are unparalleled and unique. A live preacher, if only he gets far enough away from his study and his Bible to know the world and what is going on in it cannot watch the footsteps of the prophet-statesman who swung the destiny of the people of Israel three thousand years ago, without feeling that the inspiration still vouchsafed to the man of God *is never designed* to be employed exclusively in fitting men to get out of the world respectably and to live "beautifically" *in the world to come.* The Lord's prayer teaches us to pray: "Thy will be done on earth." For you that means, *first of all:* "Thy will be done in Chicago." And there is no point from which such a keynote can be sounded so effectively as from your pulpits. It is encouraging to know that the feeling is growing that Christian fidelity means *patriotism* just as much as it does *piety:* means being a good citizen just as much as it does being a good church member, and that "Nearer My God to Thee," and "Star Spangled Banner" are *both Christian hymns* in the mouth of an all-around Christian.

I am simply reading these that you may see the situation and the interest with which these things are being put forth.

The movement with us began *in a church,* and the appeal all the way through has been to that which *the church* and *the synagogue represent.* The strength of the game throughout has been men's responsiveness to the authority of the ten commandments.

There is no event recorded in the old Bible story that *for sanctity* would rival *the enterprise* of *regenerating Chicago,* and no situation in which there was more occasion than here for the ringing out of the voice of some local Elijah, and the more of them the better. The whole question that confronts you just now is a question of righteousness versus iniquity, honesty versus knavery, purity versus filth, and if the clergy cannot come out *en masse* and take a direct hand in the duel, what under heaven is the use of having clergy anyway?

One more:

> There is a moral leadership that it belongs to the clergy to exercise and that it is wickedly delinquent if it fails to exercise. An appreciation and a vision of the eternal realities that load the instant, makes out a very large part of the genius of statesmanship, and it is that appreciation precisely that distinguishes the preacher, if so be he is gifted with divine equipment. In the old days of Israel, the statesman was the prophet and the prophet was the statesman, and within certain limits, it even yet lies in the intention of nature and of God that the *two offices should coalesce* and that the man who knows the secrets of

> God should shape the moral purposes and inspire the moral councils and activities of his *town* and *time.* and I venture to say to my brethren in the Christian ministry that I speak with the assurance of definite knowledge when I say that there is no influence that will more immediately operate to bring back the world to the church than for the church and its modern prophets to come back to the world and fulfill to it their mission of gentle authority and moral governance.

This is enough to set the whole field before you, that the terms that relate only to the salvation of the soul in righteousness and are used in the Bible that way and belong only to the church to use that way, these terms are used for worldly things altogether, and the whole of it, the whole plan of salvation, and of church work, is reduced to the level of this world and made to mean the saving of things as they are in this world. Then you see the application of the ten commandments which they make will be only to the outward man and it will be just simply the same old iniquity over again – cleanse the outside of the cup and the platter, and the inside will be as it always has been with the Pharisees.

Some time ago you saw the statement published in the *Sentinel,* which Dr. John L. Scudder, of Jersey City, New Jersey, made with reference to the position and the work of the Young People's Society of Christian Endeavor. I will read a clause or two from this, and will then call your attention to another statement made within the last week or two, from a direct representative of one of the managers of the Young People's Society of Christian Endeavor movement. First introducing the subject, I read some of the statements made by Dr. Scudder as published in the New York *Sun* of November 5, 1894.

> Almost every church in America has its Young People's Society of Christian Endeavor, and these societies, extending into every hamlet in the land, have declared their intention to enter politics. This is a significant fact when we remember that these organizations number several hundred million followers and are composed of young people full of energy and enthusiasm. This means that the church is going into politics, and is going there to stay. Furthermore, it means that the church is to become a powerful political factor, for in these societies it has a perfect and permanent organization, extending through county, state, and nation and will act as a unit on all great moral questions.
>
> I do not take it that the churches are to form a separate political party; on the contrary, they will stand outside all parties but they will cooperate and as one prodigious organization make their demands upon existing parties and have their wishes fulfilled. Before election every local union will assume temporarily the appearance of a political convention, ratifying such candidates only as will carry out the desires of the respectable portion of the community. They will secure written pledges from the candidates and hold them to their pledges and if they fail to keep their pledges, those particular politicians will be doomed.
>
> I hail with the utmost joy the coming of this eventful day in the history of the church. At last the politicians will find that we Christian people are not a parcel of fools; that we know enough to cooperate, command several millions of voters, and hurl our combined forces against the enemies of righteousness, law, and order... Now, when

> Christian people combine and hold an overwhelming balance of power, when they pull together and refuse as a body to vote for any man who will not carry out their principles, then, and then only, will they be respected and become politically powerful. Why should there not be Christian halls as well as Tammany halls? What objection to a sanctified caucus? Why not pull wires for the kingdom of God? If sinners stand together and protect their interests, why should not the saints do the same thing and whip old Satan out?

Here is the latest from the Christian Endeavor Department of the *Christian Statesman.* It is conducted by a Christian Endeavor officer and the particular series of lessons that are being taught now and studied is on "Christian Endeavor Good Citizenship." Just a few sentences from this:

> The politics the Christian Endeavor movement is striving for is Christian politics and if party politics, Christian party politics. We are to conceive of it as a section of Christian living, of which the social life, the business activities, the family duties, and the distinctively church work are other sections. Politics as a Christian duty to be thoughtfully considered along with social, business, and home duties. In politics, Christianity takes exactly similar ground. Of two good candidates the church has no right to decide between them, but from every pulpit let there thunder tremendous protests against candidates who have the Ten Commandments on the other side.

That may be a misprint for "leave" the ten commandments on the other side, but you get the thought.

Wherein is a discussion of Christian politics less suitable for the pulpit or prayer meeting than a discussion of Christian business or society or home duties? Politics has its peculiar temptations, and the Christian spirit is indispensable. If only to save a multitude of young men who enter it every year from moral ruin, we must purify it. But also to save the country and our sacred American institutions.

Then what does their salvation reach? What only does that salvation from the whole plan of it concern? Only this world, the things of this world. It does not go beyond that. The minister is to understand, "if he can get far enough away from his Bible" – and that is a very appropriate expression – that he is not to work for people getting out of this world in a respectable way and enjoy happiness in another world; he is to work for his own town and his own city, his own state, and the nation, to redeem, to save, to regenerate all these. That is the situation.

Further:

> Christian Democrats will find great duties in voting and party organization, which are deeper and broader than any details of party movements. With their conservative attitude to all changes, they have an important place in Christian civilization. Let them, like good men and true, study their duty, and with faces toward the Judgment Day fully discharge it. So their fellow-Christians in the Republican party, with a different

> attitude to governmental policies, yet both alive to exalted responsibilities, to Christian patriotism and steady moral development of the nation. Here would be an easy and natural union among Christian citizens.
>
> The church is the best place for the agitation of moral and spiritual good, and this union in every church of all Christian citizens, with sections in it of the closer organization of each party, would promote thorough efficiency where these smaller bodies are most influential, that is, in their own party. Leaving out all details of party action, or leaving these to the general meeting in a hall convenient of all the sections of any designated party, we have good citizenship activity which every church may wisely assume. This is the only sort which will accomplish any good. In Christian Endeavor it is high time more definite plans be pushed. We cannot simply go on giving addresses and holding rallies, with nothing practical beyond. On the principles of Christian Endeavor, and in line with its genius, we urge inter-partisan plans. *The Christian spirit must have a place in politics* and the ten commandments and the Sermon on the Mount must rule.

The Civic Federation of Chicago, modeled after Parkhurst's New York machine, is following the same course that he has, as far as they are able, so far as he followed it in New York. And we have a report from the head of that federation, Rev. Dr. Clark of Chicago. He has written an official report which was published in the *Interior*. I had a copy of the paper, but it was mislaid. May be we can find it again before we get away from the subject entirely, and have some of his statements also; but one of them particularly is on the same line as this; that is, the Christian's relationship to the state, the Christian's relationship to politics, the Christian's role in molding and shaping and reforming the state. And one of the chiefest principles of politics that he lays down in the platform upon which he stands is the Supreme Court decision of February 29, 1892, that "this is a Christian nation." And as this is a Christian nation he asks in expectation, What is there for a Christian to do but to work according to that idea and carry out the principles of this Christian nation in a Christian way, shaping and moulding it upon the forms of Christianity? Here then are all these elements working all these plans to get control of the law and the law-making power.

Now one other sentence from Parkhurst's speech that I left to the last that opens up a field that is worthy of our thinking upon and watching from this day till the end.

> The questions that are most deeply agitating the public mind this year, and that will continue to agitate it probably for many years to come are not national ones but municipal. We have reached a period that may be designated the "renaissance of the City." The remarkable concentration of population at urban centers [that is, city centers] has operated to accentuate [to put an accent upon it, to emphasize] the municipality, and to such a degree has this concentration reached and so largely are material values and intellectual energies actuating all these points that we may almost say that the real life of the nation is lived and throbs itself out at these centers and that the nation is going to be increasingly what our municipalities make it to be, determine it shall be.

The argument is this:

> That such vast concentration of the people into cities, so many large cities are being built up in the country, that these cities are holding such a position in the country that they shape the course of the nation, and it no longer lies among the people of the open country outside of the cities, but the way the cities go, that is the way the nation goes, and the mold that the cities take, that itself molds the nation. Even leaving out religion altogether, the great cities of the country carry the political tide of the country, whichever way it may turn. Now you see these church leaders understand this, and therefore are working to control the cities, thus worming themselves into power there, and then through that to rule the nation.

Thus you see all the way through, every one of these statements that I have read is simply the statement over again of the system that made the papacy, and has characterized the papacy from the first step that was taken by the church in the days of Constantine until now. Anyone that has gone over that history knows that each one of these statements I have read is just exactly the same thing over again.

Has anyone here who has gone over that history had any difficulty at all in seeing the image of the papacy in the situation as laid out here in the statements which I have read from their own words? No, sir. Anyone who has gone over that history cannot fail to see the image there, working the precise way, for the precise purposes that the papacy did; and the whole image stands working right before us.

Then how can any one of us mistake the fact that the image of the beast stands full-formed, as it were, before the country today, and working with all its insinuating might – not with all the power of the law yet; it has not that fully in its hands yet, but with all its insinuating policy, and by all of these encroachments, little by little, taking possession here, working itself in there, to get control of that which controls the nation, and then mold and shape the nation.

Look at another phase in this that shows the image.

Those who have read the history of the papacy and its making, the beast and its making, know that the whole contest and all the contests that the papacy had were fought out in the cities. Rome, Alexandria, Constantinople, Antioch, Jerusalem, Carthage, Corinth – the principal cities – were the ground-work and the theater upon which the papacy fought her battles and gained control of the Roman Empire and wormed herself in all cases.

The country people – I was going to say they were a *secondary* consideration but they were practically of no consideration at all. A country bishop was a very inferior order of being. A city bishop stood much higher. The gradation of the bishopric was according to the gradation of the great cities. And the bishop of the chief city, which was Rome, held the chief power; he could there, and thereby, control more of the elements that were needed to build up the power of the papacy. And thus Rome became the seat, and its bishopric the head, of the papacy – the beast.

Now do you not see the precise likeness, going right over the same ground in this country, trying to secure control of the largest cities – New York, Chicago, Philadelphia, Boston, St. Louis, Cincinnati, San Francisco; all of them have this same thing working – municipal leagues and the clergy leading in it all, working to control the cities, to get these into their hands, and so to control the nation.

Are not the same principles at work here now as were at work in the original making of the beast? Is it possible for us to close our eyes to the fact, and fail to see that we are in the presence and the working of that wicked thing? And is it not high time to sound aloud the message of warning against the beast and his image, with the loudest voice that the power of God can give?

I will read one more statement. This is from the *Herald and Presbyter* of Cincinnati, January 3, 1895. The object, the chief, the grand, the all over-topping object, that they propose to use this power for when they get it through the shape of these municipal governments is shown to be *the enforcement of Sunday*. The article from which I read is entitled "Enforcement of Law."

> Law is a rule of human action or conduct. Moral law is that perceptive revelation of the divine will which is of perpetual and universal obligation upon all men. It is therefore binding upon the conscience and with the Christian should not require statutory enforcement. But it has developed, in process of governing society, that all men will not obey the ten commandments, which are of universal application, and hence it has been found necessary to attach pains and penalties and provide for their enforcement by using the strong arm of the civil government.

This, as anyone can see, is the very position and teaching and argument of the papacy. We shall have occasion to read some other such things when we come to the next phase of this matter in the next lesson.

> One of the ten commandments, which has the commendation of our lawmakers and which has been engrafted on the statute books of nearly every state is that which provides for the proper observance of the Sabbath. Our lawmakers thought it necessary to restrain evil doers and those who would violate the sanctity of God's holy day by special prohibitions and penalties for violation of the same. In our city the open violation of this law has been so continuous and so defiant as to awaken Christian men to a sense of their duty to the State and the Municipal Reform League was organized.

"Municipal Reform," that is, city reform, what the "Civic Federation" in Chicago and the "Society for the Prevention of Crime" in New York are pledged for.

They are the same *thing* but are not called by the same name in all the cities. But what caused it to be organized in Cincinnati? Why, the disrespect for Sunday. What in Chicago was the chief thing? Disrespect for Sunday.

> The first movement was to secure the closing of the theaters on the Sabbath. In this work the law was sufficient and the police force of the city able to enforce the law, but there was found to be one man more powerful than the law, the police force, or the elements of reform in this city, and that was the mayor. The violators of law were so numerous that if each one called for a jury it was impossible to try offenders. The courts were blocked and justice obstructed.
>
> The League came to the relief of the Court with the law at their backs and proposed that the police be instructed to make arrests of persons found in the act of violating the Sabbath law. This would have made the law prohibitory and closed the theaters, even if offenders were not fully punished. The mayor came to the rescue of the theaters and forbade officers to make arrests till after the offense was *complete* and the entertainment over.
>
> The League appealed to the Police Commissioners on the ground that the police ware not bound to obey unlawful orders. A majority of the Commissioners decided that the officers must obey all orders of the mayor, that this was necessary to proper discipline. Now then, what are law-abiding citizens to do? They are told that Cincinnati is better governed than any city of its size in the country, and yet Boston, New York, Philadelphia and Baltimore are able to close their theaters on Sunday. There is some talk of impeachment proceedings against the mayor, while others favor petition to the governor to remove the Police Commissioners, and an appeal to the polls on the issue whether the chief magistrate of a city can place his feet on the statutes of God and man, and defy the moral sentiment of society.

So you see, this demands the enforcement of Sunday laws first. If this is not done to their satisfaction, they demand "municipal reform." The city is going to ruin, and so you must have a different element to save the city. But what would they want to save the city for? Oh, to enforce Sunday laws, in order that Sunday may be saved, in order that the nation may be saved. So don't you see the one great thing at the last that is aimed at in all these movements in everything is the enforcement of Sunday, and we know that that is the making of the image of the beast and the enforcement of the mark of the beast.

Therefore, from all this evidence it is perfectly plain that the country is now in the living presence – the living, acting presence, of the image of the beast, and his endeavor to force the mark.

Sermon 2

February 6, 1895

Our lesson tonight will be the study of the papacy, as it was last night on the image of the papacy. I would say, now as then, all that I am doing at present is setting before you the evidence, stating the case; the arguments will come more fully after we see what is to be built upon them.

The statements I shall read tonight will all be from Catholic authorities – Catholic speeches and Catholic papers.

First I shall read from some of the Catholic speeches in the Catholic Congress in Chicago in 1893, printed in the Chicago *Herald* of September 5, 6, and 7. They are simply parallel statements with those that were brought forth in the previous lesson from the other side, or rather from the other part of the same side, and by putting these together, as we did those others together and having the two lessons, it will be easy enough for you to mark the parallels, almost word for word you will find in some of them, and they are *identical* in *principle* and in *purpose*.

I will first read from an address delivered to the Catholic Congress at Chicago September 4 on the "Influence of Catholic Citizens," by Walter George Smith, as published in the Chicago *Herald* of September 5, 1893.

> The church and the state, as corporations or external governing bodies, are indeed separate in their spheres, and the church does not absorb the state, nor does the state the church, but both are from God, and both work to the same ends, and when each is rightly understood, there is no antithesis or antagonism between them. Men *serve* God in *serving the state* as directly as in *serving the church*. He who dies on the battlefield, fighting for his country, ranks with him who dies at the stake for his faith. Civic virtues are themselves religious virtues, or, at least, virtues without which there are no religious virtues, since no man who loves not his brother, does or can love God.

That is in the same line, you will remember, with the statement of last night, that "Nearer, My God, to Thee" and "Star Spangled Banner" are "both Christian hymns" to one that understands this thing. You can see that this makes the government wholly religious, equally with the church.

Another statement from the same speech:

> The church [what he means is the Catholic church] in all ages has been the most democratic of all organizations; the church alone has taught the true theory of the fraternity and equality of all men before God, and to her precepts must mankind look for the foundation of their measures of relief from present dangers.

What he refers to is the present danger in social affairs, labor against capital, and the controversies at present rife in the United States.

Another statement from the same paper from a speech by Edgar H. Gans entitled, "The Catholic Church in America," is published in the Chicago *Herald* of September 5, 1893. Speaking of the spirit of liberty as exemplified in the United States and gathering the statement concerning this spirit of liberty from a quotation from Webster, the speaker says:

> The Catholic church welcomes this bright and beautiful spirit and takes it to her bosom, for *she is its foster mother*. With tender devotion has she nourished it through the ages. Time and again has she rescued it from the bold and impious hands of despots, whether they be kings, emperors, or a popular majority enthroned. Within the church of God is the *only true sovereign* and the source of all power. The sovereignty of the people comes from him as a sacred trust, and they must use this trust for the common weal.

We shall find presently from the pope's encyclical that he, in the place of God, is the guardian and the source of this sovereignty.

We now read the closing statement of this same speech of Mr. Gans'. The statement is identical with one which we read last night:

> We have among us our prophets of Israel, divinely commissioned, as were the holy men of old, to guide, instruct, ennoble, and *elevate the nation;* and *the American people* will have achieved their highest glory when they seek the words of wisdom and truth from their lips – *when they voluntarily submit to the gentle ministrations of the priests and the bishops of the holy Catholic church.*

These statements need no comment. Your recollection of the statement we read last night will be clear enough to make the connection.

We now read from a speech by Bishop John A. Waterson, of Columbus, in the Catholic Congress, and published in the Chicago *Herald,* November 6. His speech is upon Leo and Satolli, and he says this, speaking of Leo:

> By his personal dignity and goodness, the practical wisdom of his teachings and the firmness of his acts, he is giving the world to understand that the pope is a great thing in the world and for the world. [Loud cheers.] And intellects heretofore rebellious are accustoming themselves to think that, if society is to be saved from a condition worse

in some respects than that of pagan times, it is from the Vatican the savior is to come. [Renewed cheering.]

Another statement in the *Herald* of September 7 is by Katherine E. Conway. Her paper was entitled, "Making America Catholic," and she said this:

> Your mission is to make America Catholic. This was Archbishop Ireland's greeting to the assembled delegates at the Catholic Centenary Congress in Baltimore four years ago. And this was the charge with which he sent them back to their homes. Patriotic and religious enthusiasm were at flood tide, and all hearts were willing to respond like the first Crusaders to the call of Peter the Hermit, "God will it."

These addresses show that the aim and work of the papacy are precisely what those are of which we read last night.

Now I turn to some other statements made last fall in connection with the then coming encyclical of the pope. A letter from Rome dated October 14, 1894, printed in the *Catholic Standard* of November 3, 1894, has this:

> The United States of America, it can be said without exaggeration, is the chief thought of Leo XIII in the government of the Roman and universal Catholic church.

I would like to comment a little upon this as we go along. Why is it that Leo thinks so constantly of the United States? Oh, it is concerning the government of the Roman and universal Catholic church.

Then what he proposes to use the United States for is for some purpose in the government of the Catholic church throughout the world.

> He is one of the choice intellects of the Old World who are watching the starry flag of Washington rise to the zenith of the heavens. A few days ago, on receiving an eminent American, Leo XIII said to him, "But the United States are the future; we think of them incessantly." The inattentive politician, the superficial observer, in Europe as in America, is astonished at this persistent sympathy for the American people and care for its general interests. But those who know the ardent soul of the pope, restless for what is good, eager for all that is great and fruitful; the philosopher who sweeps over the whole intellectual, social, and religious horizon; the statesman who judges matters by the light of central and governing ideas, these all read in the heart of the holy father the motives for his unbending resolutions and his devotion to American ideas. This ever-ready sympathy *has its base in the fundamental interests of the holy see.*

Now the fundamental ideas of the holy see are the ideas upon which the whole structure rests, and this sympathy for America has its base in these fundamental ideas concerning the interests of the holy see of "the Roman and universal church."

> This ever-ready sympathy has its base in the fundamental interest of the holy see, in a peculiar conception of *the part to be played,* and the position to be held by the Church and papacy *in the times to come.*

This is explained more fully presently that the papacy is watching the times to come with an all absorbing interest. She proposes to prepare herself in every way to meet the things that are to arise, as she says, in the times to come; and she proposes to use the United States by which, and through which, to clothe herself and prepare herself to meet successfully these things that are to arise in the times to come. So I will read further upon that same point now:

> The interest is the necessity in which Rome finds she is, to direct her general course according to *the signs of the times* and the transformations on the agitated surface of the world. The peculiar conception is the deep-rooted feeling that the Church of Europe must renew its instruments and its method of adapting unchanging principles to changeable surroundings and new conditions… In this evolution the Church, in the eyes of the Pope, has a mission to fill. To fulfill this mission, she must adapt herself to the changes which have come about the action of universal forces. State Church, official Catholicism, privileges, legal and close relations between two powers, connection of the clergy with a political party, feudal ecclesiastical organizations, all the external framework of the Church must be transformed, renewed, perhaps be done away with entirely. That is the central dominating thought which marks the whole latter half of the present pontificate from the time of the incident of the Knights of Labor and encyclical *Rerum Novarum* to that of the encyclical to the French people. In the first half of his reign Leo XIII had pacified, appeased, healed. He had been the pope of peace and rest. After sealing that charter, he became the pope of action. But how can this new type of ecclesiastic be created?

Where can he get the clergy, the form of ecclesiastic through which this scheme can be carried out and be made successful for Europe and for the world? Because Europe has to be rejuvenated, remodeled, re-enlivened. Where is she going to get the model upon which to remold Europe?

> From whom shall he be copied? What civilization, what country, what philosophy will provide him? Would it not be hazardous to create him at one stroke? Would it not be better to join forces with a nation which has a type in part, where, at least, it exists in the rough? Would it not be enough to mark the outlines boldly to finish it and make use of it? *This type is the American type;* it is American democracy, with liberty, with common law, a full and exuberant life, without restraining bonds, and without a historic bureaucracy.

The foundation of all endorsements of Sunday laws in all the courts is "the common law." Common law is the direct descendant of canon law. When the papacy was the state and the state was subject to the rules of the papacy, canon law was then what common law is now. And the states which profess to have been separated from the papacy still build up religious observances upon "the common law." And now that the whole judicial structure of the United States is built in support of Sunday, upon common law, the papacy steps in and is glad to find a model so ready made to her hand upon which she can remodel her ecclesiastical forms for Europe and all the world.

Another thing; I will read that sentence over:

> This type is the American type; it is American democracy, with liberty, with common law, a full and exuberant life, *without restraining bonds*, and without a historic bureaucracy.

The papacy is very impatient of any restraining bonds; in fact, it wants none at all. And the one grand discovery Leo XIII has made, which no pope before him ever made, is that turn which is taken now all the time by Leo and from him by those who are managing affairs in this country – the turn that is taken upon the clause of the Constitution of the United States: "Congress shall make no law respecting an establishment of religion or prohibiting the free exercise thereof." Leo has made the discovery that the papacy can be pushed upon this country in every possible way and by every possible means and that congress is prohibited from ever legislating in any way to stop it. That is a discovery that he made that none before him made and that is how it is that he of late can so fully endorse the United States Constitution.

We all know of course that that was intended to be the expression of the American people always, that religion should have no place in governmental affairs and no connection whatever with it. But the papacy is never satisfied without taking possession of everything in the government and running it in the interests of the church and Leo XIII has found out that this can all be done under the cover of that constitutional statement which was intended to prevent such a thing forever.

Thus the papacy in plain violation of the Constitution will crowd herself upon the government and then hold up that clause as a barrier against anything that any would do to stop it. And every one that speaks against this working of the papacy, behold! he "is violating the Constitution of the United States" in spirit, because the constitution says that nothing shall ever be done in respect to any religion or the establishment of it. When a citizen of the United States would rise up and protest against the papacy and all this that is against the letter and the spirit of the constitution, behold! he does not appreciate "the liberty of the constitution. *We* are lovers of liberty; *we* are defenders of the constitution; *we* are glad that America has such a symbol of liberty" as that. Indeed, they are.

> That is why Pope Leo XIII turns all his soul, full of ideality, to what is improperly called his American policy. It should be rightly called his *Catholic universal policy.*

What, then, is his policy in the United States? It is universal policy.

That which is done in the United States by the papacy is done with the idea of influencing all the world and bringing all the world into line with the papal ideas, and to build all once more upon the basic and fundamental principles thereof.

> It is in this perspective, wide as a great world, and lasting as a whole epoch, that the coming American encyclical must be viewed. To make the delegation [of Satolli] independent and sovereign [which he does] with a supreme ecclesiastical tribunal.

And that means a great deal more than many people have dreamed of yet; for Satolli has already set forth the doctrine that the clergy in the United States are not subject to civil jurisdiction. That means indeed a supreme ecclesiastical tribunal.

> To support Monsignor Satolli and make his mission permanent and successful, to point out the means of increasing influence and liberty, to continue the policy of moderation and adaptability, which has brought peace to the nation, to deal, in a word, with *all the important questions of the day* and to fix *for good* the ecclesiastical type – the model of life, which Leo XIII wishes, little by little, to bring within the reach of the weakening peoples of the old world – *that* is the sublime inspiration of the encyclical to the Americans.

Now this statement with reference to his watching the signs of the times, this recasting of the papacy, even undoing, if necessary, the establishments and the forms that have been in successful use for ages – all this in view of what the papacy is to do in the times to come – reminds me of the Jews' translation of Daniel 8:23. Where the Authorized Version says, "In the latter time of their kingdom, when transgressors are come to the full, a king of fierce countenance and understanding dark sentences shall stand up." The Jews' translation says, "A king with an impudent face and understanding deep schemes."

I want to know, then, if that does not point out the papacy as we are reading it right here tonight from these documents? "A king of impudent face and understanding deep schemes."

Bishop Keane, on his return from his visit to Rome last October, says in an interview published in the *Catholic Standard* of October 13, 1894, upon the same subject:

> Bishop Keane talked very freely about his recent trip abroad and especially about the great interest the pope takes in America and the affairs both temporal and spiritual of this country. The pope believed the political welfare or properly the temporal welfare, of the world to be guided by God equally with the spiritual welfare. It is his policy to conciliate the two as much as possible. In carrying out his purpose the pope wishes to adapt the church as much as possible to the existing conditions which characterize the world at present and to provide for those which characterize its future. The world he likens to the man, in that the church represents the soul and the state the body. A man would be foolish to cultivate the soul and pay no attention to the body and likewise the church cannot afford not to take cognizance of the conditions surrounding it. As the body of the man

> grows, his soul develops; and as the age of the world advances, the conditions surrounding the church are subject to equal changes. Consequently, it is the purpose of the pope to keep the temporal power and the spiritual power from conflicting.

The pope then still holds his claim to be God's agent in the conducting of these affairs. He sets up what he declares to be God's will respecting the church and respecting the temporal and spiritual powers and then *he* is the one who, for God, is to manipulate them and say how they are to go on together; he is the one who is to keep them from conflicting.

> The pope recognizes the fact that democracy is the coming state, and as such the most prominent exponents today are France and America. Consequently, he regards these countries with a great deal of interest. This is *especially true of the United States,* where the pope believes the *stronghold of Catholicism of the future* lies.

Now turn to the words of the pope in his encyclical as published in the *Catholic Standard* of February 2, 1895. This encyclical needs to be read over several times before its real purpose is caught, therefore I have read these statements that preceded it, that you may catch the quicker what is said there upon this subject. Several points are discussed in it, but only what is said on this subject is what we shall now read. After addressing, "Venerable brethren, health and apostolic benediction," he says:

> We have now resolved to speak to you separately, trusting that we shall be, God willing, of some assistance to the Catholic cause among you. To this we apply ourselves with the utmost zeal and care, because we highly esteem and love exceedingly the young and vigorous American nation in which we plainly discern latent *forces for the advancement alike of civilization* and Christianity.

Speaking of the landing of Columbus, he says:

> Like as the ark of Noah, surmounting the overflowing waters, bore the seed of Israel together with the remnants of the human race, even thus did the barks launched by Columbus upon the ocean carry into regions beyond the seas as well germs of mighty states as the principles of the Catholic religion.

Speaking further of the landing of Columbus:

> Now, perchance, did the fact which we now recall take place without some design of Divine Providence. Precisely at the epoch when the American colonies, having, with Catholic aid, achieved liberty and independence, coalesced into a constitutional republic, the ecclesiastical hierarchy was happily established among you.

That is to say, just when liberty and independence were gained and this nation started, the ecclesiastical hierarchy of the Catholic church was also started in this country. The two things belong to the same time; that is what he is pointing out.

Another point upon that is thus made:

> And at the very time when the popular suffrage placed the great Washington at the helm of the republic, the first bishop was set by apostolic authority over *the American church.*

These expressions are not put in there without a purpose. The papacy intends that the Catholic church shall be recognized as the American church henceforth.

Again I read:

> The well-known friendship and familiar intercourse which subsisted between these two men seems to be an *evidence* that the *United States ought* to be enjoined in *concord and amity with the Catholic church.*

In another passage, after stating what the bishops did in their synods and by their decrees, he says:

> Thanks are due to the equity of the laws which obtain in America and to the customs of the well-ordered republic, for the church among you, unopposed by the Constitution.

The constitution as it reads was made for the direct purpose of opposing Rome and to save the country from the domination of Rome. Those who made the Constitution and the history of the time in which it was made, said this:

> It is impossible for the magistrate to adjudge the right of preference among the various sects that profess the Christian faith without erecting a claim to infallibility which would lead us back to the church of Rome.

So to keep the people of the country from the domination of the church of Rome, they said in the constitution, the government must never have anything to do with religion. But Leo has discovered that that lack of *opposition* in the constitution is the church's best hold, her greatest opportunity.

> For the church among you, unopposed by the constitution and government of your nation, fettered by no hostile legislation, protected against violence by the common laws and the impartiality of the tribunals is free to live and act without hindrance.

And she is acting without hindrance. Now I am not saying that the constitution should be in such shape that Congress *could* legislate against the papacy. Not at all. The surest safeguard against the papacy is the constitution as it is, but under the circumstances she is making that the surest means to the dominance of the papacy. Leo continues:

> Yet, though all this is true, it would be very erroneous to draw the conclusion that in America is to be sought the type of the most desirable status of the church or that it would be universally lawful or expedient for state and church to be, as in America, dissevered and divorced.

Although the church has prospered under this constitution and has here the finest chance and prospect of any place on the earth, that is not to be taken as evidence that it is better to have the church and the state separate. Oh, no, because before he gets done with this paragraph, he teaches that they shall be joined.

Here are his words:

> The fact that Catholicity with you is in good condition, nay, is even enjoying a prosperous growth, is by all means to be attributed to the fecundity with which God has endowed His church, in virtue of which, unless men or circumstances interfere, she spontaneously expands and propagates herself, but she would bring forth more abundant fruits *if*, in addition to liberty, she enjoyed *the favor of the laws and the patronage of the public authority.*

It is not enough that she shall be free and unmolested; she must be *favored* and *supported* before she is satisfied, and although the constitution leaves her totally unfettered, that is not enough. And although she prospers under it, that is not enough. Nothing can satisfy but that she shall be supported and favored by the laws and the public authority.

Now as to the establishment of the apostolic delegation, that is, the position of Satolli, hear his words upon that. They are full of meaning, too:

> By this action, as we have elsewhere intimated, we have wished, first of all, to certify that in our judgment and affections, America occupies the same place and rights as other states, be they ever so mighty and imperial.

By the establishment of Satolli's position here, he proposes, and says by that, that America today, the United States, occupies the same place, and has the same rights as other states, however mighty and imperial they may be – as Austria, Spain, France – any of them, even as is said in this dispatch which appeared in the Lansing, Michigan, *Republican* of September 24, 1894.

> The papal rescript elevates the United States to the *first rank* as a *Catholic nation*. Heretofore this country has stood before the church as a "missionary" country. It had no more recognition officially at Rome than had China… By the new rescript [and by this encyclical also] the country is freed from the propaganda and is declared to be a *Catholic country.*

Yes, "a Catholic country," as much so as any other state, "be it ever so mighty or imperial!"

> In addition to this we had in mind to draw more closely the bonds of duty and friendship which connect you and so many thousands of Catholics with the Apostolic See. In fact, the mass of the Catholics understood how salutary our action was destined to be; they saw, moreover, that it accorded with the usage and policy of the apostolic see. For it has

> been, from earliest antiquity, the custom of the Roman pontiffs in the exercise of the divinely-bestowed gift of the primacy in the administration of the church of Christ, to send forth legates to Christian nations and peoples.

To whom do the pontiffs send legates? To missionary countries? No. To protestant countries or peoples? –No. To heathen countries or peoples and nations? No, to "*Christian nations and peoples.*" How did the papacy find out that this was "a Christian nation" to which she could send a legate? Why, the Supreme Court of the United States said it "is a Christian nation." And no sooner had it done so than the legacy was commissioned and the delegation was sent and established here permanently.

> Legates ... who, supplying his [the pope's] place, may correct errors, make the rough ways plain, and administer to the people confided to their care increased means of salvation… His authority will possess no slight weight for preserving in the multitude a submissive spirit.

Then telling what he will do with the bishops and how he will help them and preserve their administration and diocesan affairs, it says this is all done that all "may work together with combined energies to promote the glory of *the American church* and the general welfare."

> It is difficult to estimate the good results which will flow from the concord of the bishops. Our own people will receive edification, and the force of example will have its effect *on those without* who will be persuaded by this argument alone that the divine apostolate has passed by inheritance to the ranks of the Catholic Episcopate.
>
> Another consideration claims our earnest attention. All intelligent men are agreed and we ourselves have with pleasure intimated it above, that *America seems destined for greater things.*

You see he is watching America for these greater things in view of "the times to come."

> Now it is our wish that the Catholic church should not only share in but help to bring about this prospective greatness. We deem it right and proper that *she should* by availing herself of the opportunities daily presented to her, *keep equal step with the Republic* in the march of improvement, at the same time striving to the utmost, by her virtue and her institutions, to aid in the rapid growth of the States. Now she will attain both these objects the more easily and abundantly, in proportion to the degree in which the future shall find her constitution perfected. [That is, the church's constitution.] But what is the meaning of the legation [that is, Satolli's position] of which we are speaking? or what its ultimate aim, except to bring it about that the constitution of the church shall be strengthened, her discipline better fortified?

There is the whole situation laid out. The church sees herself in need of a new formation, a new molding of machinery and of the framework by which she carries forward her work and imposes her doctrines and dogmas upon the peoples of the earth.

The United States is leading the nations, and she joins herself to this in view of the times to come and by reclothing herself, remodeling herself, intends to use this nation as the chief agent in her schemes. Here is a most forcible figure of this in the letter from Rome before quoted from the *Catholic Standard* of November 3, 1894:

> Now to the mind of Leo XIII so receptive to the broad and fruitful ideas of Cardinal Gibbons, of Monsignors Ireland and Keane, Europe is going through the process of casting off its slough.

Europe here relates to the papacy as the chief of all and she proposes to cast off her slough, as the snake casts off its skin, and applying the argument and allowing the papacy to speak for herself, it is a very appropriate figure, because the Scripture says that she is actuated by that "old serpent." It is correct, and she casts off her old rough, worn skin and is coming out in such a new skin, so beautiful and so rosy that thousands of Protestants think it is another thing altogether, but God says it is the same old serpent, whether it be in the same old skin or not. It is the same old serpent in her new skin, working the same way for the same purposes for bringing the nations under her hand and she now proposes to do it, and will do it.

I must read a few more statements and make a few more comments. I read from the *Catholic Standard* of November 3, 1894, as follows:

> There is an awakening, a metamorphosis, uneasiness and hope. The tradition is that in ancient Rome there were such strange expectations while the tragedy on Golgotha was being enacted and even now mysterious voices may be heard announcing that Great Pan is dead. What new order will arise? Will humanity be once more its own dupe? and will the old evils appear again under new names to people the world once more with false gods? Who knows?

The idea is suggested there that nobody knows what the answer will be. Now he tells:

> What we do know is that a *world is in its death agony.*

Is it not time that Seventh-day Adventists knew that thing full well too? The papacy knows that the world is in its death agony. do you know that? If you know it, is it not your place to tell it to the world, as well as it is the place of the papacy to tell it to the world? What has God given us this message for all these years but that we may show that the world is in its death agony and that we may tell the people so, that they may turn to the Author of life and be saved when the agony brings the last result? The papacy knows this, and she is acting in view of it. I will now read the rest of the sentence:

> What we do know is that a world is in its death agony, and that we are entering upon the night which must inevitably precede the dawn.

Of course we are. "Watchman, what of the night? Watchman, what of the night?

The watchman said. The morning cometh, and also the night." Continuing, I read:

> In this evolution, the church, in the eyes of the pope, has a mission to fill.

This is in view of the times to come. What is she looking for? A world in its death agony. All nations uneasy, society racked, everything going to pieces as it is. The papacy sees all that is going on and expects it to go on until the finish, and out of the agony and the tearing to pieces that comes with it, she expects to exalt herself once more to the supremacy over the nations, as she did of old. And she is going to do it; we know that. The Scriptures point that out.

She sees precisely what we see. We see the world in its death agony. We see society racking itself to pieces. We see thrones trembling. She sees that too, and she proposes to exalt herself upon what comes through all this at the end. We see that coming. We know she is going to do it, for her triumph comes out of this death agony. She gains new life herself and then glorifies herself upon it, living deliciously . . . saying in her heart, I sit a queen and am no widow and shall see no sorrow. Therefore, shall her plagues come in one day. Death and mourning and famine. And she shall be utterly burned with fire, for strong is the God who judgeth her.

Are we not, then, in the very whirl of events that brings that thing before the whirl shall stop? We are in it; the whirl is going on. What are we here for but to tell the people that the world is in its death agony and to call upon them to flee to Him who is the life of all?

Has not the papacy had experience in just that thing? Has not the papacy seen, practically, the world once in its death agony? The Roman Empire was the world; all civilization was embraced within its limits, was under its control. She saw the Roman Empire go to pieces; she saw universal anarchy there. As the world then stood and then was, she saw the world once in its death agony, and out of that death agony of the world she exalted herself to the supremacy that she had in the Dark Ages and wrought the mischief that cursed the world so long. She sees the same elements working again – the same movements again going on among the nations, and she congratulates herself. "We did it once. Once I rose upon the ruins of that thing. I will do it again. That demonstrated to the world in that day that I was superior to all earthly things. This will demonstrate to the world in this day – large as it is – 'I am, and there is none else beside me.' I shall be a lady forever. 'I sit a queen and am no widow and shall see no sorrow.'" That is her tone; that is what she is watching for; and God has opened this up to us in the prophecies that are before us and he wants us to call to all the people that the world is in its death agony. She raised herself upon the ruins of the death agony of the Roman world, and after the pattern of her old experience, she proposes to do the like thing now. She will succeed; that is certain. And it is likewise certain that her success will be her certain ruin, and therefore, "Come out of her my people, that ye be not partakers of her sins and that ye receive not of her plagues."

Sermon 3

February 5, 1895

We have looked at the evidences which reveal to us the existence and active working of both the beast and his image in the United States – both are even now grasping for supreme power, governmental power, to be used in enforcing the same thing, the mark of the beast. Our message is against that. "If any man worship the beast and his image and receive his mark in his forehead or in his hand, the same shall drink of the wine of the wrath of God." It is not enough, however, for us to tell the people that the course that these others are following is wrong, unless we show to them that this is so; it is not enough for us to say it, unless we can cause them by the Scriptures to see it; and therefore the lesson we will study now is the reasons why that thing is wrong.

We will begin with Philippians 3:20, reading the Revised Version. "Our citizenship is in heaven, from whence we look for the Savior, the Lord Jesus Christ." This is the Lord's statement concerning every Christian. Every Christian's citizenship is in heaven. The Authorized Version is, "Our conversation is in heaven," but that word "conversation" does not mean simply our words and the conversation which we have one with another in talking about neighborly affairs, or whatever it may be, but our *manner of life,* our *course of conduct,* our *walk,* is in heaven.

Now as our citizenship, the citizenship of every Christian, is in heaven, what has any citizen of heaven or of the heavenly government rightly to do with the political or governmental affairs of any other government or any other kingdom? In fact, what has a citizen of *any* government rightly to do with the political concerns or management of any other government?

These people of whom we have been reading in the previous lessons, profess to be citizens of the heavenly kingdom, profess to be those whose citizenship, the Scripture says, is in heaven, but they are constantly involving themselves in the political workings of the governments of this earth. They profess to have a citizenship in heaven and yet they manipulate the affairs of the kingdom of earth! They profess to be citizens of the kingdom of God, yet they propose to regulate the affairs of the governments of men. But that is a thing that never can rightly be done.

If a citizen of Great Britain should come into the United States, still retaining his citizenship in the government of Great Britain, and should take part, or attempt to take part, in the political affairs of this government, his action in that respect would be resented by every citizen of the United States. It matters not with what party he might wish to ally himself and work; they would not have it. They would say to him, That is none of your business. You do not belong here. You are a citizen of another government. If the laws of this country do not suit you, that has nothing to do with the case. The political systems of this country suit us, and if things do not suit you, just let them alone, or else change your citizenship from the government to which you belong, and bring your citizenship here, and *then* begin to discuss the laws and how they should be made and what they should be.

You know that that is so. You know that that is the way that a citizen of another country would be treated by all the citizens of this country if he should undertake to manipulate, to control, or have any part in the political concerns of this country. That is not denying his right to live here; he may do that, but all do deny his right and his very citizenship in another country denies his right to have anything to do with the citizenship of this country or with the political affairs of this country.

As the Christian's citizenship is in heaven, that itself, the very principle of it, prohibits him from taking part in any of the political concerns of any other government, even though it be the government of the United States. And that is so. It exists in the very nature of the case. It lies in the very principle of citizenship itself. Not to dwell too long on any one text, although each text that shall be read will tell the whole story, turn next to 2 Corinthians 5:20:

> Now then we are ambassadors for Christ, as though God did beseech you by us: we pray you in Christ's stead, be ye reconciled to God.

This is not simply the ordained minister, for all who receive the grace of God are to minister that; they are ministers of that grace. So it is written: "As every man hath received the gift, even so minister the same one to another, as good stewards of the manifold grace of God." Even if it were confined to the ministry, this text would not be out of place in this connection, because it is the ministry that takes the lead in all this work of the beast and his image and is managing the whole movement, leading the people under their charge into these devious and evil ways.

So then, "We are ambassadors for Christ." An ambassador is one sent, and accredited by one government as the representative of that government to another country. Now the principle of ambassadorship prohibits him from any interference whatever with the political concerns of the government to which he is accredited. If the British ambassador to the United States that is tonight in Washington city – or the ambassador from France or any other of these countries – should express an opinion upon, or take any part in, any of the political concerns of this country, his sovereign would be immediately notified that he was no longer an accepted person here, and would be called upon to withdraw him from the position of ambassador in this country.

That has been done at least twice in my recollection. In one of Grant's administrations the Russian minister to this country touched in some slight way upon some political issue, a mere insignificant one so far as any particular turn of politics was concerned. Yet he was sent out of the country at once, recalled. In the campaign between Cleveland and Harrison the first time, you remember the British minister to this country, Sackville-West, received a letter from a Mr. Murchson of California, who pretended – whether it was correct or not – to be a British subject, and in the letter were some questions and observations upon the then current issues of the presidential campaign. The British Minister answered the letter and expressed an opinion. The letter was published and a dispatch was immediately sent to the court of St. James, demanding his recall, and he was recalled.

These are cited merely to illustrate the recognized principles of ambassadorship among nations, among men.

"We are ambassadors for Christ." These church leaders who are building up the beast and his image profess to stand in the place of and profess to be ambassadors for Christ, yet they not only express opinions, but they lay down laws, they manipulate campaigns, they mold politics, and shape the whole political course of the governments among the nations and the people to whom they are accredited, and thus violate the first, the last, and every principle that is involved in ambassadorship.

Here then are two distinct reasons given in these two plain scriptures, the same principle expressed in two ways that demonstrate that the course of these professed citizens of the heavenly kingdom, these professed ambassadors for Christ, is absolutely wrong. And our preaching the message and the warning against the worship of the beast and his image, against the evils which are simply the result of the violation of the principles here laid down – our opposition to that, our warning against it, must be one of *principle,* and not merely in theory, nor from policy. Unless our proclamation against it is founded upon principle and is loyal to principle, our proclamation will amount to nothing. If we hold in theory only that it is wrong and make the proclamation against it even in the words of Scripture and in practice ourselves violate the principle, our proclamation will amount to nothing. So that our connection with this must be with *the principle* and that *in* principle and in loyalty *to* the principle and that *from the heart* – not in theory, not assenting to it merely. The principles of Jesus Christ speak to the heart. They take hold of the heart and are of value only as they have hold upon the heart. If they do not have hold upon the heart, the man who professes these principles will violate them in his actions, even though he be a Seventh-day Adventist.

"Our citizenship is in heaven," and of all people *our* "citizenship is in heaven, from when we look for the Savior, the Lord Jesus Christ."

Again: John 18:36:

> Jesus answered, My kingdom is not of this world. If my kingdom were of this world, then would my servants fight, that I should not be delivered to the Jews.

If His kingdom were of this world, then for what kingdom would His servants fight? For a kingdom of this world. For what kingdom would they contend? For what would they work? For the kingdom of this world. Then the man who fights for a kingdom of this world, who contends for supremacy and power in the kingdom of this world, denies His connection with the kingdom of Jesus Christ, for *His* kingdom is not of this world. But that is what these men are doing who are leading in this movement of which we have read in two preceding lessons. They seek to take possession of the kingdoms of this world, to rule the governments of this world, to fight, actually to fight, for the governments of this world, to work to put themselves in places of position and relationship to the governments of this world, and therefore they proclaim with the loudest voice they possibly can that they are of this world and not of the kingdom of Christ at all.

Another scripture in connection with the same thing is found in Luke 22:24-26: "There was also a strife among them, which of them should be accounted the greatest." There was also a strife among them which of them should be accounted the greatest in the kingdom which they expected to come upon this earth – the kingdom which they expected Christ to set up and which they expected would be a kingdom of this world, and in which they would have a place. There was a strife among them as to which should be accounted the greatest, and which would have the greatest place in that expected kingdom. It was a mistaken idea, to be sure, with respect to the kingdom, but the lesson that he gave them upon it is applicable in all cases of the kind.

> And he said unto them, The kings of the Gentiles exercise lordship over them, and they that exercise authority upon them are called benefactors.

Factors, agents; benefactors, agents of good! That is what these church leaders now profess to be; agents of good to the country, to the people; to be working the redemption of cities, states, and nations – thus these would now be called benefactors. "But ye shall not be so." "So" what? These exercise lordship over them and exercise authority upon them. "Ye shall not be so." Where? Why, ye shall not exercise authority and lordship over one another in the church, in the place where you do belong. How, then, about exercising authority and lordship over people in a place where you do not belong at all?

Another verse in connection with the one we had a moment ago, "My kingdom is not of this world":

> Giving thanks unto the Father, which hath made us meet to be partakers of the inheritance of the saints of light: who hath delivered us from the power of darkness, and hath translated us into the kingdom of his dear Son. Col. 1:12, 13.

What we want to study there is the contrast between this light and the darkness. "Delivered us from the power of darkness." That is not simply the power that darkness itself exerts upon us, but the idea is, delivered us from the dominion, the rulership, the government of darkness; brought us out from under the jurisdiction of the power of darkness, and "hath translated us into the kingdom of His dear Son."

Now we read in Ephesians 6:10-12:

> Be strong in the Lord and in the power of his might. Put on the whole armor of God, that ye may be able to stand against the wiles of the devil. For we wrestle not against flesh and blood, but against principalities, against powers, against *the rulers of the darkness of this world*.

There are defined the dominion, the rulership, and the authority that rules the darkness of this world. Now we are to contend against that. And only those can contend successfully who have been delivered from the power of that darkness and translated into the kingdom of His dear Son.

In this I am not saying that the kings and other rulers of the political governments of this world are the "rulers of the darkness" referred to in the text. The text is not quoted for that. The "rulers of the darkness" here referred to, we all know to be the spiritual powers of darkness. But the text says that these spiritual powers are the rulers of the darkness *of this world*. And it therefore shows that this world is *in* that darkness and is *of* that darkness and shows therefore that kingdoms and governments being of this world only are in and of the darkness. That is what the text is quoted for.

Now read in Eph. 5:8: "Ye were sometimes darkness." When? Why, when we were subject to "the rulers of the darkness of this world," when we were in sin. "For ye were sometimes darkness but now are ye light in the Lord: walk as children of light; proving what is acceptable unto the Lord."

Governments, nations, political organizations are of this world only; they belong to this world only. And the world is under the dominion of darkness. "Darkness shall cover the earth and gross darkness the people." Are governments and municipalities of the kingdom of God or of this world? They belong to this world and to this world alone. That is the side of darkness. But he who is translated out of darkness, delivered from that darkness and translated into the kingdom of God's dear Son is of another world; he belongs to another world. He is connected with another world, and that world indeed is the heavenly world. The city to which he belongs is the heavenly city. There is his citizenship – in the dominion and the world of light.

Then what connection has that kingdom of light with the kingdoms of darkness? What has that government which is in the light and is of the light, to do with governments that are in the darkness and of the darkness? What have those who profess, as these

National Reformers do, to belong to the dominion of light, to [do with] the kingdom of light? What have these rightly to do with the affairs of darkness and the rulership and the dominions that pertain only to this world of darkness? "What fellowship hath light with darkness?" That question belongs here. And the same thought is expressed right here in connection with the text we are studying.

Read now the whole connection:

> Ye were sometimes darkness, but now are ye light in the Lord: walk as children of light (for the fruit of the Spirit is in all goodness and righteousness and truth), proving what is acceptable unto the Lord. And have no fellowship with the unfruitful works of darkness, but rather reprove them.

How much of the world is to be embraced under the dominion of the beast and his image? All the world. What is our message? "If any man worship the beast and his image." That is our message *to the world*. To how much of the world is that message due and applicable? All the world. Then what has that message to do but to do this very thing – to "have no fellowship with the unfruitful works of darkness, but rather reprove them?" Will that message be a reproving message to everyone that is engaged in the work of the beast and his image? It will.

Thus the work of the beast and his image is violative of the principle of citizenship of the kingdom of God, or any other kingdom; violative of the principle of ambassadorship of Jesus Christ or any other ambassadorship; violative of the principle that Jesus Christ laid down for His disciples as to seeking place and authority; violative of the principle of His that separates the government of God from the governments of this earth – that separates between light and darkness. It is simply an attempt to blend light and darkness and is always and only darkness that will seek to blend the government of light with the governments of darkness.

There are several other texts that I want to read. John 17:14 and onward, Christ's prayer for His disciples: "I have given them thy word, and the world hath hated them."

In another place He says to them:

> If ye were of the world, the world would love his own, but because ye are not of the world but I have chosen you out of the world, therefore the world hateth you. Remember the word that I said unto you, The servant is not greater than his Lord.

Now the 18th verse: "If the world hate you, ye know that it hated me before it hated you."

Then turn to another place and you find the statement of Christ: "The world cannot hate you, but me it hateth, because I testify of it, that the works thereof are evil."

When the beast and his image govern the world and here are a people that are testifying against it, testifying that its works are evil, then what will follow? That people will be hated. But if one does not testify to the world that its works are evil, is the world going to hate him? Oh no, the world will love its own.

Now read on in the 17th chapter of John and the 14th verse: "And the world hath hated them, because *they are not of the world, even as I am not of the world.*" There is the standard; there is the measure of compassion that tests our relationship to this world. That is Jesus Christ. "They are not of the world, *even as I am* not of the world."

> I pray not that thou shouldest take them out of the world, but that thou shouldest keep them from the evil. *They are not of the world,* even *as I am not* of the world.

Here are these National Reform church leaders, *professing* to be not of this world. If that profession be true, they will act as Jesus Christ did when He was in this world with respect to governmental affairs on the earth. That is what we are talking about now. The beast and his image are of the world. If these church leaders are right, if they are of the truth, if they are of Christ's truth, then they are no more of the world, and no more interfering and taking part with the affairs of this world, or seeking to control in political affairs, than Jesus Christ did Himself in the world.

And to what extent did He do it? He never touched it. Were there not evils in His day that ought to have been corrected? Evils in city government? Evils in colonial government? Evils in imperial government? Why in the world did He not set about to redeem Jerusalem and Rome by political wire-working? Why didn't He? Because He *was not of this world.* Then as certainly as these are engaged in it, they demonstrate that they are not of Christ, nor of the truth of Christ, but are of this world. And they being of this world, yet professing the name of Christianity, seek to run Christianity in the mold and the form of this world, and that is antichrist.

Let us read a text in which we have a definite statement upon this subject. In the book of Luke, 12th chapter, 13th verse to the 21st: "One of the company said unto him, Master, speak to my brother, that he divide the inheritance with me." Here is a man whose parents had died, leaving an inheritance. His brother, it seems, had not dealt fairly with him, and he calls upon Jesus to speak to the brother and have him act right in the matter. That was, in principle, asking Jesus to take the position of a magistrate or an arbitrator in affairs of this world, concerning things that pertain to the government of this world, to sit in judgment upon that case and decide what was right and direct accordingly. It is a case that contains the whole principle which is involved in the evidences which we read in the extracts given in the two preceding lessons. "And he said unto him, Man, who made me a judge or a divider over you? And he said unto him," (not simply to him, but that was a text from which Christ would teach him and all the rest a lesson):

> Take heed, and beware of covetousness, for a man's life consisteth not in the abundance of the things which he possesseth. And he spake a parable unto them, saying, The ground of a certain rich man brought forth plentifully: and he thought within himself, saying, What shall I do, because I have no room where to bestow my fruits? And he said, This will I do: I will pull down my barns and build greater, and there will I bestow all my fruits and my goods. And I will say to my soul, Soul, thou hast much goods laid up for many years; take thine ease, eat, drink, and be merry. But God said unto him, Thou fool, this night thy soul shall be required of thee: then whose shall those things be, which thou hast provided? So is he that layeth up treasures for himself, and is not rich toward God.

Now for the application of another point upon ambassadorship.

Ambassadors are rightly sent from one government, one kingdom, to another. He is not sent there, as we found in studying the former point, to manipulate, to interfere, or have anything at all to do with the affairs of the government or of the people of that government as they stand related to that government. He is sent to that country, to that government, to attend to the affairs of *his own* government *as they may arise* in that government or in that country. That is what he is here for.

There are subjects of Great Britain in the United States, and there are in this country interests that concern Great Britain, in connection with her subjects here. She sends her ambassadors here, a personal national representative, to attend to the affairs of Great Britain and of the subjects of Great Britain, as these things may arise within the territory of this government. And to *these things alone* is he to turn his attention and devote his time – to the affairs of his own country, as they may arise in the country where he is.

So was Jesus Christ sent as the ambassador of God to this world. He was in the country of Judea, the government, the dominion, and the jurisdiction of Rome. He was asked to attend to the affairs and take jurisdiction in matters that pertained to that other country. But instead of yielding to the invitation, He stuck closely to the affairs that belonged to *His own country.*

They asked Him to act as a judge and a divider in the things that belonged altogether to the government in whose territory He was, and where the man was. But He was not there to attend to these things. He was there to attend to the affairs of *the kingdom of God,* the affairs of the government which sent Him. And instead of crossing the line, and interfering with the affairs that belonged properly under the jurisdiction of this world, He, as became Him, was loyal to the kingdom to which He belonged, and to the King whom He represented, and accordingly He adhered strictly and attended closely to the affairs of that government of the kingdom of God, as they arose in that kingdom of this world.

God has people in this world. He has interests in this world. His people have interests in this world. That is true. Therefore, God rightly has ambassadors in this world, but they are here to attend to the affairs of *the kingdom of God* and the people of God, as the affairs of the kingdom of God may arise in the course of things in this world, and not at all to any affairs of the kingdoms of this world. And the ambassador for Jesus Christ that goes over the line and undertakes to attend to the affairs of this world, abandons his own government, breaks his allegiance to his own King, and unlawfully and illegally invades the province of another government. That is why the wickedness of this thing is so great; that is why it made the beast in the first place; that is why the violation of these principles makes the image of the beast in the second place.

Now I want to ask a question: Taking only the texts which we have studied tonight and the principles that lie in them – not that are brought to them but lie inevitably in them – taking those texts alone, and if these principles of the church had been strictly adhered to, as they were by Jesus Christ in this world, would there, or could there ever have been a papacy? Could there have been such a thing as the beast? Could there ever, then, have been such a thing as the image of the beast? No, sir. That is evidently true.

Then upon that, as the violation of those principles inevitably made the beast in the first place, the violation of those principles in the second place could not possibly do anything else than to make the image of the beast. It was not because the people, the professed Christians, in the Roman Empire were worse than any other professed Christians that ever were, that made the papacy; it was not that. It was the violation of the best principles that ever came into the world, that made the worst thing that ever was in the world. And when God had called the world once more unto Himself by the principles of Christianity, through the work of the Reformation and set forth once more the principles of Christianity as against the beast, that made Protestantism as it was. And when these professed Protestants violate these principles, it brings the same identical thing, in the perfect image of the original thing that was made by the violation of the principles in the first place.

Then it has been demonstrated before all the world on these two occasions, that the violation of those principles revealed in the verses which we have read, can do nothing else than curse the world with the very papal beastly spirit. Then what thing is most to be avoided by everyone that names the name of Christ? It is the violation of those principles, and if it comes home even to Seventh-day Adventists themselves, the thing to be done is to wed ourselves eternally to the principles and hold to them, because those principles violated by Seventh-day Adventists will work the workings of the papacy, as well as by Protestants or by Catholics.

So I say again, It was not because the professed Christians of the Roman Empire were worse than any other people on the earth that made the papacy as bad as it is.

It is not because the Protestant church leaders in this land are worse than anybody else that the image of the beast has been made and is carrying on its cruel workings, but it is because those people violated the principles that have been laid down for the good of the world and the violation of them can do nothing else than to curse the world. And if they are violated by Seventh-day Adventists even, it will be a curse – a curse wherever it is done.

Once more, and then we will have to close this lesson at about half way through: John 17:9: "I pray for them." That is, His disciples, whom He said to the Father, thou hast given me out of the world. "I pray for them: I pray not for the world." Then can the man whose affections and attention, and his working and labor are upon this world and engaged in the affairs of this world have the benefit of that prayer? No, sir. "I pray for them: I pray not for the world, but for them which thou hast given me, for they are Thine." Given me out of the world. Taken from the world. Given them to me. I pray for them; they are not of the world, even as I am not of the world. Then every man who would have the benefit of that prayer must be separated from the world, from the things of this world, from the affairs of this world – his affections off from anything that is in the world or of it, as certainly and as entirely as Jesus Christ Himself, for "they are not of the world, even as I am not of the world."

Sermon 4

February 8, 1895

OUR lesson closed last night with the example and the action of Christ, which He gave to us when solicited to cross the line defining the boundary of ambassadorship. We will begin this evening with John 20:21.

> Then said Jesus to them again, Peace be unto you: as my Father hath sent me, even so send I you.

When Christ was solicited to perform the office of a judge and a divider over men, He refused. Now He says, "As My Father hath sent me, even so send I you."

And we read in another verse telling what the situation of the Christian is in the world. 1 John 4:17, "As he is, so are we in this world." These verses, however, are only saying in another way the same truth which we studied last night. "They are not of the world, even as I am not of the world."

And from the experience which we have heard this evening from Brother Holser and Switzerland, would it seem to be going too far to take all these scriptures as they read and accept the principle that is involved in them as it there lies? As stated in the present week's *Review and Herald,* our publishing house was founded in Switzerland for the reason that there was supposed to be the most liberty and that there we would have the most opportunity to do our work for the longest time. Also in the United States it has been considered that this was the home of liberty. That is true, it *was.* But *now* the United States and Switzerland are the two countries where there is more persecution and where more of these evils go on than in Russia itself. Does not that of itself, from the experiences we have heard tonight, demonstrate sufficiently, as a lesson to us, that when we have any connection with these as they appear to us and lean in any respect upon them, we are leaning on a broken reed, and that the sooner we find that our *only* refuge, our *only* confidence is in God and our *only* allegiance is to His kingdom, to His laws, and to the principles which are there given, the better off we will be?

This principle, stated in another way is, not how near we can conform or connect ourselves with earthly governments and kingdoms, but it truly is how far we can keep away. We are not to see how near we can go without compromising, but how far we can be away *to be perfectly safe.* That is the principle. The ten commandments are prohibitions. One of them says, "Thou shalt not kill," and in saying that the commandment does not describe to us the line which tells how near we can go to killing a man without doing it, but in telling us that we shall not kill a man, it tells us that we shall not think a thought which, if carried out to its logical conclusion could hurt a man at all. In saying, "Thou shalt not commit adultery," He does not tell us just how near we can go to that without doing it, but He tells us that we cannot think on that subject without doing it.

> Ye have heard that it was said by them of old time, Thou shalt not kill, and whosoever shall kill shall be in danger of the judgment, but I say unto you, That whosoever is angry with his brother without cause [the Revised Version leaves out "without cause"] shall be in danger of the judgment, and whosoever shall say to his brother, Vain fellow, shall be in danger of the council, but whosoever shall say, Thou fool, shall be in danger of hell fire.

A man who goes so far as to think of another that he is a fool and decides the question that he is a fool and then passes the sentence in words, "Thou fool," has committed murder, and the only thing that waits for him is hell fire.

But what is the Savior talking about? He is teaching them what it means when it says, "Thou shalt not kill." And when God said, "Thou shalt not kill," He forbade the thinking of a thought or the speaking of a word which if carried out to its utmost possible limit, could lead to killing or to doing harm.

> Ye have heard that it was said by them of old time, Thou shalt not commit adultery; but I say unto you, that whosoever looketh on a woman to lust after her hath committed adultery with her already.

Has done it. What? All he did was to look and think. That is all. But he has committed adultery, so that in forbidding to commit adultery, He forbids a look or a thought which, if followed up, could possibly lead to it. The law of God is intended to control the actions, by controlling the very *spring* of *the thoughts.* That is the principle upon which the Bible deals with mankind. And in this principle that we are studying – the separation of religion and the state, God expects us to take our position upon a principle, which it is *impossible* to push by any possible means to a union of church and state or of religion and the state. If we take a position upon that subject which, if followed, could possibly lead to a union of church and state, then we are wrong – we have not the true principle. If we accept a point or make a statement which, if carried out to its utmost possible bearing, could lead to a union of church and state, then that thing is teaching a union of church and state. And if we, therefore, would be exempt from it, if we would keep clear of it, in such a way that our words, our teaching, our proclamation to the world, shall be the testimony of God against the beast and his image and the testimony of the truth as it is in Jesus, we are to find a position and hold it, which it is impossible, by any sort of dealing, to cause to *lean* toward a union of church and state.

Now we have found, and you agreed last night, and everyone must agree, that if the principles which lie in these texts which we read last night had been followed always by all who name the name of Christ, it would have been impossible for there ever to have been a papacy in the world, and if the principles involved in these texts had been followed by Protestantism from the day that Luther sounded the trumpet of God until now and should continue so, it would be impossible for there ever to be such a thing as the image of the beast.

Well then we all know that the violation of the principle lying in the texts which we read last night, made the papacy; it makes the image of the papacy, and it is impossible for the violation of the principle ever to make anything else. The first step over the line involves all that ever has come, from the first step that was taken in the development of the papacy until now.

There is another verse that we might read in this connection. Mark 12:29,30. When asked which is the first commandment in the law,

> Jesus answered him, The first of all the commandments is, Hear O Israel; the Lord our God is one Lord, and thou shalt love the Lord thy God with all thy heart and with all thy soul and with all thy mind and with all thy strength.

That takes *all of the man, all the time,* to be devoted to God. How much then is there left with which to serve Caesar? "Render therefore unto Caesar the things which are Caesar's and unto God the things that are God's." A little *money* from the Christian – the levied tribute – belongs to Caesar. The Christian himself belongs to God. How much of the Christian is God's, by the Christian's recognized right? Of course all men are God's by creation and by purchase, but the Christian recognizes God's right to him, and it takes a complete surrender to God to be a Christian. To get into that position a man has to be born again or else he cannot see the kingdom of God, and that kingdom is not of this world. Then as certainly as obedience to the commandments of God calls for all the man to be surrendered to God, so certainly there is none of the man left for the service of Caesar.

Look a moment at the verse we have just read. "With *all* thy mind."

When that law is fulfilled in me, I want to know how much of my mind I am going to have left for running politics, for wire-pulling in municipal affairs, for working to elect this man or that man or to see who will nominate me for office or to see what position I can have in the city or in the state?

"Thou shalt love the Lord thy God… with all thy mind."

But if I divide my mind and put part of it on these things and give the rest to the Lord – what about the double-minded man? "Unstable in all his ways."

"Let not that man think he shall receive anything of the Lord." "No man can serve two masters." Ye cannot serve God and this world; ye cannot serve God and Caesar.

As before suggested, this is not saying that the tribute is not to be rendered to Caesar; Christ has commanded that, but that is but a little money which itself is coined and stamped by Caesar, but our service, ourselves, all there is of us, belong to God. Christians are *subject* to the powers that be, but they *serve* only God. And even this subjection to the powers that be upon the earth is out of conscience toward God. It says so. God must have all the heart.

Now I am talking still on the subject of the beast and his image and all these movements that have been set before us is the first two lessons, which show the standing of the beast and his image as they are in the United States. We are studying the reasons why these things are wrong which these persons are doing; why it is that the churches interfering in the political workings of the cities and through that of the country and through this proposing to control the nation – we are considering why it is and studying why it is wrong. For, as I stated before, it is not enough for us to tell people that it is wrong. We must show to them that it is wrong and show them by the Word that it is wrong, that they may know from God which is the right and *by that* which is the wrong.

Now there is another consideration that we shall study in this connection. In the Scriptures you know that the church is called the body of Christ, and Christ is the head of the church. We need not take time to turn and read those scriptures; there are so many of them and you are all familiar with them. Then with the church being the body of Christ and He the head, is not the church, practically and indeed literally, Christ in the world? But Christ taught, the Scriptures teach, a separation of church and state. Christ says, "I am not of this world."

This blackboard happens to be standing here, so I will use it, taking the figure we had last night as between the darkness and the light. This world is darkness, the rulers of the darkness of this world. "Ye were sometime darkness, but now are ye light in the Lord. Walk as children of light." Now let that blackboard represent the dark world without this white mark upon it. When Christ came into the world, the light shone into the world. From Galilee there was the word of the prophet: "The people which sat is darkness saw a great light." Let that white line on the blackboard represent the line between the darkness and the light. On this side is the light. Here is where Christ is. There is still the dark world, the world of darkness. Now He says His kingdom is not of this world. The kingdom of God is the kingdom of light and of glory. He is the King there, and "the kingdom of God is within you." Now on which side of that line is the church? Wherever Christ is. For we found that He is the church. The church is Himself in the world. So then here in the light is the church, here is Christ. Over there in the darkness are the states, the governments, that are altogether of this world.

No government that ever was on the earth will enter heaven. Now Christ is separated from them. He refused, absolutely refused, to exercise the office of judging or dividing, to do the thing that pertains, and by right, to these.

Another thing. He had "all of these kingdoms of the world" offered to Him once, anyway. Why didn't He accept that offer and thus become the head, by gift, of all the governments and kingdoms of this world and then manipulate them and by political means "regenerate society," "redeem cities," reform the mayors, governors, presidents, kings and emperors and thus "save" the world? Why not? That would have only confirmed the world in eternal ruin.

Christ did not accept them. He could not do so. He was offered the governorship, the possession, of all the kingdoms of the world once. He would not have it. But lo, here we find these church leaders in our day actually grasping for it and working to obtain it. If all Christians from the day of Christ until now had acted in that respect in regard to the kingdoms of the world, in their measure as Christ did in His, could there have been a papacy? No. Could there have been an image? Impossible. Then where is the place for Christians to stand on that question? Where He stood, refusing to have anything to do with the kingdoms of this world.

Now there is one other consideration we must notice tonight, and that is that these church leaders, these National Reformers, are doing all this to "regenerate the city," to "redeem the State," to "save the nation in the interests of society for the prosperity of kingdoms and nations and the advancement in civilization, and this in turn is to rebound to the prosperity, the glory, and the exaltation of the church." And they say, If this clear-cut line that separates between the church and the state shall be maintained, what will become of civilization? Then how is the church to influence the world?" They argue that the church certainly is in the world to do good to the world in some way. Here are these cities, states, kingdoms, and nations, that are corrupt, and the church must have some influence upon them, and if she is to be completely separated from them, how is she to influence them in any way for good? These are the queries that they raise, and the arguments which they make.

Well, the answer to all that is, that by totally separating from them is the *only* way in which she can ever possibly influence them for good. The church will influence the world; it will influence kingdoms; it will influence nations and the peoples thereof *when,* and *only* when, it is faithfully the church of Christ and is not of the world, even as He is not of the world. When she is not this, she will influence them – that is true – but *only to their undoing.*

Now I lay it down as a principle that *the aim of Christianity is not to civilize anybody.* Christianity aims alone at *Christianizing* men. And it is better, a thousand times, to have *one* Christian savage, than to have a *whole nation* of savage Christians.

This appears paradoxical, I admit. Therefore, allow me to explain, for it is correct. The great boast of the papacy is that she is the civilizer of nations – even the mother and the ground and the stay of civilization. Let a papal missionary go into a tribe or nation of savages. He may get the king or the chiefs to accept the Catholic teaching. He may indeed succeed in getting them to put on clothes and in turning them to the building of houses, fencing fields, and tilling the ground, thus turning them to a civilized instead of the savage way of living. He may even get them to forego warfare – except for "the faith." In this sense they are civilized. And upon this she calls them all Christians. They are taught to consider themselves Christians. Other heathen and other savages look upon them as Christians and count them so. And so here she has "a Christian nation." But as a matter of fact, in essential disposition they are unchanged. In heart they are still savages and upon occasion, especially in behalf of "the faith" will show themselves absolutely savage. There is abundance of evidence of this, for never was there on the earth more savage savagery, even among savages, than there was for ages in the Roman empire in the height of the dominion of the papacy. It is impossible for men to be more savage than were those champions of orthodoxy. And that is what I mean by the phrase, "savage Christians."

Now on the other hand, let a Christian minister or a Christian individual go into a nation of savages, as they run wild in the forests and present the gospel of Jesus Christ in the love of God. Let one of those savages be converted to Jesus Christ. He may still wear his savage clothing or lack of clothing; he may not know anything about building a fence or building a house or anything of this kind, that is signified in the term civilization, but *he is a Christian.* The savage is taken out of his heart. Yet as the world goes, as men look at things and as relates to civilization, he would pass only as a savage. But he is a Christian and in being Christianized, in the very nature of things, he is civilized, and as certainly as he continues to live the outward forms of civilization will appear in due time. That is what I mean by the phrase "Christian savage." And that is what I mean when I say that that *one* Christian savage is worth more than a whole nation of these savage Christians.

If civilization were the aim and the object of Christianity, then there was no place for Christianity in the world where it started and at the time it started. I want you to think of that. Were not the Jews civilized?

But if it be counted that the Jews were not up to the proper standard of civilization to suit these National Reformers, then let us turn to Greece and Rome. What was the position of Greece and Rome at that time with regard to civilization? They had such a standing in civilization and all that pertains to civilization as that today civilized nations are but copyists of the civilization, the art, the splendor, the laws, and forms of government of the Greeks and the Romans. And for that reason I say that if civilization is the subject of Christianity, if that is, in any sense, the aim of Christianity and of Christian work, then there was no place for Christianity in the place and at the time when it started in the world; for there was a stage of civilization that the world has never since reached. But what were the people? They were heathen. And the gospel was sent to those civilized heathen as much as to any savage heathen that was upon the earth. And if there could be any difference, these civilized heathen needed the gospel more than did the savage heathen.

Now as a matter of fact, the gospel will have a great deal to do with civilizing people, *provided* that no effort is made *by means of the gospel* to civilize people. That is to say: If the gospel, which is put in the world solely to *Christianize* men, is used only to *civilize* men, you will not even civilize them; whereas, if that which is put into the world solely to Christianize men, shall be used *solely for the purpose* of Christianizing men, it will both Christianize men and *as a consequence,* it will civilize them.

It is the same old story all the time. If you take the things that God has given for the most supreme purpose that could be mentioned or thought of and use them for another purpose, you will miss the purpose for which you use it; while if you will use them solely for the purpose for which God gave them, *then* you find that purpose accomplished, and you get all the blessed fruits of that and also all those other things in addition. The Bible is full of illustrations of this principle, but it is all summed up in this word, "Seek ye *first* the kingdom of God and his righteousness, and all these things shall be added unto you."

Therefore, Christians are not to aim at civilizing men but solely at Christianizing them, and then the civilizing will take care of itself. Christians are not to seek to civilize men in order to Christianize them. The Christian seeks to Christianize people in order to *save* them. And I say again, these National Reformers, in working for what they call the advancement of civilization, in the interests of civilization, trying to have the state connect with the church, are simply working for the ruin of civilization that is already here. This effort will end only in turning the elements of civility, even as far as they are, into the most savage deviltry, in the image of the beast.

Then we are never to allow ourselves to be deceived by any such argument as that. Point out the fact and show by holding steadfast to the straight up and down line, heaven high, between the church and the state, that the church of Jesus Christ – Jesus Christ working in the world by all members of His body, which is the church, for the Christianizing of men, for their *salvation*. Teach all, that with the church devoting *all* her powers, *all* her mind, and *all* her strength, to *that one thing,* she will influence the world and nations and kingdoms – I was going to say, infinitely more than she will the other way, but she will not influence them at all the other way for good. In this way she will influence them only for good, whereas to go a hair's breadth awry from that only turns the influence which would be for good into nothing but that which is bad.

The one is Christ, the other is antichrist. The work of the church, the aim of Christianity, is not civilization but SALVATION *through faith in our Lord Jesus alone.*

Sermon 5

February 11, 1895

After meeting had closed last night, a question was asked which requires notice in the same line of the last remarks we had, as to the influence of Christianity in civilizing people beyond the limit of those whom it Christianizes. That is a fact, and a good illustration is before us in Christianity in the Roman Empire, which will answer the question, and also illustrate the principle.

When Christianity started in the Roman Empire, there was no such thing known as rights of conscience. In fact, there was no such thing known as the rights of the individual, of any kind, and as the rights of conscience are the chief of all rights, of course this was the least known. Christianity means nothing if not the rights of conscience. That was its one claim that overtopped everything else, of course included everything else, as it entered the Roman Empire. The contest between Christianity and all the power of the Roman Empire was upon the Christian's claim of the right of conscience, the empire of Rome denying it, because the empire did not know anything about it.

Rome said, "What the law says, is right."

And what the law says, from law itself as it is in itself, from that alone do we get the idea of right and wrong. What the law says to be done, that is right, and what it prohibits, that is wrong, and *that* is the *reason* as to *why* it is right or wrong.

But the Christian said, What *God* says is right, *that* is right; and what God says is wrong, that is wrong.

To Rome, the State was god; and therefore the maxim, "The voice of the people is the voice of God." And as the law was the voice of the people, so the law was the voice of the Roman god.

Therefore, when the Christian denied the Roman god and asserted the rights of conscience toward the *true* God, he himself became judge of the right or wrong of the law, which to the Roman mind was in itself the test of wrong or right. That contest went on for 250 years before it was settled in favor of the rights of conscience. And by that time the principles of Christianity had so impressed the pagans, who made no profession of anything but paganism, that the rights of conscience were sacred. So that when the apostasy seized the civil power and began to use it in behalf of what they called the Christian religion, then *pagans* pleaded the rights of conscience!

There is the whole story. Christianity, the principles of Christianity, *Christianized* multitudes of people. The Christianizing of these people fixed in them, in its integrity, the rights of conscience, and there it was so fixed that they would die rather than yield. That was genuine Christianity. These were Christianized, and by their integrity, at the expense of every consideration in holding to that principle, pagans themselves were impressed by it, to the point to which they pled it when occasion offered. There is where Christianity Christianized one multitude and civilized another.

This illustrates the principles which we are studying: That Christianity, if held faithfully by those who profess it, will exert upon those who are not Christianized by it, upon those who make no pretensions to Christianity at all, an influence for good, that will elevate them above savagery and above the base principles and ways of civilized paganism.

Macaulay discovered the principle, too, and expressed it in a sentence that is one of the most powerful human statements there is in literature in favor of Christianity. In writing of India, in a certain place he makes this remark: "*A man needs not to be a Christian to desire that Christianity should be spread in India.*" That tells the whole story. Now a Christian wants Christianity spread in India for Christ's sake, for the sake of souls who will be Christianized. The man who is not a Christian can well wish for Christianity to be in India, for the sake of the poor heathen that would be elevated, even if they do not become Christians. That is the thought.

But the mischief has always been and it is yet that Christianity is not taken and held *for what it is* by those who profess it; God is not given large enough place in the profession of it by those who profess it, and by not being given large enough place, He does not have any chance to demonstrate the real power of Christianity in these people who do not give Him the place that belongs to Him in which He would demonstrate the divinity of Christianity with power that would convince.

Then men finding the loss of that divine power and influence they go about to do by themselves and by human power the things that would be done by the Lord if only they would give Him the place that belongs to Him in their profession. That is why professed Christians must put themselves forward and propose to legislate or get into office or manage and dictate to those who *do* legislate or *are* in office. And all to give things "a Christian mold," and make it influential in elevating the people and bring cities, states and nations around to the right way. But that is putting *themselves* in the place of Jesus Christ; that is putting themselves in the place of God. And that is the papacy over again; that is the beast or his image one or the other, as the case may be, wherever you find it. Let those who name the name of Christ do it in such integrity, in such absolute surrender to God, as will give to God *all* the place and Him *alone* all the place that belongs to Him. Let the influence all be His; let the power all be His; let Him alone be looked to and depended upon to do all in all. *Then* Christians will see the power of God so manifest that they would be ashamed to put themselves forward to give mold or shape to the influence of Christianity.

When people do not give the Lord the place which belongs to Him and therefore do not see what they expect to see, it is very natural that they should begin to think that they are better than the Lord and could do better than He does and so they must take hold and do the thing their Christianity fails to do. But that, I say again, and you see it plain enough, is only to leave God out, and put themselves in His place. And by leaving God out, they leave out His power, and by putting themselves in His place, they put into exercise *their own* power, and that is worldly, earthly, sensual, and at the last devilish.

Now we take another step in this study of our proclamation of the message against the beast and his image, we will take this step starting again with the principle of ambassadorship. "We are ambassadors for Christ."

And as we found in the other lesson, an ambassador is not sent to another country to pry into the affairs or attend to the political concerns of that country, but to attend to the affairs of his own country as they arise in that country.

We are ambassadors for Christ. The whole attention of Christians is to be on the things of their own country, the affairs of their own kingdom, and to attend to these as they may arise in the country on the earth where they may be sojourning. For as certain as we are Christians, "we are strangers and sojourners"; our country is yonder, where *we* belong.

The particular study that we are taking up tonight is a study of the rights which we have as Seventh-day Adventists, as ambassadors of Christ, as citizens of the heavenly kingdom, in the nations and countries upon the earth where we may be sojourning – the rights that we have in opposing the things which we shall have to oppose, and which soon we are to meet.

The experiences which we have heard Brother Holser relate tonight cannot be studied any too carefully by Seventh-day Adventists in the United States. God is giving to *us* the principles and preparing us *beforehand* for what is as certain to come as that the sun shall rise. In His providence the Lord prepared the brethren and sisters in Switzerland for crises that have come since they were waked up on that thing, as Brother Holser has told us, and if we in this country do not accept the principles and put our thoughts and our endeavors upon these principles to understand what God is teaching us in these times and by these things, the crisis will come upon us and find us unprepared, and the danger is that we will miss the point altogether and fail right in the place where God wants us to make a success. We cannot afford to do that.

An ambassador, then, in the country where he may be sojourning, is to attend to the affairs of *his own kingdom* as they may arise there and as they may affect the subjects of his own kingdom. Therefore, if that kingdom or that government in which he may be sojourning undertakes to enact any laws or take a political course that will infringe the rights of the people of his own country, he has the right and it is his duty to protest. He has the right to call attention to the principles that will be violated by the government in passing such a law and taking such a course. Yet that government is independent and sovereign in its own realm and may enact such laws as to it seem expedient. And these laws may affect the citizens of his own country and may bring hardships upon them. But in the enforcement of these laws it is the place and the rights of the citizen or ambassador to see to it and insist that the procedure *at every step* in the case shall be strictly in accordance with its own jurisprudence and with all the principles upon which the laws are based.

Every Christian has the right to protest against any earthly government making any laws on the subject of religion! That is out of their jurisdiction. That invades the realm of the kingdom of God and infringes the rights of the people of the kingdom of God. Therefore, every ambassador of Jesus Christ has the inalienable right to protest against any such thing by any government on the earth.

But upon their power and their asserted right to make laws, these governments do go ahead and make laws respecting religion and then they arrest us and bring us before their tribunals for violating these laws. And when they do that, we have the right to insist that they shall strictly conform to their own laws and the constitutional principles upon which the governments rest. This the Christian, the heavenly citizen, has the right to do *in addition* to the right to protest against their right to make any such laws at all.

There is another thought we may look at before turning to the Scripture illustration of this principle. As for the governments of earth, on their own part they count us their citizens or subjects, even after we have become citizens of the heavenly country. That is, earthly governments do not recognize the transference of our citizenship from that government into the heavenly one; and this brings a conflict many times. If every government would recognize this transference of citizenship and every man that professes to be a Christian from its roll of citizens or subjects, there would not be so much difficulty on this point nor so many controversies arising.

But these governments do not do that; they propose to hold on to the man even after he has transferred his citizenship, and sometimes they will assert their right to hold him, just as we have learned in the lesson this evening already. They assert their right to control citizens of the heavenly kingdom as though they were still citizens of their former kingdom. We have transferred our citizenship to another country – I am talking now of Seventh-day Adventists – and are citizens of the heavenly country. But on the part of the United States we are still counted as citizens of the United States, because the Constitution says that all persons who *are born here* or are *naturalized* "are citizens of the United States and the States in which they may reside."

Though by our own *choice* we are citizens of heaven and not citizens of the United States any more, the United States still holds us as citizens.

Some of these days we are going to come in conflict with United States law as well as State law – not because *we* are doing wrong but because *they* are doing wrong. We shall be arrested, prosecuted, and required to respect the law and to obey the law. When they do that, as ambassadors for Christ and citizens of the kingdom of God, we have this double right to protest against their right to make the law, because it infringes on the rights of the people of the kingdom of God, to which we belong, and we have the right also to insist that every step they take shall be strictly according to the fundamental, constitutional principles upon which the law is professedly based. Now I ask you to think of this when you get it in the Bulletin. Please read it over, because there is a great deal that concerns us in these principles.

For there we have an account that goes over this very ground and illustrates to us this principle of holding the government to its own principles, when once without our choice it has taken us under its jurisdiction and proposes to deal with us.

Now I will turn to the Scripture illustration.

Saul of Tarsus was born a citizen of the Roman Empire, as we are of the United States. When he met Christ, he was born again, and thus became a citizen of the kingdom of God. Then he was *the Apostle Paul.* His dependence was upon the King of his own country from that time on; his allegiance was to Him; his trust was in Him; he left everything to Him to be managed. But there came a time when the Roman government took him under their jurisdiction and when she did, he required her to take every step according to the principles of Roman citizenship and Roman law.

In Acts 21:27 and on to 25:11, there is an interesting story which let us now take up and study. Out of deference to James, "the brother of the Lord," and the others in Jerusalem who had been in the gospel before him, Paul allowed himself to be persuaded to take a course that was wrong (see Sketches from the Life of Paul) and which brought him into the place and position where the mob broke loose upon him as related in chapter 21:27. Read it.

Now who let loose that mob upon Paul: God did it? For the Spirit of Prophecy tells us that at the moment when he was talking with the high priest as to the offering that should be made, which was a blood offering, a sin offering which would be practically a denial of Jesus Christ if it had not [sic] been done, the mob broke loose and saved him from doing it. The Lord saved him from the consequences of the effort of the brethren to get him to compromise in principle, out of deference to whom he yielded that far.

But how did he get into the hands of the Roman authorities? When he saw that the mob desired to kill him, methinks I hear him calling loudly for the Roman governor to save him from the mob: "Call the Roman governor. Hurry up, and bring in the troops. They are going to kill me. I am a Roman citizen. I appeal unto Caesar. Hurry up, hurry up, call down the captain of the temple, the Roman officer. Don't, please don't, let them murder me."

Did I hear aright? Did he do that? No, no, no. And why not? The captain of the temple was right there and near enough to hear him call if he had done it. According to Roman law wasn't he a citizen? And therefore was it not his place to call on the Roman power to protect him? He didn't do it anyway.

No. He was the Lord's. He was in the hands of God, and he would let the Lord take care of him. So the Spirit of Prophecy tells us that God took him here and kept him from that day until the day of his death, nearly all the time in prison, so that the Church lost his loving personal ministry because of that compromising attitude into which the brethren had asked him to go.

Well, now he is in the hands of the Roman authorities. Did he ask for it? No. Did he start it? No. Did he assert his Roman citizenship as a claim on which he should be taken and protected by the Roman authorities? No.

He asked of the officer permission to speak to the multitude. It was granted, and taking his place on the stairs he made the speech in chapter 22:1-21 where he said that the Lord had said to him, "Depart, for I will send thee far hence unto the Gentiles." At the word, "Gentiles," their fury broke out again and they yelled, Away with such a fellow from the earth, for it is not fit that he should live. And as they cast off their clothes and threw dust into the air the captain took him away and, thinking from the turmoil about him that he must be some desperate character, ordered him to be scourged. But this was forbidden by Roman law to be inflicted on Roman citizens. And now as he is in the hands of the Roman authorities, he has the right to insist that they shall proceed according to their own law, and therefore he said, "Is it lawful for you to scourge a man that is a Roman and uncondemned?" This word stopped the proceeding.

The next day the captain, desiring to know what all the row was really about, had the Sanhedrin assemble and sent Paul before them; he had barely began to speak, when the high priest commanded some to "smite him on the mouth." "The Paul said unto him, God shall smite thee, thou whited wall: for sittest thou to judge me after the law, and commandest me to be smitten contrary to the law?" Thus, he holds these to the law which governed them in their procedure against him. He was not there from his own choice. They had brought him there without any of his effort. And he had the right to insist that they should conform to their own law and proceed according thereto, and this he did.

While he had said, "I am a Pharisee, the son of a Pharisee: of the hope and resurrection of the dead I am called in question," this set the Pharisees and Sadducees against each other. And as with the Sadducees trying to kill him and the Pharisees trying to rescue him, he was about to be pulled to pieces, the captain sent down the soldiers to take him by force from them.

Next, certain ones entered into that curse upon themselves neither to eat nor drink till they had killed Paul. By Paul's nephew this was made known to him and to the captain. In consequence the captain ordered out four hundred and seventy soldiers and by them sent Paul away by night and had him brought to Caeserea and delivered to Felix the governor.

A few days afterward the high priest and the Sanhedrin went down to Caeserea to prosecute Paul and did do so, hiring Tertullus, an orator, for their spokesman. After the hearing, Felix deferred the case till Lysias might come down. With numerous hearings and delays, two years passed, and Festus succeeded Felix as governor, with Paul still in bonds to please the Jews.

Festus passing through Jerusalem, the Jews brought Paul's case up and asked to have him brought up to Jerusalem – intending to kill him as he came. Festus however refused, and told them to send down their prosecutions and accuse him at Caeserea. They sent their prosecutors down with Festus, and the next day after his arrival "sitting on the judgment seat commanded Paul to be brought."

The Jews "laid many and grievous complaints against Paul, which they could not prove [chap. 25:1-7], while he answered for himself, Neither against the law of the Jews, neither against the temple, nor yet against Caesar, have I offended anything at all."

"But Festus, willing to do the Jews a pleasure, answered Paul and said, Wilt thou go up to Jerusalem and there be judged of these things before me?"

"Then said Paul, I stand at Caesar's judgment seat, where I ought to be judged: to the Jews have I done no wrong, *as thou very well knowest.*"

He was not at "Caesar's judgment seat" by any choice or effort or desire of his own. Caesar had taken him and *had kept him* all this time without finding any fault in him. Against no one had he done any wrong, and this the governor "very well" knew. The Roman governor therefore had no right to deliver him to the Jews merely to please them.

Therefore, Paul continued and put a climax to the whole case in these words:

> For if I be an offender or have committed anything worthy of death, I refuse not to die; but if there be none of these things whereof these accuse me, *no man may deliver me unto them.* I APPEAL UNTO CAESAR.

The Roman governor as a Roman had no right to deliver a Roman to the judgment of the Jews. That Roman citizen, being in the hands of a Roman governor, under Roman jurisdiction, by *their* own choice, had the right to insist that the Roman authorities should obey their own law and confirm their own principles, and instead of delivering him to the Jews, they should keep him and try him and conduct the whole case according to Roman law.

There is the secret of Paul's appeal to Caesar. It is a divine example worked out on the principle of giving to the Christian a double right as ambassadors of God and citizens of the heavenly kingdom, *first,* to protest against any interference on the part of any earthly government with the laws of the people of the kingdom of God or the kingdom of God itself; and *secondly,* when they do interfere and without our choice or desire take us under their jurisdiction, then we have the divine right as ambassadors and citizens of another country to demand that they shall follow in strictness the law which governs them in their own realm.

God will take care of us under the law and in the realm of which we are citizens and in the kingdom to which we belong. He will attend to that, and he will conduct all these affairs according to his own righteous ways. And in the country where we may be sojourning when they do take us under their jurisdiction, we have the right to demand that they shall deal with us according to the principles of their law.

Sermon 6

February 11, 1895

THERE are two or three other scriptures that we will notice in the line of study that we have been following the past three evenings, and we will begin where the lesson stopped last night – Acts 25:11, with the words, "I appeal unto Caesar."

We followed the record last night from its beginning up to that point and found that in the common view of that subject, Paul never did appeal to Caesar. After Caesar had *taken* him, Paul held Caesar to his own principles and laws.

The particular principle that we are studying now is the right of a citizen of the kingdom of God, an ambassador of Christ, to require other kingdoms and authorities to conform strictly to their own rules and the laws that govern themselves in their dealing with him.

The 16th chapter of Acts is another, beginning with the 16th verse; they were at Philippi.

> It came to pass as we went to prayer a certain damsel possessed with a spirit of divination met us, which brought her masters much gain by soothsaying; the same followed Paul and us, and cried saying, These men are the servants of the most high God, which shew unto us the way of salvation. And this she did many days. But Paul, being grieved, turned and said to the spirit, I command these in the name of Jesus Christ to come out of her. And he came out the same hour. And when her masters saw that the hope of their gains was gone, they caught Paul and Silas and drew them into the marketplace unto the rulers.

And these were *Roman* rulers too, because Philippi was a Roman colony and had special privileges from the emperor.

> And brought them to the magistrates, saying, These men, being Jews, do exceedingly trouble our city and teach customs which are not lawful for us to receive, neither to observe, being Romans. And the multitude rose up together against them, and the magistrates rent off their clothes and commanded to beat them.

And they said, No, we appeal to Caesar. Didn't they? They did not. But they were Roman citizens, were they not? Why didn't they appeal to Caesar then? Were they not about to be abused and beaten? What would you have done? No, we need not say,

What would you have done, but, What are you going to do? That is the question now.

> And when they had laid many stripes upon them, they cast them into prison, charging the jailer to keep them safely, who, having received such a charge, thrust them into the inner prison and made their feet fast in the stocks. And at midnight Paul and Silas prayed and sang praises unto God, and the prisoners heard them.

Then follows the account of the earthquake and the conversion of the jailer and his household, and their baptism.

Now the 35th verse:

> And when it was day, the magistrates sent the sergeants, saying, Let those men go. And the keeper of the prison told this, saying to Paul, The magistrates have sent to let you go: now, therefore, depart and go in peace. But Paul said unto them, They have beaten us openly uncondemned, being Romans, and have cast us into prison; and now do they thrust us out privily? Nay, verily, but let them come themselves and fetch us out.

They violated every Roman law that governed themselves in their city; now they want us to go sneaking out of this place. No, sir. You come and take us out. You put us in here; take us out.

> And the sergeants told these words unto the magistrates, and they feared when they heard that these were Romans. And they came and besought them, and brought them out, and desired them to depart out of the city. And they went out of the prison and entered into the house of Lydia, and when they had seen the brethren, they comforted them and departed.

There is another passage: 2 Cor. 11:23-25, speaking of those who are boasting of their standing and so on:

> Are they ministers of Christ? (I speak as a fool), I am more; in labors more abundant, in stripes above measure, in prisons more frequent, in deaths oft. Of the Jews five times received I forty stripes save one. Thrice was I *beaten with rods.*

Now that beating with rods was the Roman punishment. Of course the Jews were limited by the law to forty stripes save one. Five times he got that, but this beating with the rods was not simply Jewish whippings but Roman scourgings – beating with the Roman rods, and *he a Roman citizen.* And we have no record anywhere that he ever appealed to Caesar under any such circumstances or any circumstances at all. When Caesar had taken him and kept him over two years in prison and then wanted to deliver him up to the Jews, then to Caesar or Caesar's lieutenant, he said, "No sir. I stand at Caesar's judgment seat, where I ought to be judged. I appeal unto Caesar."

Question from the audience: "Why did he even then appeal to his Roman citizenship instead of to his heavenly ambassadorship?"

What I am saying is that he *did* depend upon his *heavenly ambassadorship* and upon his heavenly King, until the Roman power had taken him under its jurisdiction, and then he simply held the Roman authorities to the Roman law. But in the common idea that has been held on this subject, you would get the idea that Paul appealed to his Roman citizenship on every occasion when there was any danger, when the fact is that he never did it at all.

Three times at least he received Roman scourgings and made no use of his claim to Roman citizenship, made no appeal whatever to the civil power. But when he was taken into their hands and held under their control and kept within the power of Rome, *then* and *not till then* did he make any use of the Roman power. But then when the Roman captain was about to scourge him, which was unlawful, Paul said, "It is not lawful for you to scourge a man that is a Roman and uncondemned.

Under these circumstances and under no others did he ever make any appeal to or any use of the Roman power or make any use of his Roman citizenship. For when he went preaching the gospel and wherever he went he was mobbed, he was stoned, he was "shamefully entreated" and yet in the whole record there is no hint of his ever in any case making any appeal to any earthly power or any use of his Roman citizenship. Now if this was all written for our example and for our learning, then is this what we are to learn and is it not about time we were learning it? He put his trust in God, the Sovereign of the kingdom to which he belonged and where his true citizenship lay. Why shall we not do the same.

Daniel was in the country of Babylon and Medo-Persia. That is true. And whenever the time comes that one nation shall come with its armies against the country where you are or may be sojourning and shall take you with a great multitude of people and bind you and carry you off to their own country and keep you as slaves of the king, and the king shall put you in his palace, in his service – then you can decide easily enough, I think, whether there is not a difference between that and voluntarily *seeking* for political position. This is the record in my Bible about Daniel and how he got there. And when your turn comes and you get into such a place as that, I don't suppose anybody would find any objection to your serving the king in the place he puts you. But as long as you are at liberty to keep out of such places as that, I do not think you can cite Daniel as a justification for your deliberately going in there, in the face of the plainest teachings of Christ.

If I were taken captive, as Daniel was, and was appointed by the king, as some of Daniel's people were, to brickmaking or building the walls of Babylon round about, I suppose I should work in the brickyard. Then, if the king should take me out of there and send me to school, as he did Daniel and some of his brethren, I think it is altogether likely I should go on in school and study to the best of my ability. And after I had done that, if he should take me out and put me in his palace as a doorkeeper, I should perform the office of doorkeeper; if he should finally even bring me into his court to stand before the king, as the record is of Daniel and his three brethren, I should stand before the king. And if I should be honest and faithful enough and God should give me wisdom to interpret deep things to the king, as God gave to Daniel, and the king should appreciate God's blessing in that enough to honor God for it and should at last put a chain of gold around my neck and put me in position next to the king, I should stand there.

But I am satisfied that until that time does come and such circumstances as that do arise, I would not be justified in running for political or any other kind of office, nor in taking any political steps to get somebody else elected, nor in taking any part in city government or State government nor in national government nor in politics of any kind. Jesus Christ did not, and He says, "ye are not of the world, even as I am not of the world." "As My Father sent me, even so send I you," and "as He is, so are we in this world."

Joseph was sold by his brethren, was bought and made a slave, was carried into Egypt as a slave, sold there as a slave and served as a slave. His integrity to God and faithfulness to His law got him into prison and there he remained quite a while. His faithfulness there, his quiet demeanor, and the atmosphere of the Spirit of God that was with him gave him favor in the sight of the jailer, who put him in charge of the doors and the other prisoners round about – what now would be called a "trusty" in the penitentiary. And God was with him still. The time came when God would prepare for the salvation of Israel – that is, Jacob and his family and all Israel to come – and He gave to Pharaoh remarkable dreams, as He did to Nebuchadnezzar in the days of Daniel. The king sent for Joseph, and he interpreted the dream for Pharaoh. Pharaoh wanted somebody to take charge of the matters that had to be arranged to prepare Egypt against the famine that was to come. Said Pharaoh, "Who knows as much about this as the man who knows all about it? Therefore, the one that knows about this, the one that has explained it and told us what is going to come is the one to take charge of it and carry it out. I put everything in Egypt into his hands, only in the throne will I be above him." Everything in all Egypt Pharaoh gave to Joseph's care.

And if you ever get into such a position as that through *such experiences as that,* I do not think that even I would raise any objection to your performing the duties of the place to which you are thus called. But I do deny that these experiences, as my Bible gives them, have any bearing whatever upon the course of Seventh-day Adventists now anywhere on the earth, who are out of jail, free to choose where they will go and what they will do.

Now I want to state a little further upon the principle that no Christian, being a citizen of the kingdom of God, can of right *start* any procedure in connection with civil government. *After* it is started by the government itself, that is another question, and we have studied that. I repeat therefore, that upon the principles which govern kingdoms and governments, the very principle of the law that underlies the whole subject of government, whether it be law in heaven or law in earth, a Christian cannot *start* any procedure in connection with civil government.

And of all Christians, Seventh-day Adventists cannot do it. The very keeping of the Sabbath forbids it. For to submit a case to a court, he submits it to the procedure of the court. Now every court in the land can go strictly according to law and to all the rules of the courts and hold court and try the case *on the Sabbath.* The Sabbath-keeper cannot attend court on the Sabbath. But he has started the case himself, and in starting the case he submits the case to the procedure of the court. Yet if the court in regular proceeding even without any design calls the case *on the Sabbath,* he will be required to attend on the Sabbath. He cannot do this though and keep the Sabbath. But to refuse, while starting the case himself, is only to trifle with the court. This the court cannot allow, and therefore may levy a fine for nonattendance. But if the fine is paid, it is paid for keeping the Sabbath. If it is not paid and he goes to prison instead, he cannot justly count it persecution, because without any fault on the part of the court it is only the straight consequence of his own action in starting the case. Therefore, the very words, "Remember the Sabbath day *to* keep it holy," forbids the starting of any case in court, because that commandment forbids us to start on a course that may prevent the keeping of the Sabbath holy.

And before I read, as I shall read that, I want to say that what I shall read is to meet an objection that is in the minds of a good many, that these things that are being brought out here are very wide of the mark. I have not heard any denial yet that the principle is there or that the principle is all right, but it is the following up of the principle that some do not accept. Well, if you acknowledge a principle *as* a principle which you are not willing to follow wherever it goes, then you would better give up the principle.

In order that all may know that this is not new, I shall read from the *American Sentinel* of 1893. Of course the article was not dealing with the subject *in the way that we are talking on it tonight,* but it is the same principle and the whole principle is there, and the certain consequences of the violation of the principle are also there.

I read from the *American Sentinel* of July 6, 1893, and I shall read perhaps the most of the article upon that subject:

> The Sunday managers resorted to the United States courts and got swamped the first thing. They called upon the courts to decide the question. The courts did decide the question. And now they refuse to accept the decision. They submitted their cause to the courts and now refuse to accept the decision *because it was not on their side.* Well, then, as they are determined to have their own way anyhow, what in the world did they want with the courts in the first place?

Unless you are ready to accept the decision of a court of this world, you cannot *voluntarily* make any appeal to it. As certainly as you do, you are pledged, by every principle of government heavenly or earthly, to accept the decision, and if it is against you there is nobody to blame but yourself. And I say that that has been there all these two years and yet in 1894 some Seventh-day Adventists went right over that ground and found themselves caught just as certainly as these National Reformers did. However, the Seventh-day Adventist did not refuse to accept the decision. They accepted the decision, but it was at the expense of their paying a fine for keeping the Sabbath. Under the circumstances there was nothing else to do. I read on:

> Well, then, as they are determined to have their own way anyhow, what in the world did they want with the courts in the first place? Ah! They only wanted to use the court as a tool in enforcing *their own decision* and their own will upon the people of the United States.

And if this had been written in this month of February 1895 of some procedure of Seventh-day Adventists, every word of it would have been exactly as it is; it need not be changed a particle.

Now I am not bringing this as a charge, or a reproach or an accusation against any Seventh-day Adventist or to find fault with any. I am only stating the fact. I am only sorry it is so; as sorry as I can be that it is so. But in the Bible it is written, "Now all these things happened unto them for ensamples: and they are written for our admonition, upon whom the ends of the world are come." And when we ourselves, in violation of the principles which we profess go over the ground of National Reformers themselves and get caught just as certainly as they did, then shall not we take warning from these examples as much as from those of our brethren in A.D. 35 or 40 in Judea? This principle is just as applicable in Maryland or any other state of the Union as it is in Judea or in Illinois. I say again, I am not finding fault. I know all make mistakes. All that I am saying is, Shall we not learn lessons from *our own* mistakes as well as from those of other people? I need not tell where this occurred. It is not necessary that this should be known. The fact is all that is needed, for the *place* will be just *where you are,* if you do not become better acquainted with principle than many now are.

Calling attention again to the *Sentinel,* there comes in there a little history about their case as to what it was in the court, which I need not read. Then coming back to the principle, we continue:

> Of course it is always understood that *especially* the party which *initiates* legal procedure shall accept in good faith the final decision. With the other party it is not necessarily so, for he may be dragged into it and forced into court by the course of the initiative and he is not bound to accept any decision, because the whole procedure may be one of persecution and therefore wrong from the beginning.
>
> But with the initiative it is not so. It is in the nature of things, it inheres in the very idea of legal government that the party who resorts to the law, the party who begins legal procedure, shall accept in good faith the final decision. Otherwise there is no use of legal

government; violence becomes the only procedure, and might the only source of appeal. And that is anarchy indeed.

Then unless you, as a citizen of the kingdom of God, are ready to accept the decision of an earthly court, you cannot take the initiative; you cannot start the case, because to start the case and then not to accept the decision is the principle of anarchy itself – it annihilates government. But Christians are not in the world for that purpose. We are here for another purpose. We are to recognize *and to respect* without any question the systems of government that are already established, *as they are established* by those who have established them, and not to inculcate a principle nor to follow a course that can only annihilate the very foundations of the governments that are here.

Now it is the everlasting truth that the Sunday party did take the initiative and have kept it from the first inception of the act of Congress clear up to this final decision of the court. And now, instead of accepting the final decision in good faith, they do not accept it at all, but resort to violence. The party of the second part, the party that was dragged unto the procedure and into court, freely announces beforehand that if the decision is against them, they will accept it in good faith and so conform to it. The party of the first part, the party which takes and holds the initiative from the beginning, openly disregards and refuses to accept the final decision and boldly announces their purpose to pursue such a course as will make the fair "a financial failure." And these are the ones who so scathingly denounce the course of the directory as "anarchistic" ad "rebellious."

The sum of the whole matter is this: It is essential to the very idea and existence of legal government that the party who takes the initiative in legal procedure shall accept in good faith and so conform to the final decision. Not to do so but to act the same as though there had been no decision *after the final decision has been rendered* is in itself to renounce legal government and is essentially anarchistic and rebellious. The Sunday-law party is and has been from the beginning the party of the initiative in this legal procedure. This party, instead of accepting in good faith the final decision, ignores it entirely and resorts to violence – the boycott – after that decision has been rendered. It therefore follows inevitably and the demonstration is complete that the action of the Sunday managers in this matter is truly the action and the only one which is indeed "anarchistic in conception and rebellious in execution." This is the logic of the situation, and it is the exact truth. Their very action only further illustrates it, and their calling other people "anarchists," "rebels," "traitors," "atheists," and so on, can never disprove this abiding truth.

This is the same conclusion to which we were forced last year by the logic of their course in securing the act of Congress requiring the closing of the Fair. It is the only just conclusion that can ever be reached from the basis of ecclesiastical dictation or control in the affairs of the government. And this for the plain and simple reason that on the part of the ecclesiastics it is never intended that they shall pay any respectful attention to any law or any decision that does not suit them. Therefore, the only purpose for which they ever resort to either legislation or judicial procedure is that the governmental authority may be at their disposal with which to execute upon the people their arbitrary will. And this, in itself, is at once to sweep away all really just or properly legal government.

> And all this only makes the more manifest the divine wisdom which commands the total separation of the ecclesiastical and the civil powers, which forbids the Church to have any connection with the State. It also demonstrates the wisdom of the men who made the government of the United States, in embodying in the Constitution and the supreme law the divine idea for governments – the total separation of Church and State. And this which has been done and is now being done by the churches is only a hint and the beginning of the sea of troubles into which the government will be plunged and indeed finally sunk by this gross disregard of the governmental principle established by our fathers and announced by Jesus Christ.
>
> So long as the Church keeps herself entirely separate from the State, she can consistently and *rightly* disregard any and all legislative acts, judicial decrees or executive powers put forth upon religious questions [or that touch religious practices]; because she ever denies the right of government to touch religion or any religious question in any way.

And this is *present* truth. It is present truth for us as well as for the National Reformers.

> But when she forgets her place and her high privileges and herself actually invites governmental jurisdiction of religious observances, she then, by so doing, and in justice forfeits her power of protest and her right to disregard governmental commands in things religious, while in fact and in practice she refuses to let it go, so that whenever the government does not do according to her will, she openly and intentionally disregards the very authority which she herself has invoked. She thus becomes the chiefest example and source of lawlessness and the swiftest instrument of governmental ruin.

And with us especially as we have seen, this principle covers all cases. Shall we learn what the principle is indeed and stick to it? That is the question for us all.

Sermon 7

February 13, 1895

The lesson tonight will be directly connected with the lesson that closed on page 33 of the Bulletin, that is, the close of the second lesson, the one on the position and aims of the papacy, and that you may get the connection clearly, I will read a few lines from the last of it, taking again the sentence that was quoted from the letter from Rome, that what we do know is, that a world is in its death agony, and that we are entering upon the night which must inevitably precede the dawn, and that in preparation for this agony of death of the world, the papacy is casting off the old slough, putting on a new form in every conceivable way in order to fulfill her mission in these times that are to come, as was read.

[Here was read on page 33 from the quotation, "What we do know is that a world is in its death agony" to the end of that lesson.]

Now we will study that a little while in the Scriptures. And these scriptures, like all others that we are quoting and studying here, are scriptures with which we are all perfectly familiar; scripture which all have often quoted and of which we expect the fulfillment. And the first one is in Rev. 13:8:

> All that dwell upon the earth shall worship him, whose names are not written in the book of life of the Lamb slain from the foundation of the world.

That shows that the papacy is to have control of this whole world and all that is in it, and of everybody that is in it, except only those whose names are written in the book of life of the Lamb – those who belong to the kingdom of God and are separated from this world. So that, as an actual fact, the papacy does – that Scripture shows it, too – have possession in the times when these things shall culminate, of all those of this world, because Christ's disciples are not of this world. There stands the word – not that God wants it so, but it will be so in spite of all that He wants to the contrary – that all whose names are not in the book of life and retained there will worship the beast. They will do it; it matters not what they have their minds made up to do or not to do; that thing they will do. They cannot help doing it, because not having their names in the book of life of the Lamb, they will be of this world entirely and therefore will be of the papacy entirely, because whatsoever is of this world is of the papacy in the times in which we live. This shows that the power of the world is brought once more into her hand.

Now a verse in the 7th chapter of Daniel. This power will be used by her for the only purpose for which she ever used any power in the world or for which she ever shall use it – to compel all to do her bidding. All that she ever used any power for was to force upon everybody her dictates. All that she wants with power now is to do that, and everything that she is doing anywhere on the earth is devoted to that one point of getting back her power over the world. The evidences of this that have been given in the lessons we have already had are before all, and I need not cite any of these.

And so it is written, 21st and 22nd verses:

> I beheld and the same horn made war with the saints and prevailed against them, until the Ancient of days came, and judgment was given to the saints of the Most High, and the time came that the saints possessed the kingdom.

That is at the coming of Christ, of course. So that when it is written that "all that dwell upon the earth shall worship him," it is also written of the same time that this power which she shall have gained and is now gaining over the world and in the world is used for the purpose of compelling all to do her bidding – to compel all to worship the beast. And those who will not do that, she makes war against, till the day that they enter into the kingdom of glory at the coming of the Lord.

Another verses, Revelation 17:1, 2:

> And there came one of the seven angels which had the seven vials and talked with me, saying unto me, Come hither; I will show unto thee the judgment of the great whore that sitteth upon many waters.

Now before reading the second verse, I wish to call a little more attention to the first verse.

The angel that reveals this judgment and explains it and the time in which it comes is one of the angels that has the seven last plagues to be poured out. This shows that the revelation of this judgment is in the time immediately preceding the plagues, for it is one of the angels to whom was given one of the vials of the plagues to be poured out. So that when the time comes that the plagues are imminent and are as it were hanging over the world, then this chapter will be understood, *then* it will shine forth by the revelation of Jesus Christ, the revelation of the angel which He sends.

This, being one of the angels having the vials, he does not say, Come here and I will show thee *the woman;* he does not say, Come here, and I will show thee the great whore; but "Come hither; I will show thee THE JUDGMENT of the great whore."

Then again: As it is one of the seven angels that have the seven last plagues who reveals this, *that* shows that the revelation will be in the time when the plagues are just hanging over the world and are ready to fall. And as the revelation is *the judgment* of her and not the revelation of herself that shows that the revelation and this chapter which describes it and the times which are connected with it – that *there* and *then* will be the time of the revelation of these things that the angel has to tell.

Now I am not starting on a study of the seventeenth chapter of Revelation, nor undertaking to explain that chapter. I am reading this simply to get the time when the thing is to be, and now for the second verse:

> The judgment of the great whore that sitteth upon many waters; with whom the kings of the earth have committed fornication, and the inhabitants of the earth have been made drunk with the wine of her fornication.

When? When does this angel appear? Just before *the judgment of her* falls. Who is he? One of the seven that have the plagues. So that, by this double count, this is plainly just before the judgment of her. When is it, then, that the kings of the earth are referred to in this verse? At the same time, assuredly. At that time what will be the condition of the kings of the earth – not *some* of them, but *them* – as respects this great harlot? O, they have all held illicit connection with her. And the inhabitants of the earth at that time have all been made drunk by her. Then that tells the same thing that the other verse does, that "all that dwell upon the earth shall worship him, whose names are not written in the book of life."

Well, after the angel goes on describing this *judgment* of her, or rather the events that immediately precede the judgment, then another angel joins. Rev. 18:1:

> After these things I saw another angel come down from heaven, having great power and the earth was lightened with his glory. And he cried mightily with a strong voice, saying, Babylon the great is fallen, is fallen, and is become the habitation of devils and the hold of every foul spirit and a cage of every unclean and hateful bird. For all nations. . .

How many of them? All. When? In this time when one of the seven angels with the seven plagues appears and tells of the judgment of Babylon.

> For all nations have drunk of the wine of the wrath of her fornication, and the kings of the earth have committed fornication with her.

How many of them? –All of them.

> And the merchants of the earth are waxed rich through the abundance of her delicacies. And I heard another voice *from heaven*.

Do not forget then; it is a voice *from heaven* saying it.

> Saying, Come out of her my people, that ye be not partakers of her sins and that ye receive not of her plagues. For her sins have reached unto heaven and God hath remembered her iniquities.

What has He remembered her iniquities for? What does that mean, that God hath remembered her iniquities? Back in Egypt it was said of the Lord, "I have remembered my covenant with Abraham, Isaac, and Jacob; I have remembered the promises I made to your fathers. And I will deliver you with a stretched out arm and with *great* judgments." Ex. 6:5,6. When he "remembered" that the thing *was done* that had been promised formerly. "God hath remembered her iniquities." And this shows that this remembrance of her iniquities means the visiting of the judgment upon her iniquities.

> Reward her even as she rewarded you and double unto her double according to her works; in the cup which she hath filled, fill to her double. How much she hath glorified herself and lived deliciously, so much torment and sorrow give her; for she saith in her heart, I sit a queen and am no widow and shall see no sorrow. Therefore, shall her plagues come in one day, death and mourning, and famine. And she shall be utterly burned with fire, for strong is the Lord God who judgeth her.

This is still the description which the angel gave when he said, "Come hither; I will show unto thee the judgment of the great whore."

> And the kings of the earth, who have committed fornication and lived deliciously with her, shall bewail her, and lament for her, when they shall see the smoke of her burning, standing afar off for the fear of her torment, saying, alas, alas, that great city Babylon, that mighty city! for in one hour is thy judgment come.

Thus when Babylon triumphs, she is destroyed "in one hour," the shortest period of time that is measured in the Bible, aside from the resurrection moment, which is the "twinkling of an eye." So that when this judgment does fall, it falls in that way, and *before it falls,* these warnings are given, and God gives us signs by which we may know and mark the way up to the time when that is the thing, and *the one thing,* that comes next.

Now before our eyes in the daily papers, in the situation even as we have examined it in the previous lessons, the papacy is *now* carrying on the very movement that is here marked out and is succeeding at every step. In former lessons we have merely touched evidence as relates to the United States. Brother Robinson gave me a copy of *Present Truth* a day or two ago, and there, on the first page, are quotations from Catholic papers of London, touching the nations of Europe that are counted as not being exactly Catholic and how that these are falling more and more and one by one back into the hands of the papacy.

In the *American Sentinel* two or three weeks ago you had the evidence, taken from Catholic papers, as to Germany and Switzerland. The Catholic Church holds the balance of power in Germany – a Catholic for Chancellor of the German Empire, and the Catholic Church party in the *Reichstag* holding the balance of power, so that the government cannot do anything it wants to without their will and permission and they hold for the repeal of all the laws that have been enacted against the papacy or else nothing goes. And they are getting what they want as the days go by.

Switzerland has a Catholic for a president, and of him the *London Universe* says that he "is as papal as a Swiss guard." It is not strange therefore that the experiences which we have heard from brethren in Switzerland should be manifesting themselves against the truth of God and against the Lord.

The other day I saw a German paper in which the editor and proprietor spoke of a trip he had taken through Europe and, passing through Holland, he saw the parade of Catholics in celebrating the recovery of Holland to the Catholic Church.

In England, for the papacy to get control, only one thing remains of all the things that were done in making England a Protestant country and establishing the succession of sovereigns – all that remains is just that one requirement, that the sovereign shall be a Protestant. The oath to sustain the Protestant succession is gone. And the one remaining point that requires a Protestant succession has become so weakened that the papacy herself is in expectation that even this will soon be so modified that it may be at a moment set aside and she have control once more. About a year ago, the pope, in receiving a band of pilgrims from England and giving them his blessing said to them that there were many signs in favor of England's once more returning to the Church.

These are simply – well, they are more than *signs* of what is going on; they are the actual *facts* in the *proceedings themselves* of what is going on. We cannot count them as *signs;* they are the *thing itself.*

In these extracts from the Catholic papers that were printed in the *Present Truth,* the United States was mentioned among the countries where the papacy is having its greatest success; and directly in the line of these evidences that we have presented already in the lessons is the fact that the United States is to be used, as the pope says, in the molding all the other nations and that this country is to shape the destiny of the other nations, and the destiny of the other nations is always intended to be simply the return of the world to the papacy and to do her will and to promote her interests in the earth.

So then we stand in the presence and a long way forward, too, in the presence of the events that are bringing the fulfillment of these prophecies to the point when all nations indeed shall be actually joined once more to her. And when she shall have succeeded in all this movement that is being carried on, when these things are fulfilled, THEN her judgment falls. When that point is reached, when that time comes, in which she stands at the place where she can congratulate herself that all these nations are joined to her once more and she has lifted herself to the supremacy out of the turmoils and the agonies, the anarchy and the violence of every kind, to the supremacy, as she did once before, when this is fulfilled, that is the last thing that we shall see before her judgment falls.

A few years ago we preached the coming of the Lord, as we do yet. We preached everywhere the coming of the Lord, the *soon* coming of the Lord, even in the generation that is upon the earth and that generation a long way forward in its life.

Yet at the same time we told all the people to whom we preached that the Lord was coming, that He *could not come* until the United States government had recognized the Christian religion and had set up Sunday instead of the Sabbath. We told them, in other words, that he could not come until this government had made the image of the beast. Then, after having told them that the Lord is coming and coming soon and that the generation is far spent in which He will come, we had to tell them that *this thing* had to come *before He* could come, and then we turned to point out to them the steps that were taken and the progress that had been made toward that recognition of religion in the United States and the setting up of Sunday instead of the Sabbath. These things we told them were the signs by which they might mark the way up to that thing that should be done, and as soon as it should be done, then we would know the coming of the Lord was to be looked forward to as never before.

Now that has been done. We cannot in truth tell the people that the United States is *going* to recognize the Christian religion. We cannot tell the people any more that the United States government is *going to* put away the Sabbath of the Lord from the fourth commandment and put Sunday in its place. No man can do that and speak truly. Everyone that speaks the truth on that has to say *that has been done* and point the people simply to the official record in the proceedings of the government that shows it and there it stands. Therefore, as this is truly so, this text applies as never before, "*Now* is our salvation nearer than when we believed."

We also told the people that when that thing should succeed, the papacy would rise in triumph at the expense of the Protestants who were doing that and without their expectations and put herself in the place and would receive strength and influence and power from it to mold the world once more to her hand.

Well, we cannot say anymore that the papacy is *going to* do that. The only thing we can now say is. She *is doing* it, and point the people now to *the facts* which show that she *is* doing it and that that is her one grand scheme for the whole world, to be worked through this power which she already has upon the United States.

But the success of that scheme, the completion of that plan of hers, is simply the fulfillment of this prophecy that we have read, that all the nations would be joined to her; all would be worshiping her; the inhabitants of the earth connected with her; all the world under her hand; all worshiping her, and the power of all the world in her hands to pour out in wrath against those who fear God. The Scripture sets forth in prophecy precisely the thing that everyone of us sees and cannot help seeing, that the papacy is doing. And the very point that the prophecy sets out is the very point at which the papacy aims and toward which she is working and which, when she reaches it, will see the prophecy fulfilled, "I sit a queen and am no widow and shall see no sorrow." And when that plan of the papacy is completed and the prophecy and the papacy meet at that point, then, says the word, "In one hour" from that point her judgment comes; "She shall be utterly burned with fire: for strong is the Lord God who judgeth her."

Where then are we but in the very days when the judgment of the great whore in the plagues of God are hanging over the world? There is where we certainly stand.

Then see this: As at the first we were obliged to point the people to the signs that marked the coming of the image of the beast and as we are now beyond that and can cite those things no more; *so now* we are in the time when event after event simply marks the steps which we are to take in passing to the coming of the Lord; and a good many of those steps are taken and we are beyond them.

And in this time what word has the Lord put there to be given to the world? "Come out of her, my people." What for? Why, "that ye be not partakes of her sins and that ye receive not of her plagues."

The success of this movement of the papacy that is being carried on *is its ruin;* her success is her ruin. Her triumph is her destruction, in an hour. Then whoever would not be ruined must separate from her, leave here entirely. And whosoever would not see his fellowmen endangered and ruined must, in the fear of God and the love of souls, say to them, "Escape for your life; for ruin is about to fall."

Her ruin will be how widespread? How much does it embrace? How much is under her control? How many are worshiping her? How far does her wrath extend? And how many are made drunk with the wine of the wrath of her fornication? *All the world.* Then when the judgment falls upon her, how widespread will be the judgment? *worldwide.* When the ruin falls, how complete is the ruin? Utterly. It is said that he cometh up out of the bottomless pit, and "goeth into perdition." "Perdition" means *utter destruction;* she goes into utter destruction.

Then as certainly as her influence is worldwide; as certainly as all nations are joined to her and the inhabitants of the earth are drunk with the wine of the wrath of her fornication and as certainly as that all that dwell upon the earth are worshiping him, whose names are not written in the book of life of the Lamb; so certainly all this shows that everyone will fall in the ruin and will be ruined by the ruin, whose name is not in the book of life.

Then, also as certainly as we stand here, so certainly God has given a message to us in the midst of these events and that message is to warn the world that it is indeed "in its death agony," that out of that death agony the papacy triumphs, that her triumph is her certain ruin, and that whoever will escape must "*come out of her.*"

Now I think we have time to bring a word here that will illustrate this thing so forcibly that all can see it. There was a Babylon of old. God caused the prophet to write out her judgment. In the 50th and 51st chapters of Jeremiah there is written out, in prophecy, the judgment of Babylon. I am not going to read a description of it; all can read it at your leisure, because there is a great deal in it for us even now, but we will read the last verses of the 51st chapter, beginning with the 59th verse:

> The word which Jeremiah, the prophet, commanded Seraiah the son of Neriah, the son of Masseiah, when he went with Zedekiah [margin: on behalf of Zedekiah] the king of Judah into Babylon in the fourth year of his reign. And this Seraiah was a quiet prince. So Jeremiah wrote in a book all the evil that should come upon Babylon, even all these words that are written against Babylon. And Jeremiah said to Seraiah, When thou comest to Babylon and shalt see and shalt read all these words; then shalt thou say, O Lord, thou hast spoken against this place, to cut it off, that none shall remain in it, neither man nor beast, but that it shall be desolate forever. And it shall be, when thou hast made an end of reading this book, that thou shalt bind a stone to it, and cast it in the midst of Euphrates; and thou shalt say, Thus shall Babylon sink, and shall not rise from the evil that I will bring upon her, and they shall be weary.

Look at Rev. 18:21, in connection with this, in the judgment of Babylon, the description of it:

> A mighty angel took up a stone like a great millstone and cast it into the sea, saying, Thus with violence shall that great city Babylon be thrown down and shall be found no more at all.

Is there any correspondence between these two stones? Assuredly there is. Then that sinking of old Babylon pointed to the sinking of Babylon now; the judgment of Babylon in old time pointed to the judgment of Babylon in this time.

Now we notice Jeremiah 51:45: "My people, go ye out of the midst of her." God's people were in that Babylon; He had a people there. He did not want them to be there when the judgment of Babylon fell and caused her ruin; therefore, He said, "My people, go ye out of the midst of her and deliver ye every man his soul from the fierce anger of the Lord."

What is the word now? As the angel is about to cast that mighty stone into the sea and say, "Thus with violence shall that great city Babylon be thrown down and shall be found no more at all," the call is, 'Come out of her, my people, that ye be not partakers of here sins and that ye received not of her plagues. For her sins have reached unto heaven and God hath remembered her iniquities… For strong is the Lord God who judgeth her.'"

Reading again in Jeremiah of the old Babylon:

> And lest your heart faint and ye fear for the rumor that shall be heard in the land; a rumor shall both come *one year* and *after that* in *another year* shall come a rumor, and violence in the land, ruler against ruler.

The people in Babylon were to have two rumors as the sign for leaving Babylon. Two rumors of what? Two rumors of her fall, two rumors of her destruction. A rumor was to come one year that the armies of the Medes and Persians were on the way! But were they to be afraid that the ruin would be then and was everyone to go as quickly as he possibly could? NO. He could go if he chose, but the ruin was to be in another year.

So when the first rumor was to come, then was "*the preparation*" to "get ready" to go, so that when the second rumor should come, then they had to go or her ruin would be their ruin.

Accordingly, the Medo-Persian army started from Ecbatana in the spring of A.D. 539 – the year before Babylon fell – and went partly on the way and then stopped and stayed until the next spring. When the army started, of course the first rumor spread rapidly to Babylon. That was the first sign that everybody there should *prepare* to get away just as soon as they could. They could in a sense take their time for the actual going, but they must prepare and *be ready* at the *second* rumor, for when the second rumor came they *must* go or perish. When the next spring came, the "other year," the armies started again on the way to Babylon. Then came the second rumor of Babylon's ruin, and *the ruin came* with the second rumor, and whoever would escape the ruin had to flee when the rumor came.

Now look at modern Babylon and the two rumors of her fall. In 1844 there came the first rumor of the fall of Babylon. Rev. 14:6-8:

> I saw another angel fly in the midst of heaven, having the everlasting gospel to preach unto them that dwell on the earth, and to every nation, and kindred, and tongue, and people, saying with a loud voice, Fear God, and give glory to him; for the hour of his judgment is come: and worship him that made heaven, and earth, and the sea, and the fountains of waters. And there followed another angel saying with a loud voice, Fear God, and give glory to him, for the hour of his judgment is come, and worship him that made heaven and earth and the sea and the fountains of waters. And there followed another angel, saying, *Babylon is fallen, is fallen,* that great city, because she made all nations drink of the wine of the wrath of her fornication.

There was a rumor of the fall of Babylon; that was the *first* rumor. Now read Rev. 18:1-4:

> I saw another angel come down from heaven, having great power and the earth was lightened with his glory. And he cried *mightily* with *a strong voice,* saying, *Babylon the great is fallen, is fallen,* and is become the habitation of devils and the hold of every foul spirit and a cage of every unclean and hateful bird… And I heard another voice from heaven, saying, Come out of her, my people, that ye be not partakers of her sins and that ye receive not of her plagues.

When that second rumor comes, the rumor ceases only with the judgment which is her ruin. Are we in the time of the second rumor of the fall of the second Babylon? Oh, we are; we certainly are. Then as certainly as that second rumor of the Medo-Persian army in ancient Babylon meant her certain ruin, as certainly as that is true, so certainly we are in the midst of the second rumor now; and whoever will escape that ruin must go. "Come out of her, my people."

And therefore, as certainly as we to whom that message has been given have any care for the souls of men, any fear of God, or any love for the message which Jesus Christ has given us, what is there alone for us to do but to tell the people what is going on; what Babylon *has* done, what she is doing, how ruin hangs right over her? Tell them the ruin is there, the second rumor has come, she is to sink to rise no more, nor be found anymore at all. But God does not want any man to sink with her. He would have every soul turn away from her and turn to Him for the life and salvation there is in Him; therefore, He calls, "Come out of her my people, that ye receive not of her plagues."

There is where we are; there is the rumor abroad. Oh, *is* it *abroad?* That is the question. Is it *abroad?* Have you been sounding it abroad? How long have we been in the time of the loud cry? More than two years. Have you been sounding that rumor these two years, brethren? Have you all been giving the message which has been given you to sound, urging the people to escape from the ruin that is impending and that they must flee to God if they would escape the ruin?

Well, then, shall we not go from this Conference to sound that rumor with the loudest voice that God can give? Is there anything else to do? How can there be anything else to do? And of all things how can there be anything else thought of by those to whom God has given the message and upon whom He has laid the responsibility of sounding that rumor? "Come out of her, my people."

Sermon 8

February 13, 1895

Our study tonight will be merely a continuation of the lesson of Friday night: What Babylon is, how much it embraces, and what it is to come out of her. We may not get through all of this in this lesson, but from the evidences we had Friday night, it is plain enough that there is nothing else to do but to inform the world of the ruin that hangs over it and to sound aloud the call that God has given to save people from the ruin. The thing for us to do is to lift up the cry, to sound aloud the warning and the call, and the Lord will see to it that the people are convinced that that is the thing to do. Whether they *will do it* or not is for them to decide afterward. But the Lord will see to it that they shall know that that is the thing *to do*.

Therefore, I stated last night, especially when we read for the first time the words, "I heard another voice from heaven, saying, Come out of her, my people," that it is the voice that comes *from heaven* that calls the people out. And therefore, those human instruments who will make the call by the word of mouth will have to be so connected with God that in that call the people will hear the voice from heaven. We must be so connected with God that when that word is sounded, "Come out of her, my people," the Spirit of God will say to them, That is the thing to do. Those who will give the warning must be so connected with God that when the voice shall present the words of God which show the situation as it is at present, the Spirit of God will impress those who hear with the actual conviction that that is the truth, that we are in the time and that the thing to do is to come out of her.

But I say still that whether they will do it or not is for them to decide. God never takes up a man and drags him out. An illustration of what I am saying is in the instance where Peter and John were in jail in Jerusalem and the angel of the Lord let them out and in the morning they were brought before the Sanhedrin. Acts 4:13. When the Sanhedrin "saw the boldness of Peter and John and perceived that they were unlearned and ignorant men, they marvelled and they *took knowledge of them*, that they had been with Jesus."

In the words and by the presence of these two disciples of Christ, those priests and rulers were convinced of Christ's mission and that these men were in the right.

"And they took knowledge of them, that they had been with Jesus." Yet, instead of surrendering to the conviction, they hardened themselves against it and commanded the disciples to be sent away. Then "they conferred among themselves, saying, What shall we do to these men? for that indeed a notable miracle hath been done by them is manifest to all them that dwell in Jerusalem, and we cannot deny it. But that it spread no further among the people, let us straitly *threaten them,* that they speak henceforth to no man in this name. And they called them and commanded them not to speak at all nor teach in the name of Jesus. But Peter and John answered and said unto them, Whether it be right in the sight of God to hearken unto you more than unto God, judge ye. For we cannot but speak the things which we have seen and heard. So when they had *further threatened* them, they let them go, finding nothing how they might punish them."

They were willing to punish them, but they did not find just how under the circumstances, but the point is that they were doing all this threatening and had this desire to punish them, *against their own convictions* that the disciples were right.

And that is where God intends His people to stand now. We have a message to the world now, just as important as that of the disciples then. And our position is not the right one until we find such a connection with God that when we do speak the truth, wherever we go and tell the people the message that He has now given us to tell, the Spirit of God will be there to witness to the people that that is so, and say to them, That is right and that man is speaking the truth. All that we can do is to tell the message to the people. We cannot bring them out, and God will not bring them out by force. He wins men by telling them what is right and making His goodness pass before them. And this God will do when the human instrument by which He works stands so related to Him that His Spirit can speak in the words, in order that in the human words the people shall hear the "voice *from heaven."*

I am satisfied that everyone, – and I am not satisfied as a mere persuasion but I know it is a fact – everyone who will yield to the truth of God as the Lord reveals it today and as He will reveal it to every man, will be brought by the truth into just the place where the Spirit of God can work with him in this way all the time.

Now we know that for more than two years we have been in the time in which God said, "Arise, shine, for thy light is come." That is the truth, and we all know that we are there. But we cannot raise ourselves. We cannot get up; it is the truth of God that must *raise* us. The power of God must have a place, and that will raise us. We have to "Arise" before we can "shine"; that is settled. We cannot shine down where we are; we are not in the right place; we must be *up.* We must *arise* in order to shine, because up there is where the light is. We are down too close to the earth – Seventh-day Adventists, all of us, are too close to the earth; we are too far down, too close to the darkness; we cannot shine as God wants us to shine. And therefore He says, "*Arise,* shine."

But I say again, it is no use for us to try to raise ourselves and I also say again that as certainly as any Seventh-day Adventist here in this Conference or anywhere on the earth will surrender his whole will and body, mind and heart – everything – to God, taking His truth for what it is, God will see to it that the truth shall raise him to where he will shine. Therefore, let us honestly, right here, enter upon the study of this thing in the place where we are, and the work there is to do, in such a way as to see what God has to give us of His truth, which will raise us to the place where He can do what He pleases with us and where, when He uses us and speaks by us, the people will know the power of God is there and will hear the voice from heaven? Unless that be so, we cannot give this message; that is all.

It is no use for us to undertake to tell the people, "Come out of her, my people," when there is no power in our words that will bring them out; no power connected with us that will cause the thing to be done. It would be simply speaking into the air. But we are in a time that is too vastly important for us to be talking into the air. God wants us to talk to men in such a way that in the words that we shall speak, He shall speak to the heart.

We are not sufficient of ourselves to do this. There is the record: "Our sufficiency is of God." We can rest with all our weight upon that statement, "Our sufficiency is of God." That simply says to us that God will *make us sufficient;* He will furnish our sufficiency.

Let us look, then, a little further at how much is embraced in Babylon. In other lessons you remember we read certain texts which from this side, as it were, showed that all the world is going to honor the beast, the papacy, and do her bidding – all except those whose names are written in the book of life. But there are some further texts on this subject that we can read. Turn to Rev. 17:8, particularly the last part of the verse. I shall read all the verse, however:

> The beast that thou sawest was and is not and shall ascend out of the bottomless pit and go into perdition, and *they that dwell on the earth shall wonder,* whose names were not written in the book of life from the foundation of the world, when they behold the beast that was and is not and yet is.

They shall wonder when they behold the beast that was and is not and yet is. Now there are going to be some people that will not wonder at that a particle. All the world will be wondering at it, surprised at it, astonished at it, and considering it in wonder, but there is going to be a set of people who will not be in any way concerned about that and these are going to be the ones whose names are in the book of life. They are the ones who do not worship the beast and his image. I read that verse particularly to connect with the thought of the other evening, that "all that dwell upon the earth shall worship him, whose names are not written in the book of life"; all kingdoms of the earth committed fornication with Babylon; the inhabitants of the earth are made drunk with the wine of the wrath of her fornication, and this showing also that all the world is connected with her and out of this wonder she will, and indeed by means of it, raise herself to the place where the scripture shall be fulfilled.

Let us just here ask a question: Taking this just as these scriptures speak it, "All the kingdoms of the world" are joined to Babylon in fornication, in illicit connection. The inhabitants of the earth are made drunk with the wine of her fornication. What is it then, what alone must it be, to come out of Babylon? Nothing short of coming out of the world itself.

There is another word here, too. Turn to Revelation 18, and we will read and see how much there is connected with it. We read up to the 10th verse Friday night. Now begin with the 11th verse:

> And the merchants of the earth shall weep and mourn over her, for no man buyeth their merchandise anymore.

Now I am going to read this slowly, and when it is ended, I want you to see how much of the traffic of mankind she does not control.

> The merchandise of gold and silver and precious stones and of pearls and fine linen and purple and silk and scarlet and all sweet wood [that would be fine, fancy, costly, decorative woods], and all manner of vessels of ivory and all manner of vessels of most precious wood and of brass and iron and marble and cinnamon and odors and ointments and frankincense and wine and oil and fine flour and wheat and beasts and sheep and horses and chariots and slaves and souls of men.

That is controlled by Babylon. How much then of the traffic of the world is left? None. Then when the time comes for the general boycott to be set up, it is going to be easy enough for her to say a man shall not buy or sell, because all the traffic of the world is under her hand. Nobody can buy or sell who does not do as she says. But when she controls all of this and God says, "Come out of her," it is plain that obedience to that call will carry us right to the place where His will is accomplished in a complete separation from her. The very fact that our names are in the book of life and our refusing to do the bidding of Rome, brings us out absolutely and sets us in such a place that we shall have no sort of connection with her, not so much as for anything to eat.

Let us study this a little further. When our allegiance to the truth of God, our giving ourselves *to God,* leads to that place where we are absolutely separated from anything on the earth to eat or drink, how in the world are we going to live? Ah, there is the promise: "Bread shall be given him; his water shall be sure." Well, then, as in our allegiance to God we will be *forced* to absolute separation of every kind from the world and all that is in it; is it not *now* high time when we ourselves *by our own choice* shall be utterly separated *in heart* and *affection* from the world and all that is in it?

Further, here are *the kingdoms of earth* that are connected with her too, and they are going to be used by her to execute her will upon the people of God. Then, when that thing is done, it will force a separation from all connection with them or any dependence upon them for anything. But when that time comes, how in the world will we get along? How will we be protected, what shall we do, when mobs attack us and people commit outrages upon us? What in the world shall we ever do for protection? How can we live in the world then? Would it be safe to be so separated from the governments of earth that we could not prosecute any who offer violence to us? That we could not hold the law with its penalties as a menace over the heads of those who would stone our churches or tear down our tents or do us harm in other ways? Well, that time is going to come anyway, when we shall be outlawed and all these kingdoms under the power of the beast will be simply tools for executing her wrath upon us. Not only is this time *going* to come, but it is *now at hand.*

But when the very shaping of things by Babylon shall *force* us into that position, what shall we do? How shall we ever live? Well, from our side of the issue, what is it that is to bring us there? It is only allegiance to God that will ever put us there. Very well, then, will allegiance to God help us *when we get there?* Will allegiance to God furnish us the protection that we shall need when that time comes? You all say, yes. Well, if allegiance to God should *in heart* bring a man to that place *now,* do you think it would be too much of a risk for him just to break loose and put his trust altogether in God *right now?* Do you think anyone would be going too far *just now* to put his allegiance upon God and his trust in Him for protection, just as fully *as though there was no government on the earth at all.*

Everybody whose name is in the book of life is going to be *forced* there by the very powers of earth themselves. Then why should not we let the word of God and His power *lift* us there now? I would rather have the work of God and His power *put* me in a place than to have the course of evil and the powers of the earth *force* me into it by the very force of circumstances. I would far rather cheerfully choose wholly the Lord and His way at once, than to linger and linger with my affections and trust and dependence upon the powers of earth, perfectly willing to have it this way longer, but because I cannot have it so and get into heaven, I will finally allow myself to be broken loose and take the consequences – and go to heaven. No, sir. I would far rather "cut loose" from the world and everything in it or about it and put my trust steadfastly upon God, just as though there was nobody in this universe but God. I believe there is a text that covers this whole ground.

Turn to Jeremiah 17:5:

> Thus saith the Lord: Cursed be the man that trusteth in man, and maketh flesh his arm, and whose heart departeth from the Lord.

If my heart leans for support in any confidence toward something or somebody that is not God, where is my heart? Surely it is departing from the Lord. Now look at the next verse:

> For he shall be like the heath in the desert, and shall not see when good cometh.

Brethren, we want to be able to see when good cometh. But what will hinder a man's seeing when good comes? Trusting in man, making flesh his arm. Looking to any man, to any invention of men, to any combination of men, will do that. "Maketh flesh his arm." Depending upon any organization of flesh, any combination of flesh, and making that my arm, will keep me from seeing when good comes? Why? Because my heart is leaning on somebody besides God. I may try to satisfy my conscience that I can use that as an instrument of God to hold me up, but the Lord does not put it that way. He makes a clear distinction between God and man, and between trusting in the Lord and trusting in the arm of flesh. I would rather lean altogether upon God and have Him *use* flesh if He wants to, to hold me up, than to lean upon the flesh to be held up and expect God to do it that way, for when we lean upon the flesh, on the organization of flesh and the power of this world and of man and expect to give God the credit for it – the truth that is we will give the combination or whatever it is we are leaning on the first place. But God must have the first place. And therefore when we lean altogether upon Him, He can use whatever instrument He pleases to hold us up or to do whatever He chooses with us. But the one important thing in it is that he that trusts in man and makes flesh his arm *shall not see when good comes*. And that is an awful risk to run in our time.

> He shall be like the heath in the desert and shall not see when good cometh, but shall inhabit the parched places in the wilderness, in a salt land, and not inhabited.

And that scene of desolation – a salt land and not inhabited – will be about the place where Babylon finds herself at last. But ah! Look at the other side: "Blessed is the man that *trusteth in the Lord*." In the Lord through man? No. In the Lord through the arm of flesh? No, sir. In the Lord Himself, and whose hope the Lord is.

> For he shall be as a tree planted by the waters and that spreadeth out her roots by the river and shall not see when heat cometh but her leaf shall be green and shall not be careful in the year of drouth, neither shall cease from yielding fruit.

There is going to come a dreadful drought. But God has fixed it so that a man need not be afraid of the year of drought, nor careful at that time. He has been careful before the drought comes; his trust is in God, and when the drought comes, his trust is in God still. But note the difference. The one who trusts in man and makes flesh his arm shall not see when *good* cometh, and this man that trusts in the Lord shall not see when *heat* cometh. This is the better way. Let us take it. When calamities come, they will not affect this man; he will not care for them at all.

Now let us turn to the 16th chapter of Revelation and read another thought that seems to me to be expressive of how much Babylon covers. Rev. 16:13, 14. I am not reading this for the point of *time* when the verse applies; I am reading it simply to get the limit of Babylon's dominion, how much is covered by her, how much is under her dominion:

> I saw three unclean spirits like frogs come out of the mouth of the dragon and out of the mouth of the beast and out of the mouth of the false prophet. For they are the spirits of devils working miracles, which go forth unto the kings of the earth and of the whole world to gather them to the battle of the great day of God Almighty.

16th verse: "And he gathered them."

19th verse, after the seventh plague, when the end comes: "The great city." What great city? Babylon, all the way through.

> The great city was divided *into three parts* and the cities of the nations fell and great Babylon came into remembrance before God, to give unto her the cup of the wine of the fierceness of his wrath.

So then, the great city, Babylon, is divided into three parts. Now do those three unclean spirits that come out of the mouth of the dragon, out of the mouth of the beast and out of the mouth of the false prophet have anything to do with these three parts into which the great city is divided? I believe they have. I believe that they definitely point to that. I believe that the dragon, the beast, and the false prophet express these three parts into which she is divided when the time of her ruin comes. And we all know what the dragon, the beast, and the false prophet are, and the three unclean spirits working miracles coming out of their mouths, going forth to the whole world to gather them. Therefore, from this it is also clear that Babylon controls the world, the whole world. Then what does it mean to come out of Babylon?

Another situation: 2 Timothy 3:

> This know also, that in the last days perilous times shall come. For men shall be lovers of their own selves, covetous, boasters, proud, blasphemous, disobedient to parents, unthankful, unholy [–and through the whole category there of nineteen sins] having a form of godliness but denying the power thereof.

Now what made Babylon the mother? I mean what produced her first? The church leaning upon the arm of another, separated from her own husband, turning to another, leaning upon the arm of another than her rightful Lord – that is what made Babylon. The church, pretending to be the church of Christ, joining herself to another lord, makes the adulteress, the harlot. And thus came Babylon the great. And as she is the one that has led in all that wicked course and set the wicked example for all the rest to follow, she is described as "the mother of harlots."

Then when God in the Reformation would have healed Babylon and she would not be healed, Christianity started in the world independent of her again. But when the professed Protestant churches have followed her ways and turned away from *their* rightful Lord and put their trust, their hope, upon earthly governments, earthly kingdoms, and joined themselves to these, they are the daughters; then there is Babylon and the daughters, the beast and the false prophet. So that you see the profession of religion without the power of God, the profession of godliness without the power of it, and those professing it, seeking and depending upon the kingdoms and nations of the earth for the power that they know they lack themselves – *all* this is fitly described as the combination of the form of godliness without the power. Babylon, the mother and daughters, embraces the world in the last days, and Babylon, the mother and daughters, is the form of godliness without the power.

Therefore, it is plain that the third chapter of second Timothy does describe Babylon. The third chapter of second Timothy is in that place a description of Babylon, just as much as Rev. 18 is in that place a description of it. And when the passage from 2 Tim. 3 closes by saying, "Having a form of godliness, but denying the power thereof: *from such turn away,*" that cry, "From such turn away" is in that place the call out of Babylon just as "Come out of her my people" is in its place the call out of Babylon.

The form of godliness without the power is the bane of any profession of religion. And now it is the bane of all of them in the world. And the success of this grand scheme to bring about the union of all denominations and the unity of the faith, which is being diligently worked from the pope of Rome up to many professed Protestants is only to put the seal of completeness upon it.

Down in Ohio last August at the camp meeting of another denomination the leading minister of the camp, preaching the Sunday sermon to thousands of people on the millennium and the hope and the prospect of its coming, giving as one of the great signs of the millennium the patent fact that "Protestants and Catholics are all wheeling into line," and hundreds of the people responded, Amen.

Now that is an actual fact, not only a fact as to that meeting but that sort of scheme that has been framed in the minds of those who are going more and more into Babylon, is a fact, and the scheme will be worked by them in all its parts to bring the millennium and the kingdom of God at last by preparing the way for the king. And thus when the Savior comes, He will find the whole combination of the kingdoms and churches of the earth gathered together into one body, professing to be Christianity, yet with none of the power of Christianity, and promising themselves and the world the grand, glorious millennium that has been for so long looked for over all the earth and the speedy coming of the kingdom of God. We know well enough also that then *their king* really will come, presenting himself as Christ and will be received as Christ. There will be some though who will be disconnected from that whole system – those who have obeyed the call, "Come out of her, my people," those whose names are written in the book of life. These will not receive the king of Babylon to reign over them. And then, as was proposed by the National Reformers away back in 1886 even, that scripture will be used against these: "These, mine enemies, that would not that I should reign over them, bring hither, and slay them before my face." That brings logically enough the death penalty, as in the 13th chapter of Revelation, upon all who will not worship beast and image. The whole combination under the dominion of the earth and the dominion of evil spirits – the dragon, the beast, and the false prophet – Satan and all the instruments of Satan in all the earth, in combination – will be set up as one grand system of Christianity, when it is all one grand system of deviltry.

What then could show a more universal reign of the form of godliness, not only without the power but denying the power? For this form of godliness will deny that Jesus Christ is come in the flesh. Every spirit that confesseth that Jesus Christ is come in the flesh, that is the Spirit of God. Every spirit that confesseth not that Jesus Christ is come – not that He *did* come, but now *is* come in my flesh – Christ in you the hope of glory, Christ abiding within, God reigning in the kingdom of God that is within you – that is what this signifies. Every spirit that confesseth not that Jesus Christ *is* come in the flesh is not of God. And this is that spirit of antichrist. And ye have overcome them, little children, because greater is He that *is in you, in* you, *in* you, than he that is in the world.

Therefore, all this shows as plainly as ABC that in the last days the whole system of the world and worldliness, will be combined into this one grand system of the form of godliness, without the power and denying the power also, and growing worse and worse. And the cry, "From such turn away," is simply another form of the cry, "Come out of her my people." And wherever this cry is heard, it means simply, Come out of the world, separate from the world and from the things that are in the world, in heart and in mind, as completely as though the world had already vanished away. "Come out of her, my people."

Sermon 9

February 13, 1895

There is another very important thing that I must notice with this division of the subject. It is a thing that is going to *force* every Seventh-day Adventist and every other Christian to a decision between Christ and this world and between allegiance to Christ and connection with the United States government. It is a proposition endorsed by all the governors of all the states and territories of the United States, to drill in military tactics all the school boys in the public schools. Some of the governors in the states where the legislatures are in session are already trying to get legislation enacting laws providing for it. A meeting in favor of the project was held in New York City the 25th of January in which speeches were made.

Let the United States government and all the states undertake to drill in military drill, filling with the war spirit all the children of the country, and what Christian can allow his children to take any part in it? And if the evil thing shall be made compulsory or shall be *required* by law, then what Christian can allow his children to be in the schools any more? The word that ushered Christ into the world was, "Peace on earth." This thing is precisely what it says in Joel, "Prepare war." Are you ready for the issue? The scheme is on foot and has spread over all the country like a flash of wild fire. It has been taken up as though it were the grandest thing that ever was, from the day it was mentioned. It has been greedily grasped and it is proposed at once to fix it in the law.

Whether this military drill, this inculcating the war spirit into all the children of the country, shall be made compulsory at the first or not the doing of it at all is enough, for the simple introduction and practice will make the thing in a sense, compulsory, for the simple reason that any boy that would refuse to take part in it would be called a coward by those who did take part. He would be ostracized. His schoolmates would pass him by on the other side. For all this is to be done in the interests of "Patriotism"; it is said to be all for the "inculcating of patriotism" and "love of the flag." Any boy that will refuse to take part in the military exercise will be declared "unpatriotic"; he will be "despising the flag." It will be said he does not "love the country," is "a traitor."

But no Christian parent can allow his child to be filled with the war spirit. It is with the Spirit of Christ, the Spirit of peace, that he must be filled. It is to Christ that his allegiance is owed.

This is certainly true. And that being so, it brings a test that will separate every Christian child and every Christian parent from the government of the United States and every state. Then is it not time we began to be separated anyway? Were the lessons last week too extreme? Did they go too far when they said, Let us cut loose? Why, brethren, the very events from the side of the enemy are forcing us right up to the line where we have to decide between allegiance to Jesus Christ and this world.

But there stands that wicked thing right before every Seventh-day Adventist and every other Christian in the United States. It will be a test as to whether he will let every earthly thing go and hold only to Christ, let them call him what they choose. That is the test. It is only another note sounded in the one universal call, "Come out of her, my people."

But where did the mischievous thing start? This particular phase of it as to putting it in the public schools started with the Papacy. Professed Protestant churches have been organizing what they call "Boys' Brigades" for two summers. But the first step that I have found toward putting it into the public schools and forcing it upon the people of the country was by the Catholic Club of Jersey City, N.J., as reported by the *Catholic Mirror* of October 6, 1894:

> The Catholic Club of Newark (N.J.) at its meeting last Wednesday night adopted a set of resolutions asking the Legislature to make provision for the introduction of military drill in the public, parochial, and other schools within this state in which boys are taught. The resolutions are as follows:
>
> *Resolved,* That in the judgment of the Catholic Club of Newark, N.J., the military resources of our country should not now be neglected but should be developed as fully as a reasonable economy will allow; and be it,
>
> *Resolved,* That we, therefore, suggest, respectfully, to the Legislature of our state that military instruction for the boys in our public schools ought to be provided for and may without a doubt be secured very cheaply through the agency of the members of the state, and be it,
>
> *Resolved,* That we also suggest to the Legislature the propriety of providing for similar instruction in all the other schools in this state in which boys are taught, and be it,
>
> *Resolved,* That a copy of these resolutions be forwarded to the Clerk of the Senate and another to the Clerk of the House of the Assembly.
>
> It is hoped that such a plan will come in vogue, as it will be of great benefit to the boys in many ways.

Lafayette Post of the Grand Army of the Republic of New York City – the one which started the movement to put the flag on every school house – has lately taken it up and has spread it abroad to the whole country.

Now look further at the situation:

Everyone that protests against that will be accused of being unpatriotic and on the other hand, the papacy will simply crowd herself forward as the most patriotic of all, because she can endorse it to the fullest measure. She can show that she is the most prominent in the movement and in favor of it. Thus this is simply another means by which the papacy will set herself at the head of everything and will rule over all.

Here is a dispatch from the Detroit *Evening News* of February 4, 1895, relating to military drill in the churches, which is an illustration of the evil thing, whether in the public schools or in the apostate churches:

> UNITED BOYS' BRIGADES
>
> Chicago, Feb. 4. The United Boys' Brigade of America, composed of companies of youths organized under military discipline in the various Christian churches of the land, has just been incorporated, with headquarters in Chicago. The incorporators are the Rev. H. W. Bolton, representing the Methodists, the Rev. P. S. Henson, the Baptists, and others. The brigade movement has for its object the development of patriotism and piety in boys, and its essential features are the drill, the study of the Bible, and missionary work. About ten years ago William A. Smith, a British soldier, organized the first brigade in Glasgow, Scotland.

Brother Robinson says it is all over England and Scotland. Are not these things near enough to us and are they not clearly enough set before us to show where these things are driving us? They are forcing a separation of the Christian from everything on the earth. Then, is it not time that we should make that separation, brethren, from choice, and in heart and with all the heart?

Babylon embraces the world, and separation from Babylon means nothing but separation from the world. And these things are so near to us and the separation so near to be forced upon every one who will be loyal to Jesus Christ, all this proclaims the all-urgent necessity that we seek God with all the heart and let our hearts be separated and we separated in heart, *unto God wholly.*

Here are a few clippings in which this military movement is discussed, which are worth reading. One from the New York *Recorder,* endorsing it fully throughout, says:

> Military drill in the schools is evidently foreordained... How much has been done already in his line and how much more may be done was amply demonstrated by the exhibition given in the Seventh Regiment Armory the other day, where not only the boys but the girls acquitted themselves with signal credit.

In the New York *Sun* of April 8, a trustee of the Twenty-third Ward school of New York City, in noticing a resolution that had been passed by a meeting of Quakers, disapproving of this military movement, says, among other things:

> The Board of Education of our city has taken up the matter, with the result that in our own state a bill has just been introduced in the Senate asking for $100,000 for the equipment of scholars of eleven years of age and upward in the public schools.

That is military equipment, of course. That is, the Board of Education of New York City as attended to having a bill introduced in the legislature of New York to equip school boys of eleven years and upward.

He continues:

> But in addition to the benefit that the nation may and will derive from this military training in the public schools, I maintain that the scholar will also be benefited, in giving him a manly, erect, and graceful bearing, and in making him more self-respecting; in strengthening the body as well as improving the mind, for there is no better exercise than drilling and marching; in learning discipline and therefore obedience and submission to lawful authority; in teaching to make him a good, loyal, and patriotic citizen, who loves his country and, if need be, ready to die in her defense – in giving him self-control and command of himself and therefore not only valuable for its effect on the mind but also on the body and, in fact, in making him strong, active and brave. I am heartily in favor of the movement, and you may count me one of its most earnest supporters.

But it is not all that way; there are some opposing voices heard. One man, writing to the Chicago *Herald* February 3 or 4, speaks in this way:

> I notice in an evening paper of recent date an article concerning the enrollment of boys into a church military organization for the purpose of fostering the war spirit and the proverbial meekness of the lowly Nazarene. Can anything be more stultifying, contradictory or grotesque than this? When the boy's education is finished in this new school, what a peculiar product he will be; what a laughable combination of saint and devil; what an impossible mixture of right and wrong; what a commentary on the Christian church, whose mission is supposed to be the inauguration of a reign of universal peace; what a confession of weakness; what a despicable trick to fill empty pews; what an insult to the memory of that noblest of characters, Jesus, whose life, acts, and teachings were the exact reverse of this! If this is Christianity, what, in the name of religion, is paganism?
>
> These church military organizations, in their utter disregard for consistency, decency, genuine morality, real justice, and, in fact, all of the Christian virtues, have no parallel in history, and the men who engineer this game – for it is only that – are the worst enemies to true democracy and republican institutions possible to imagine. This may sound radical to some, but it is true, and truth is only radical to the person unacquainted with it, and there are many such, alas, too many.

Here is a paper in which is printed the annual address of Mrs. Marion H. Dunham of Burlington, Iowa, of the Women's Christian Temperance Union; she has some excellent remarks upon this. Speaking of the increasing conflicts among the laboring classes, capital and labor, and so on, she says:

> One feature has developed which can well excite the alarm of all who love their country and that is the cultivation of the military spirit and military training.

Then, speaking of dangers enough in the regular course of governmental affairs, she continues:

> But far more serious than all of these is the fact that in a time of profound peace, threatened by no other nation, our position and power making us, in fact, impregnable to all attacks from any possible hostile power, our schools and our churches are turned into military camps, and our young boys are drilled with arms that have been used on the battlefield, and the thirst for shedding the blood of their fellow men aroused in their young hearts.
>
> In my own city [Burlington, Iowa] the girls who are serving as substitute teachers are called "cadets," and their work "cadetting," in order apparently to familiarize them with military terms and ideas, that even womanly influence shall not be exerted for peace. Our colleges are supplied with instructors by and at the expense of the government, and the Boys' Brigade of the churches, which are supposed to be organized to spread the gospel of "peace on earth, good will to men," numbers about 115,000, and the old Sunday school hymn of, "I want to be an angel, and with the angels stand," changed to:
>
> > "I want to be a soldier,
> > And with the soldiers stand,
> > A cap upon my forehead,
> > A rifle in my hand.
> > I want to drill for service
> > With military skill,
> > And master modern tactics
> > The most approved to kill."

Then it goes on and gives a revamping of that old hymn and continues:

> No foes from abroad menace us, that this preparation is needed, and whatever this movement means or portends, it is contrary to the spirit of Christianity; it is turning civilization backward to the time when might was right, and every man's hand was raised against every other.

From this we can learn another thing, and that is the real Christian minds of the country will turn away from this and protest against it, and that only opens wider the door for sounding aloud the cry, "Come out of her, my people."

Those who are favorable to Christianity even and want to see the spirit of peace spread, you can see for yourself that this movement in itself repels them and, indeed, shuts them out. It draws the line between them and the government. And just now God has a work in the earth, a message to be spread, calling upon all who would save their souls alive to separate utterly from all such evil things, to set themselves against it with all their hearts, and turning to God in the spirit of peace, they all, from the least to the greatest, may know Him who is our peace.

Here, then, is the situation as it is today on all sides: Every element of the world – whether in the papacy, in apostate Protestantism, or on the part of the government itself – everything is driving us right to the point where we are compelled to decide and separate from the world and all that is in it. Well, then, shall we not look at it from the side of God's truth and have His Spirit which will indeed separate us and clothe us with such power as will awake the world to danger and save from the impending ruin every soul who will be saved? Here is the word: Isaiah 40:9, reading the margin:

> O thou that tellest good tidings to Zion, get thee up into the high mountain: O thou that tellest good tidings to Jerusalem, lift up thy voice with strength, lift it up, be not afraid; say unto the cities of Judah, Behold your God!

God wants us to find Him now. And remember that this 40th chapter of Isaiah corresponds to the loud cry of Revelation 14 and 18.

> Behold, the Lord God will come with strong hand, and his arm shall rule for him: behold, his reward is with him, and his work before him. He shall feed his flock like a shepherd: he shall gather the lambs with his arm, and carry them in his bosom.

Thus the Lord says to us in this time, Get up into the high mountains, and lift up your voice with all your strength, and do not be afraid. Tell to the people, Behold your God. He is your refuge; He is your salvation; He is your protection.

Now let us turn again to the study of what it is to come out of Babylon. Everyone knows now that to come out of Babylon is to come out of the world and to separate from Babylon is to separate from the world. What we want to know next is, What is it to come out of the world? What is it to separate from the world? Gal. 1:4 will answer that question in a word; we shall have to read the third and fourth verses together to get the connection, but the fourth verse is the one that has the point in it.

> Grace be to you and peace from God the Father and from our Lord Jesus Christ, who gave himself for *our sins, that* he might deliver us from *this present evil world.*

As He gave Himself for our sins in order to deliver us from this present evil world, it follows plainly enough that connection with the present evil world and even the evil world itself, *lies in our sinfulness.* And therefore, to deliver from this world, we must be delivered from sin. Not from some particular sins, but from *sin itself,* the thing, the root, and the all of it. The word of God does not take a man and find out how much of good there is in him and how much bad there is in him, and then patch the good on the place of the badness and take him into heaven that way. You should not put a new patch on an old garment; Christ said so, and it is so. Then we are not to see how much good there is in us, how many good traits we have and give ourselves credit for these and then get enough goodness from the Lord to supply whatever we may lack. No. There is no goodness, not one good thing there at all. The whole head is sick and the whole heart is faint. From the crown of the head to the feet there is no soundness in it, but instead there are wounds and bruises and putrefying sores. "Who shall deliver me from this body of death?" Rom. 7:24. It is a body of *death* simply because it is a "body of sin." Rom. 6:6. To be delivered from sin, then, is to be delivered from ourselves. That is what it is to come out of Babylon.

Many people have been getting the idea that if they get out of the Methodist church or the Presbyterian church or the Catholic church and get into the Seventh-day Adventist church, then they are out of Babylon. No. That is not enough, unless you are converted, unless you are separated from this world you are not out of Babylon, even though you are in the Seventh-day Adventist church and in the Tabernacle in Battle Creek. This is not saying that the Seventh-day Adventist church is Babylon; that is not it at all. But the man who is connected with himself is connected with the world, and the world is Babylon. You have separated from sin, separated from this world, to be out of Babylon. "Having a form of godliness, without the power," is simply another expression which describes Babylon and her condition in the last days. That being so, if I, a Seventh-day Adventist, have the form of godliness without the power, I belong to Babylon; no difference what I call myself, I am a Babylonian; I have on the Babylonish garment. I bring Babylon into the church wherever I go.

Another word upon this in Galatians: Christ "gave himself for our sins, that he might deliver us from this present evil world." All of this world that ever can cripple a man or hinder him in his heavenly course is simply what is inside of him; it is simply what there is of him. Therefore, when Christ would deliver a man from this present evil world, He simply delivers him from sin and from himself. Then that man is in the kingdom of God; he is *in* the world, but not *of* the world. So Jesus says, "I have chosen you out of the world: if ye were of the world, the world would love his own." Very good; here am I. Suppose I am of the world. Then the world will love his own. That is, the world that is in me and of me will love the world and will cling to the world. It cannot do anything else, and I cannot do anything else, because I am essentially of the world itself. The world outside of me and around me will love his own, that is true; but as certainly as I am of the world, so certainly I will stick to the world and love the world; the world *within* me will love and cling to the world without. I may be calling myself a Christian at the same time, but that will not alter the case – the world will love his own. If in heart I am cut loose from this world, I am free from it, but if the world is there, I will love the world, and when the test comes, when the crisis comes, I will surrender to the world and go the way of the world in general – stay in Babylon and worship the beast.

Now turn to the third chapter of 2 Timothy. There we have the same thing taught:

> This know also, that in the last days perilous times shall come. For men shall be lovers of their own selves... From such turn away.

Then if I am a lover of my own self, from such I am to turn away. But who is it I am to turn away from? Self, assuredly. Come out of Babylon, from such turn away. It is not that I am to look at you and study you and see whether you are a lover of *your* own self, to see whether *you* are covetous and a boaster and proud and then *I* separate from *you*. Not at all.

It is not for me to look at others and say, "Oh I don't want to be in a church with such brethren as these. I cannot be the right kind of a Christian there. I think I would better go to Oakland and join the church there, or I think I would better go to Battle Creek and join the church there; the brethren here at home seem to be so kind of – oh, I can hardly describe it, but it is very unpleasant and very hard to be a Christian here. I think I will have to leave this church and join some other one." That will not answer at all, for unless you are genuinely converted and separated from the world, when you have done all that the church which you have joined is just so much worse than it was before and so much more Babylonish by just so much as *you are there.* "From such turn away." Then as I am to turn away from myself, where does Babylon lie? Where does the world lie? Altogether, in self, just as we found in Galatians, fourth chapter. Let us look at the third chapter of 2 Timothy a little further and see whether any of us are there.

"Men shall be lovers of their own selves, covetous." Can you tell what it is that will cause a man who professes to belong to the Lord and to love the Lord – what will cause him to hold back from the Lord that which the Lord says definitely belongs to Him, the tithe, for instance? Here are means that come into my hands; the Lord says that a tenth of that is His. I profess to love the Lord; I go to meeting every Sabbath; I profess to belong to the Lord myself; I profess to be consecrated, but yet I do not let the Lord have what belongs to Him. What is the root of that thing? Self. And what is the first fruit of self? Covetousness. I have not stolen anything from my neighbor or kept anything back from him, but I have held to that which belongs to the Lord. Then I am to turn away from my covetous self.

Blasphemers: We cannot take each on of these in detail. "Boasters, proud, blasphemers". A blasphemer, in the common acceptation of the term, is one who uses the name of God profanely; one who takes the name of God in vain. One of the commandments of God is set against that. But though I do not by word of mouth use the name of God profanely, if I profess the name of God, if I have taken it upon me and then take such a course as to show that the whole thing is in vain, have I not taken the name of the Lord in vain? Assuredly I have. If it is a form of godliness without the power, is not it a vain taking of the name of the Lord? And will I not, by just such a course, cause other people to blaspheme the name of the Lord? Then, as I profess to be the Lord's and yet take a course, which in the nature of things, causes the name of the Lord to be blasphemed, the blasphemy begins with me.

There is a verse which we might read upon that: 1 Tim. 6:1:

> Let as many servants as are under the yoke count their own masters worthy of all honor, that the name of God and his doctrine be not blasphemed.

There the word of God itself lays the truth right home to the individual, that he is to take such a course as that the name of God and His doctrine shall not be blasphemed; that we are to guard the name and the doctrine of God from blasphemy. But if I sanction it, if I draw it on, then it is certain that the blasphemy begins with me. I have taken the name of God in vain and wear it in vain.

Here is another test: Romans 2, beginning with the 17th verse:

> Behold thou art called a Jew and resteth in the law, and makest thy boast of God, and knowest his will… Thou, therefore, which teachest another, teachest thou not thyself? Thou that preachest a man should not steal, dost thou steal?

"Here are they that keep the commandments of God, and the faith of Jesus." Thou that makest thy boast of the law, thou that teachest a man should not steal, what are you doing? Are you cheating? Do you drive sharp bargains? If you should happen to be in charge of some of His business, are you ready to drive a sharp bargain for the Lord? Do you think that is integrity to the cause? No. It is dishonesty. It is devilry. I cannot be selfish for the Lord. This is not saying that we are not to be careful and economical, but it is saying that I cannot drive sharp bargains for the Lord any more than for myself and yet be honest. Therefore, "Thou that preachest a man should not steal, dost thou steal? or are you honest?

"*Thou that sayest that a man should not commit adultery, dost thou commit adultery?*" Do you hold the marriage relation sacred? Do you honor that ordinance? or is it to you such a thing – as has been entirely too common among our young men especially, and even those "preparing for the ministry" too, who seem to think so lightly of this solemn ordinance of God that they can go and engage themselves to some young woman that may strike their fancy at the first and then, seeing some other one that strikes their fancy a little stronger, break their engagement. And then, if they do not get married before they find another one, they are ready to repeat this course.

The seventh commandment is put in the law of God to guard the marriage institution, the marriage ordinance, and men cannot disregard the marriage institution, that solemn ordinance of God, without violating the commandment. In a single year I could put my finger on at least half a dozen young men, professed Christians, who had engaged themselves to young ladies and every one of them broke their engagement and married somebody else, because they had more fancy for the new one. And some of these were preparing for "the work of the Lord." I want to know whether it is a fit preparation for the work of the Lord to trample underfoot one of God's most sacred ordinances at the first step?

"Thou that sayest a man should not commit adultery, does thou commit adultery?" Do you honor God's commandments? Do you honor His ordinances? "Well," says one, "would you have a man marry a woman he does not love?" No, I would not, but I would have him *know what love is* and know what he is about, before he engages himself to a woman. In this course that I am describing, there is no love to start with. It is mere aimless fancy. The woman may be perfectly honest in it; it may be love on her part and in most cases it is. But on his part it is mere fancy. And if it should so happen that the marriage should be performed before another one strikes his fancy a little more forcibly than does the first, some day he will meet one that does, and then he is not sure of his position. Any man that will violate the sacred confidence that he has pledged in that way to one woman is never sure that he will be faithful to another woman. When he has trampled underfoot that sacred thing in which God has stored most happiness for human beings as such, he has no surety, even to himself, that he will be faithful in any other case of the like kind.

But what of the man, anyway, who will go so far as to win the love of a woman to betray it. The Bible, in speaking of the mutual love of two men, finds its strongest illustration in describing it as "passing the love of women." And yet a man will win that and have her love bound about him and then ruthlessly break all its tendrils and trample it underfoot. It is a violation of the seventh commandment. It is trampling underfoot the institution which that commandment guards, in taking steps which, if carried to their logical conclusion – only a few steps – will lead to the actual fact. Let me say again, I would not have anyone marry a person whom he does not love, but I would have every soul have sufficient reverence for the ordinance of God, sufficient sobriety and thoughtfulness as a Christian, to know his own feelings. I would have him possess sufficient sense to know what he is doing, to find out before God what love is before he enters this most solemn relation with its sacred obligations.

"Thou that sayest a man should not commit adultery, dost thou commit adultery?" That is the question.

"*Thou that abhorrest idols, dost thou commit sacrilege?*" But you say, "I don't worship sticks sand stones; I don't bow down to graven images." No, you do not. But how about the *fashions of the world?* What kind of hat is it that you have on? What kind of cane is it that you carry? What kind of dress is it that you cut and make? Why do you cut and make it the way you do? Is it because it is more comfortable that way? Is it because it is more pleasing to God that way? No. You know that it is rather because it is *nearer to the fashion* that way. You know that it is because it conforms more to the world and will suit the world's ways better? But this world is vanity; it is idolatry. Satan is the god of this world. "Be not conformed to this world, but be ye transformed by the renewing of your mind." "Whosoever would be the friend of the world is the enemy of God." Therefore, although I may not bow down to graven images; although I may not worship sticks and stones, yet if I follow the fashions, the ways, and the things of this world and conform to the ways of the world rather than ask God what He would have, then what am I worshiping? The god of this world. There is idolatry also. There is enmity against God.

I know of nothing more incongruous, more unreasonable, anyhow, than fashion – wanting everybody shaped on the same mold and cut the same way and to look just the same way. Why did not God make us all alike when He made us? Why did He not make us all just exactly alike? Fashion's way is precisely the devil's way. He wants to make everybody of the same cut in religion and so he must have that so fashionable that all will wear it and then have the government take it up and fix it in the law and demand that all shall wear this fashionable cut of religion. And all this concession to fashion in dress is simply training yourself to make concessions to the world's religion. Oh, it is all idolatry. Thou that abhorrest idols, dost thou commit sacrilege?

If God wanted us all to be alike and to look alike, why did He not make us all alike to begin with? Why, you sometimes see people with clothing upon them that is in no sense becoming to them but is utterly incongruous. They may have on a hat or a dress of a color that makes them look as if they were recovering from a fit of the jaundice. But that question is not thought of. All that they think is that such is the fashion now.

Now God has made us in the world so that no two of us are alike. Each one is himself; he has a personality, an individuality of his own. And the Lord intends each Christian to exert an influence in this world that no other person in this world can exert. He expects each one to so dress that the way God has made him will be represented to the world in perfect harmony, perfect congruity in every respect; so that God can use the individuality which He has created for the purposes for which He created it. Dress to suit the Lord, and then all there is about us will tell for God and the things of righteousness. But one can destroy all that God has made him or her for by professing to be a Christian and then expecting to exert an influence in the world by dressing according to the way of this world! It cannot be done. The two things will not work together at all. You cannot impress anybody in favor of Christianity in that way, because the whole thing through which the Lord would work is shut away by this tribute to idolatry. Dress the way the Lord would have you, and you will find that it is not expensive, nor will it require much workmanship or very much ingenuity always to be neatly and becomingly dressed. "Thou that abhorrest idols, dost thou commit sacrilege?" That is what I want to know. Is your mind upon God? Do you dress to please Him? Are you seeking to please Him? or are you caring for what this one will say or what that one will say? "Thou that abhorrest idols, dost thou commit sacrilege?" Thou that makest thy boast of the law, through breaking the law dishonorest thou God? For the name of God is blasphemed among the Gentiles through you, as it is written: "One of the reigning evils of the last days is that people professing godliness will be blasphemers." Are you one? Do you bear the name of the Lord in vain? From such *turn away*."

Sermon 10

February 15, 1895

I understand there are some that think I did not say enough about dress last night. I think perhaps that is so, because it is altogether likely that those who think I did not say enough about dress would be glad if I had talked about those who dress neatly and even nicely, while they themselves think they are all right.

There are people who, when they see a person dressed neatly and well take it at once as an evidence of pride. But it is just as much an evidence of pride for a person to be proud of his slovenliness, as it is for another person to be proud of his flashiness. I have seen people who were proud of their slovenliness. I have seen people who were proud of their lack of pride. They were thanking God they were not proud. But they were.

Perhaps for that reason I did not say enough about dress before, and therefore I would add this, that those who are proud of their lack of pride and in this pride think they are all right, when they might and ought to dress better or more neatly than they do, would do well to correct themselves and come up to a better standard.

However, I was not talking about dress. That was not the subject. I was talking about coming out of Babylon. I am talking against idolatry, what sacrilege is, and what the abhorring of idols is.

We had reached in the third chapter of second Timothy the word "blasphemers." We cannot take up each one of these words singly, but there are words along throughout the catalogue that are worthy to be noticed by us. One here a step or two along is *unthankful.* In these last days people, having a form of godliness without the power, will be unthankful. Unthankful is *not thankful.* Thankful is *full* of thanks. How is it with you? Where do you belong? You are a professor of religion; you profess godliness. Are you full of thanks? or are you thank*ful* when everything goes right and to suit you? But when things go so as not to suit you, then you are doubtful, fretful, impatient, and wonder what is to become of you? Are you discontented and *un*thankful when such and such things happen? Are you thankful sometimes and unthankful sometimes? If I am thankful sometimes and not thankful at other times, then am I thank*ful*? No. "From such turn away."

Those that have a form of godliness without the power and go according to feeling have their ups and downs. But God does not wish any Christian to have any ups and downs at all, only ups. He quickens us; that is, gives us life and raises us from the dead to start with, and He intends that we shall keep on going up until we land at the right hand of God.

Take the other figure: We are planted. We are called trees – trees of righteousness – rooted and grounded in the love of God, and that tree is expected to grow and *only* to grow. Not to grow and then go back. As they told me down in Florida when I was there last fall, some of their orange trees get what they call "die-back." They shoot up, outgrowing all the other trees and then die back, almost if not entirely to the ground. The next year they again shoot up that way, again outgrowing all the trees and again die back. But that is not the kind of trees God has in His orchard. He plants trees of righteousness and expects that they shall not be up and down, growing up swiftly and dying back, but that they shall grow, and only grow.

Unholy: We all know what it is alone which makes holy – the presence of Jesus Christ. The abiding presence of God alone can make any place or anything holy. But those who have the form of godliness without the presence of God are necessarily unholy. And this scripture says, "From such turn away." If I am unholy, from such I am to turn away; that is, turn away from myself. The only place we can turn from ourselves is unto God. And that brings the abiding presence of God, which makes holy and which sanctifies.

Without natural affection: How do you treat the children? Of course our children are not all perfect; they are not all born saints, because they are our children. We find many things that are awry about them in their conduct, that is true. And yet how do we treat them? How did they come by these crooked ways? How did that meanness that is there get into them? You hear many people say of certain actions or traits in a child, "Well, that child came honestly by that." Yes, that is true. In fact is there anything that the child manifests that he did not come honestly by? Surely not, for the child did not bring himself into the world. I am not in any sense saying that these traits shall be allowed to run on unchecked. But in checking or correcting them shall we treat them as though they were altogether responsible for it? or shall we consider that we ourselves are responsible in some measure for it? Which shall it be, "Without natural affection"? or shall we allow that we have something to do with it? Shall we allow that the thing is there by nature and work accordingly, not only with natural affection but with the affection of grace divine?

Truce breakers: Now a truce is made when two armies are at war. A flag is sent out by one or the other – a flag of truce it is called. A truce is a lull in warfare, a stopping of hostilities. It may be for the burial of the dead. It may be for a parley as to peace. It may be for one reason or another, but a truce is a stopping of all warfare and all contention by those who had formerly been at war. If it is for the burial of the dead, they can mix right in one with the other, sit down and talk together, everything perfect peace. But when the truce is over, the war begins again.

The Scripture says (Titus 3:2, 3), "Speak evil of no man, be no brawlers, but gentle, showing all meekness unto men." There is a truce now. But what before? "For we ourselves also were sometime foolish, disobedient, deceived, serving divers lusts and pleasures, living in malice and envy, hateful, and hating one another." That is how it used to be; and he that hates has broken the commandment which says, "Thou shalt not kill." Formerly there were contentions, strife, envy, jealousy, emulation, wrath, seditions, heresies, murders, and all these things. That is the way it was before. Now we have found Christ – professed to – and that calls for peace, and that is the truce. That is accepted among Christians, among those who have named the name of Christ.

Therefore, after naming the name of Christ and professing to be His, the man who indulges any envy, any malice, any hatred, any backbiting, any evil-speaking, any division – what is he? He is a trucebreaker. He has broken the truce that he has professed in the very name and the profession of godliness. Have you ever found in your experience among the churches in our own denomination any envy, jealousy, talking one against another, backbiting, variance, emulation, wrath, strife, divisions, or any such thing? That is truce breaking. Are you one of these? "From such turn away."

False accusers: The next expression comes inevitably, "truce breakers, *false accusers*." And the Greek for that word "false accusers" is *diaboloi,* devils, because the Greek for the devil is *diabolos* – the accuser, the chiefest of all accusers among those who do accuse.

You remember in the 12th of Revelation it says of him: "The accuser of our brethren is cast down, which accused them before our God day and night." That is the devil himself – the chief accuser. And here in the word which we are studying, it is expressed in the plural – *diaboloi* – devils. That is, they follow the ways of the devil, the chief accuser, and thus are called devils, also false accusers. Now I am not calling them devils. I am calling your attention to the fact that the Lord calls them devils. False accusers. Are you one?

Now we are studying Babylon and what it is to come out of Babylon. I have a little extract here that gives some idea of how it is really in Babylon, where the mother of harlots is, where Babylon, the mother, sits – in Rome itself. And that will be an illustration of what this signifies here and what is pointed out in the words "truce breakers" and "false accusers."

Cardinal Gibbons last year shortly after his return from Rome gave an interview to the correspondent of the New York World, and the interview was reprinted in the *Catholic Standard* in the month of October, 1894, and here is a statement from the interview:

> In talking, his eminence weighs his words nicely. Although he has no shadow of reserve when he is dealing with people in whom he has confidence, he is nice in the expression of his views. He once assured me that the pleasure he derived from seeing Rome was greatly lessened by the necessity of keeping guard upon his tongue.

> *"In the strange air of Rome,"* as he explained, *"your lightest words are caught up, commented, and misinterpreted."* "I am accustomed to say what I think, plainly and directly, in our American way," he added.

But in Rome he could not do that. How is it in Battle Creek? How is it in Oakland? How is it in College View? How is it in any church? How is it in the church where you belong? Is there such perfect confidence in you as a brother with all the others to whom you speak that no word is caught up, commented, and misinterpreted? Or is there such a thing as catching up words, making a man an offender for a word? Not taking time to understand what he said, not knowing whether you heard the thing distinctly or not, you caught some kind of indistinct sound and it did not strike you exactly right. Then you must hurry to the President of the Conference or some other brother in important position and tell him, "Oh, such and such a brother said so and so. How can you have him in the ministry? How can you support a man that holds such doctrines as that?" Have you ever seen any such thing as that? I am simply asking these questions; You can decide. You can tell whether it is so or not, and if that is the way it is in Battle Creek or any other place among Seventh-day Adventists, then where is the difference on this point between this and the very seat of Babylon itself – Rome, where your words "are caught up, commented, and misinterpreted!" If this is so, is it not time to come out of Babylon? Is it not time "from such to turn away?" and find such a connection with Jesus Christ, such an abiding confidence and faith in Him, that there shall be perfect Christian confidence among all who profess the name of Christ, that your words shall not be caught up, commented, and misinterpreted?

Now it is true that the Christian is to be so absolutely truthful, frank, and open hearted that he need not care, and is not to care, what people make out of his words. But what of those who profess to be Christians, that are ready to make such things out of his words? That is the question. And if that is so in the churches where you belong, then "from such turn away." I mean *if you are one of these,* from yourself turn away.

> False accusers, incontinent, fierce, despisers of those that are good, traitors, heady.

Heady: There is an expression that is common among people today that expresses the same thing. It is the phrase, "big head." Heady – the information all lies in the head. All they know is in their head, and they think there is so much of it that they wonder that even their head can hold it. But that is one of the characteristics of the last days. People will be heady. That is, they have their knowledge in their heads.

But God wants *hearty* people in these days. Instead of people having the big *head,* He wants them to have a big *heart.* God gave Solomon largeness of heart like the sands of the seashore, and the exhortation is to us all, in Corinthians, "Be ye also enlarged." God wants large hearted people – hearty people, not heady people. And there are no two ways about it; the Testimonies have told us often enough and plainly enough, that there is entirely too much *theory* among Seventh-day Adventists and not enough experience of the love of Christ in the heart. Too much dogma and not enough of the Spirit of God. Too much form and too little real practical experience of the power of God and of the truth working in the heart and shining abroad in the life. From such turn away. Let God have all the *heart* that He may enlarge it to the filling of it with all His fullness.

High-minded: The next word comes logically from this. It is the consequence of this, just as false accusers comes from truce breakers. These are "heady, high-minded." There is a word upon this in the 12th chapter of Romans, 16th verse: "Mind not high things, but condescend to men of low estate." How is it in our work in Bible readings, tent meetings, and so on? Are we glad when some of the rich folks come out, some of "the best society," and seem to be favorable to the truth and we do think, Now we are doing some great thing? And another man, as James described him, "a poor man, in vile raiment," comes into the tent and his appearance is not altogether in his favor. And we say to the man of the gay clothing, "O, come here. Here is a seat for you." The other man – O, we don't know him at all. How is it? James says that is respect of persons. Have you respect of persons? "If ye have respect to persons, ye commit sin, and are convinced of the law as transgressors." You cannot do it. "Mind not high things, but condescend to men of low estate." I am not saying that we shall slight the rich or those of the best society; not that at all. They are to be called to Christ and be converted just as much as anybody else. What I am asking is, Are we courting these and thinking some great thing is done when one of these shows some interest or favor toward us or the truth, while disregarding or slighting the poor and the outcast? There is no respect of persons with God. "If ye have respect of persons, ye commit sin." "Mind not high things, but condescend to men of low estate. Be not wise in your own conceits."

There is another verse in Philippians that touches the same thing, with an exhortation to us all. Phil. 2:3-6:

> Let nothing be done through strife or vainglory; but in lowliness of mind let each esteem others better than themselves. Look not every man on his own things, but every man also on the things of others. Let this mind be in you, which also was in Christ Jesus; who, though he was high, became low that he might lift up the lowest.

And that was the complaint against Him in His day. Oh, this man, why, He goes in with publicans and sinners and eats with them. "Let this mind be in you, which was also in Christ Jesus."

Lovers of pleasure more than lovers of God: I need not call any further attention to that. Brother Prescott's lesson last night is full enough on that particular point. "Having a form of godliness, but denying the power thereof: from such turn away." Now there is another text upon this particular phase of the study, as to what it is to come out of the world and wherein the world lies and wherein we are connected with the world.

Turn to James 4:4:

> Ye adulterers and adulteresses, know ye not that the friendship of the world is enmity with God? Whosoever therefore will be a friend of the world is the enemy of God.

Does not that call upon everyone to ask himself, Have I friendship for the world? Not, Have I *more* friendship for the world than I have for the Lord? Have I *any of it* at all? For whosoever will be a friend of the world is *the enemy of God.* That is written and that is so. See how he starts out with it too. "Ye adulterers and adulteresses." Let us look at that expression and see what that means in connection with Babylon. Right in that expression we can find how Babylon originated and was built up. Turn to Romans 7:1-4:

> Know ye not, brethren (for I speak to them that know the law), how that the law hath dominion over a man as long as he liveth? For the woman which hath a husband is bound by the law to her husband so long as he liveth; but if the husband be dead, she is loosed from the law of her husband. So then, if, while her husband liveth, she be married to another man, she shall be called an adulteress: but if her husband be dead, she is free from the law; so that she is no adulteress, though she be married to another man. Wherefore my brethren, ye also are become dead to the law by the body of Christ; that ye shall be married to another, even to him who is raised from the dead.

The one who professes the name of Christ stands in the place where his very profession declares that he is married to Jesus Christ, as the wife is married to the husband. Now the wife who has a husband and sets her mind upon another man and puts her dependence upon another man, what is she? You know.

Her husband is there all the time, the husband is living and living with her. Our Husband is alive, and He says, "I will never leave thee nor forsake thee." He is not like a human husband, that is sometimes called away for a long time, but even though the human husband be called away for a long time, that does not justify the wife in putting her dependence upon another man.

But there is this heavenly Husband to whom we are united, as a wife in the marriage relation. He has come from heaven to draw us away from this world, away from the god of this world and all connection with the world, unto God. Christ says, "I am not of this world." He is the second Adam. The first man – the first Adam – is of the earth, earthy; the second man is the Lord from heaven. As is the earthy, such are they also that are of the earth. And as is the heavenly, such are they also that are of the heavenly. Our Husband is of heaven and is only heavenly. When He was in the world, He was not of the world. He put no dependence upon the world. He had no connection whatever with it. As is the heavenly, such are they also that are of the heavenly.

Here are we then, joined to that heavenly husband in that heavenly relation. And the one who professes this and then has his mind, his affections, his friendship, toward the world and upon the world – what is that? That is violative of that marriage relation.

That is what is meant when the word says, "Ye adulterers and adulteresses." That is so with the individual. What then of a combination of individuals composing a church? An *individual* connected with Christ has an individual Christian experience and holds an individual Christian connection. A whole combination of these connected with Christ form the church of Christ and should have a *church* experience and a church connection. Take then one of these *individuals* who has turned away from Christ, the true husband and rightful Lord, has friendship for the world, puts his dependence upon the kings of this world. He is an adulterer, as in the text. Put with him a whole combination of persons who are doing like that, making a *church* also of that kind, that is what made Babylon the mother – committing fornication with the kingdoms of this world, the ways of this world – putting her dependence upon the governments and combinations of this world. Therefore, the next expression we see in the Scriptures describing her is where she has committed fornication with the kings of the earth and sits upon a scarlet colored beast, having on her forehead a name written, 'MYSTERY, BABYLON THE GREAT, THE MOTHER OF HARLOTS AND ABOMINATIONS OF THE EARTH." She sets the wicked example, and other churches – professedly Protestant – have followed the evil example and so have become daughters of that base lineage.

So you see that that very thing that James refers to, which causes him to use the terms "adulterers and adulteresses" – this friendship with the world by those professing the name of Christ – that is what made Babylon at the beginning and it is what makes Babylon the mother and the daughters and the whole combination of Babylon. It is the professed church of Jesus Christ, having the form of godliness without having the power. But having friendship for the world. Having connection with the world, leaning upon the kingdoms and the ways of the kingdoms of this world and not upon the strong, loving arm of her rightful Husband. Friendship with the world contains in itself all that Babylon is. It is enmity with God.

Therefore, you can see that every consideration, every principle upon which a scripture touches, demands, merely in the named principle, utter separation from the world and all there is of it. But when the world is in this condition and all going away from God and being gathered together to be pitted against the Lord, against his Christ, in the persons of those whose names are written in the book of life of the Lamb slain from the foundation of the world – of all times that ever were on the earth, now is the time when these scriptures are to have living force and living power with those who name the name of Christ and especially with those whose names are written in the book of life.

Now note: We have studied so far what Babylon is and what it comprehends. And we find that it comprehends the whole world.4 Therefore what it is to come out of her is nothing less than to come out of the world. We have lately what it is to come out of the world, and it is certain that it is to be utterly separate from the world and all that is in it, having no connection with it whatever. The next inquiry is to be, How is this to be accomplished? God has made complete provision for this. That provision is all ready for our acceptance. And now as we enter upon the study of this part of the subject, we are to know that every heart that will receive the word of God in the Spirit of Christ with the submission that is called for – the Lord Himself will cause that truth to do the very thing that is needed for every such one who will so receive it. That truth will separate us indeed; it will do this work for us. We cannot do it ourselves. We cannot separate ourselves from ourselves. But God has a truth that will do that thing, and it will separate us from ourselves, deliver us from this present evil world, deliver us from sin in the abstract – not simply from individual sins but from sin – so that sin shall not have power over us, but that the power of God will work in its place.

God has a truth in His word that will do just that thing and will lift us so above the world that we shall dwell in the light of the glory of God and of the kingdom of God. That power will be upon us and in us and about us so that we shall go forth to the work to which we are called, to do the work that God has to do and to sound loudly the message of warning and the call that is now to be given to all, "Come out of her, my people."

We cannot give that call unless we are completely out ourselves. I cannot call a man out from the world when I am not out from it myself. I cannot bring a man to see what separation from the world is. I cannot do it with the truth of God, even, unless I see and know by my own experience what separation from the world is. I cannot call people to be utterly separated from the world or anything in it and have them put their dependence absolutely upon God and nothing else, when I am connected with the world myself. It cannot be done. We can say *the words which say to them "Come out," but there will be no power in the words which reach them to bring them out, as only the power of God can, and they cannot come out themselves.*

As we read in a previous lesson, it is the "voice from heaven" that calls the people out of Babylon. Then it is certainly true that from this time forward we are to be so connected with heaven in our work, that when we speak the word of God the people shall hear the voice from heaven, which will fulfill the design of the solemn call. And in the line of truth that is to come in the next division of the subject, God will so connect with heaven everyone who will receive it that he shall find heaven upon the earth. God wants our days, especially from this time forward, to be as the days of heaven upon the earth, according to the Scripture. And He will cause this to be so with everyone who will yield fully to God and to His truth and hear the voice from heaven.

Therefore, I would ask that between this and the next lesson all will set their minds and hearts solemnly and sacredly to preparation for what the Lord has to say, for all that He will give us and for all that He will do for us. God has important truth for us which will do the great work that must be done for us, and we need to have everything surrendered to Him, saying, "Speak, Lord, for thy servant heareth." And when He speaks, drop everything, accept the word, because it is the word of God, and that word will raise us above the world. Then when God has raised us, we can shine.

Sermon 11

February 17, 1895

WE shall begin this lesson with the verse we were studying last night: James 4:4. And I desire especially that everyone shall look at the verses himself and study carefully what they say. In the times in which we are and the place to which we have been brought by the evidences that we cannot avoid and against which it is impossible to shut our eyes, I know that I never entered upon a Bible study in my life as I do upon this one tonight, and I desire that all shall surrender every faculty to the guidance of God's Spirit, with the whole spirit surrendered to God, that He Himself may lead us where He wants us to go.

> Ye adulterers and adulteresses, know ye not that the friendship of the world is enmity with God? Whosoever therefore will be a friend of the world is the enemy of God.

We wish to notice particularly the question, "Know ye not that the friendship of the world is enmity with God?" It follows therefore that the only possibility of any soul in this world ever being separated from this world and thus from Babylon is to have that enmity destroyed. For, I say again, the friendship of the world is not *at* enmity with God. If it were, it could be reconciled to God by taking away that which had put it *at* enmity with God. But it is not that; *it* is the thing itself – it "*is enmity*." And that enmity against God, that which is enmity with God, puts us at enmity with Him. Men may be reconciled to God by having the enmity taken away, but the enmity itself can never be reconciled to God. And mankind, whom the enmity puts *at* enmity with God, are reconciled to God merely by taking away the enmity itself.

We have the key to the whole situation in the fact that the friendship of the world is enmity with God. "The friendship of the world," and "the enmity" are identical; a man cannot have the enmity without the friendship of the world, for that is it – the friendship of the world is in it.

Therefore, I say yet again: The only hope of a man's being separated from the world as the Scriptures demand and as our times demand as never before in the world (if there could be any difference) is by having that enmity taken away. That is all we are to seek for; that is all there is to be done, for when that is gone we are free.

In the eighth chapter of Romans this same thing is referred to, beginning with the seventh verse. "Because the carnal mind" or as it is literally in the Greek, "The mind of the flesh is enmity against God: for it is not subject to the law of God, neither indeed can be."

That makes emphatic the thought presented in connection with the other text, that there is no possibility of that enmity being reconciled to God. Nothing can be done with it but to take it away, to destroy it. Nothing can be done *for* it at all. Something may be done *with* it, but nothing can be done for it, and for the reason that it is against God; it is *not subject to the law of* God, neither indeed *can* be. It cannot be subjected to the law of God. God Himself cannot make the carnal mind the mind of the flesh, subject to His law. It cannot be done. This is not speaking with any irreverence toward the Lord or limiting His power, but it cannot be done. God can destroy the wicked thing and all that ever brought it, but He cannot do anything *for* it, to reform it or make it better.

"So then they that are in the flesh cannot please God." Yet this world is of the flesh altogether: "But ye are not of the world" "for I" says the Lord "have chosen you out of the world." He has separated the Christian from the flesh, from the ways of the flesh, from the mind of the flesh and from the rule of the flesh. This separates from the world by separating us from that which of itself holds us to the world. Nothing but the power of God can do that.

Now let us trace a few moments the record of the time when God made man. Genesis 2. When God made man, God Himself pronounced him, with all the other things He had made, not simply good but "very good." Then man, the first Adam, Adam as he was, was glad to hear the voice of God. He delighted in His presence; his whole being responded joyfully to His call.

But there came another one into the garden and cast distrust of God into the minds of these. The serpent said unto the woman, Humph! Has God said you shall not eat of every tree of the garden? She said, We may eat of the fruit of the trees of the garden, but of the tree which is in the midst of the garden, God said Ye shall not eat of it neither shall ye touch it lest ye die. The serpent said, "Ye shall not surely die; for God doth know that in the day ye eat thereof, ye shall be as God, knowing good and evil." That is the Hebrew of it, and the Jew's translation of it also and the Revised Version, if I remember correctly.

The insinuation was to this effect: God Himself knows that that is not so, and He knows that it is not so that He has told you; this shows that there is something back of that. It shows that He is not dealing fairly with you. He does not want you to be where this will bring you. He does not want you to have what this will give you. He knows what this will do for you and not wanting it to be so, that is why He says, Do not do that. His suggestions were taken and as soon as they were entertained, she thought she now saw what before she did not see and that which in fact was not true.

As the Lord made them and intended they should remain, they were to receive all their instruction and all their knowledge from God. They were to listen to His word, to accept that word and allow it to guide them and to live in them. Thus they would have the mind of God; they would think the thoughts of God by having His word, expressive of His thoughts, dwelling in them. But here another mind, directly the opposite, was attended to. Other suggestions were accepted. Other thoughts were allowed. Other words were received, surrendered to, and obeyed so that "the woman saw that the tree was good for food." Was the tree good for food? No. But by listening to those words she saw things that were not so. She saw things in a way that they were not seen before and never could have been seen in the light of God. But yielding to this other mind she saw things in a false light altogether. She saw that the tree was good for food and a tree to be desired to make one wise. It was no such thing. She saw it so, though.

This reveals the power of deception that there is in the words and the ways of Satan who made those suggestions at that time. As certainly as one inclines his mind that way or has anything in his mind that would of itself incline that way, this gives Satan a chance to work and cause that person to see things in the wrong way, to cause him to see things as being the only necessary things, which are not true at all and not only are they not necessary, but are absolutely false in every respect.

When Eve "saw" all this, it was only the natural consequence. "She took of the fruit thereof and did eat and gave also unto her husband with her, and he did eat."

Look at the record a little further. Eighth verse: "And they heard the voice of the Lord God walking in the garden in the cool of the day and Adam and his wife hid themselves from the presence of the Lord God." What was the cause of that? There was something about them that would avoid the presence of God, something that was not in harmony with God and caused them to hide themselves rather than to welcome Him.

"And the Lord God called unto Adam, and said unto him, Where art thou? And he said, I heard thy voice in the garden, and I was afraid, because I was naked; and I hid myself. And he said, Who told thee that thou wast naked?" Now the question: "Hast thou eaten of the tree, whereof I commanded thee that thou shouldest not eat?" And he said, Yes, I have, and I am inclined to think that it was not exactly right and I am sorry. Did he? Oh, no. The question is, "Hast thou eaten of the tree whereof I commanded thee that thou shouldest not eat?" Hadn't he eaten of it? Certainly he had. Why didn't he say, Yes? As to that "why," I will go on a little further with the lesson and then ask this question again and then we can all see why.

He did not answer, Yes. Though that is all the answer there was any room for. But he said, "The woman whom thou gavest to be with me, she gave me of the tree, and I did eat." It came in at last, admitting that he was involved in it. But whereabouts did he come in? The last possible place. The woman, and even the Lord Himself, must come in for the blame before the man could allow himself to come into it at all. In all this he was simply saying, in substance, "I would not have done it if it had not been for the woman, because she gave it to me; and if the woman had not been here, she would not have done it; and if *you* had not put the woman here, she would not have been here. Therefore, if she had not been here, she would not have given it to me, and if she had not given it to me, I would not have done it. So, of course, as a matter of fact, I did eat, but the responsibility is back yonder." What was it in him and about that that would lead him to involve everybody else in the universe before himself and before admitting that he had any part in it at all? Nothing but *love of self, self*-defense, *self*-protection.

"And the Lord said unto the woman" – another clear question: "What is this that thou hast done?" And she said, Oh, I took of the tree and I ate of it and I gave it to my husband and he ate and it is too bad. No. She said no such thing. Mark: Still answering the question, "What is this that thou hast done?" (He did not ask, "*Who* did it?" but "*What* is this that thou hast done?") "And the woman said, The serpent beguiled me, and I did eat." She answered the question the same way that he did. The same thing caused her to dodge the question and involve somebody else that caused Adam to do that. Everybody else must come in but themselves.

Now I ask again, Why did they not answer the straight question straight? *They could not do it*. And they could not do it because the mind with which they were actuated, which had taken possession of them, which held them in bondage and enslaved them under its power is the mind that originated self-exaltation in the place of God and never will allow itself the second place even where God is. We all know that that is the mind of Satan, of course. But back when he started we know that the thing that caused him to reach the position where he stood at this time was exalting himself.

He turned away his eyes from God and looked to himself, gave himself credit for great glory, and the place where he was was not large enough for him and he must exalt himself. "I will exalt my throne above the stars of God. . . I will ascend above the heights of the clouds; I will be like the Most High." That was sin. The Lord called upon him to forsake his sin and his wrong course, to turn to God, to accept the ways of God once more. We know that that is so, because it is written, "God is no respecter of persons." There is no respect of persons with God. And as the heavenly family and the earthly family are all one family, as God is no respecter of persons, and as when man sinned, God gave him a second chance and called upon him to return – as certainly as there is no respect of persons with God, so certainly God gave to Lucifer a second chance and called upon him to return. That is settled. He might have forsaken his course; he might have forsaken himself and yielded to God. But instead of yielding he refused that call, rejected God's gift, refused to turn from his ways and to surrender to God once more. And in that he simply confirmed himself, in spite of all that the Lord could do in that self-assertive course. And thus *the mind* which *is in him,* thus confirmed in sin and rebellion against God is *enmity* – not simply at enmity; it is enmity itself: "It is not subject to the law of God, *neither* indeed *can* be."

Now *that mind* was accepted by Adam and Eve. And being accepted by them, it took in the whole world, because they, in that acceptance, surrendered this world to Satan and thus he became the god of this world. Accordingly, that is the mind of this world; that is the mind that controls the world. This mind of Satan, the mind of the god of this world, is the mind that controls mankind as mankind is in and of this world and is *in itself* "enmity against God, for it is not subject to the law of God, neither indeed can be."

Now that is why Adam and Eve could not answer that straight question straight. Men could answer that question straight now. But at that time they could not, for the reason that Satan had taken them under his dominion and there was no other power to control them. His control was absolute and there *at that moment* was "total depravity." But God did not leave him there. He did not leave the race in that condition. He turns next and says to the serpent, "I will put enmity between thee and the woman, and between thy seed and her seed; it shall bruise thy head, and thou shalt bruise his heel." Thus there are *two enmities* in this world: one is from Satan and is enmity against God; the other is from God and is enmity against Satan. And through these two *enmities* come the two mysteries – the mystery of God and the mystery of iniquity.

This enmity against Satan is the righteousness of God, of course. In this saying, "I will put enmity between thee and the woman," God broke the bond of Satan over the will of man, set man once more free to choose which authority he would follow, which king and which world he will have. In this word God broke the absolute dominion of Satan and set the man free to choose which world he will have. And since that time the man who will choose God's way and yield his will to the control of God can answer a straight question unto the Lord, so that when the Lord comes and asks, Did you do so and so? he can answer, Yes, without bringing anybody else into it at all. This is confession of sin. And thus came the ability to confess sin and reveals the blessed truth that the power to confess sin – repentance – *is the gift of God.*

Now the mind of Satan being the mind of this world, the mind that controls the natural man, is enmity against God, and it puts man *at* enmity with God. It cannot be reconciled to God, "for it is not subject to the law of God, neither indeed can be." The only thing to be done is to get it out of the way in some way. If that can be done, then the man will be reconciled to God, then the man is all right. He will be once more joined to God and God's word, God's thoughts, God's suggestions can reach him once more to be his guide and his all-controlling power. And as the *thing* cannot be reconciled to God, the only thing that can be done with it is to destroy it. Then, *only* then, and by that means can men be at peace with God and separate from the world. And thank the Lord He has given us the glad news that *it is destroyed.*

As to how it is done and how we can have the benefit of it, that will come in other studies. I count it glad news that God sends us that the thing is done. Then as to leading us into the benefit of it, the joy of it, the glory of it, and the power of it, that will be for the Lord to lead us. We know that this enmity – this mind of self and Satan – separated man from God, but God opened the way for man to return. The Lord gave man a chance to choose which world he will have. And this is the whole subject of our study. We are to leave this world if we are going to get out of Babylon at all. It was to give man a chance to choose which world, that the Lord said to Satan, "I will put enmity" between thee and the seed of the woman. And therefore the only and everlasting question is – which world? Which world? Which world shall a man choose? And when God in His wondrous mercy has opened the way and given us the power to choose a better world than this, why should there be any kind of hesitation?

Turn to the second chapter of Ephesians beginning with the first verse and let us read the good news that the enmity against God is destroyed so that all may be free.

Beginning with the first verse:

> And you hath he quickened who were dead in trespasses and sins; wherein in time past ye walked according to the course of this world, according to the prince of the power of the air, the spirit that now worketh in the children of disobedience.

We walked according to that spirit. What spirit is it that rules in the children of disobedience? The spirit that controls the world, the mind that originated the evil in the garden and that is enmity against God. Who is the prince of the power of the air? The spirit that worketh in the children of disobedience, the god of this world – who has nothing in Jesus Christ, thank the Lord.

> Among whom also we all had our conversation [our way of life] in times past, in the lusts of our flesh, fulfilling the desires of the flesh and of the mind.

The mind of this world, being of this world, naturally falls into the ways of this world. "And were by nature the children of wrath, even as others." We *were*.

Before reading further in Ephesians, turn to Colossians 1:21. You "were sometimes alienated and enemies in your mind." Then where did the enmity lie that made us enemies? In the mind, the fleshly mind. The mind of the flesh is enmity and it controlling us makes us at enmity and enemies – "by wicked works."

Now Ephesians 2:11:

"Wherefore remember, that ye being in time past Gentiles in the flesh, who are called Uncircumcision" – by the Lord? –No, but "by that which is called the circumcision in the flesh made by hands." Then here are some men in the flesh calling other men in the flesh certain names, making certain distinctions between themselves.

> That at that time ye were without Christ, being aliens from the commonwealth of Israel and strangers from the covenants of promise, having no hope and without God in the world.

Another passage in connection with that is in the fourth chapter, 17th and 18th verses, which we will read before reading further here:

> This I say therefore and testify in the Lord, that ye henceforth walk not as other Gentiles walk, in the vanity of their mind, [that is, in the idolatry of their mind], having the understanding darkened, being alienated from the life of God through the ignorance that is in them, because of the blindness of their heart.

Those who are in the flesh, far off from God, are walking in the vanity of their mind, are alienated from God and are separated from the life of God. Enemies in the mind; that is what we were. Reading again in Eph. 2:13: "But now" – When? I mean that. I mean we who are now here studying the scriptures, we are to yield ourselves to the word of God exactly as it is, that it may carry us where He may want us. Therefore, I ask, When? Now, right where we are.

"But NOW, *in Jesus Christ,* ye who sometime were far off." Far off from whom? Far off from God? or far off from the Jews? The previous verse says far off from God, "without God," alienated from the life of God. "Ye who sometime were far off [from God] are made nigh" *to whom?* To God? or to the Jews? – Nigh to God of course.

"Ye who sometimes were far off are made nigh to God by the blood of Christ. For He who is our peace, who hath broken down the middle wall of partition between us – that was between us – *having abolished* in His flesh *the enmity.*" Thank the Lord. He hath "abolished the enmity" and we can be separated from the world.

"Hath broken down the middle wall of partition between" – whom? Between men and God, surely. How did He do it? How did He break down the middle wall of partition between us and God? By "abolishing the enmity." Good.

True, that enmity had worked a division and a separation between men on the earth, between circumcision and uncircumcision, between circumcision according to the flesh and *un*circumcision according to the flesh. It had manifested itself in their divisions, in building up another wall between Jews and Gentiles – that is true, but if the Jews had been joined to God and had not been separated from Him, would they have ever built up a wall between them and anybody else? No, certainly not, but in *their* separation from God, in their fleshly minds, in the enmity that was in their minds and the blindness through unbelief which put the veil upon their heart – all this separated them from God. And *then* because of the laws and ceremonies which God had given them, they gave *themselves* credit for being the Lord's and for being so much better than other people, that they built up a great separating wall and partition between themselves and other people. But where lay the root of the whole thing, as between them and other people even? It lay in the enmity that was in them that separated them first from God. And being separated from Him, the certain consequence was that they would be separated from others.

"For He is our peace, who hath made both one." Made both *who* one? – God and men, certainly. "And hath broken down the middle wall of partition between us, having abolished in His flesh the enmity . . . *for to make in Himself* of *twain* [of two] one new man, *so* making peace."

Let us look that over again. "Having abolished in His flesh the enmity." Now omitting the next clause (We are not studying that in this lesson.), what did He abolish that enmity for? What did He break down that middle wall of partition for? Why? "*for to* make *in Himself* of twain *one new man,* so making peace." Does Christ make a new man out of a Jew and a Gentile? No. Out of a heathen and somebody else? No. Out of one heathen and another heathen? No.

God makes one new man out of GOD and A MAN. And in Christ, God and man met so that they can be one.

All men were separated from God and in their separation from God they were separated from one another.

True, Christ wants to bring all to *one another;* He was ushered into the world with "Peace on earth; good will to men." That is His object.

But does He spend His time in trying to get these reconciled to one another and in trying to destroy all these separations between men and to get them to say, "Oh, well, let all bygones be bygones; now we will bury the hatchet; now we will start out and turn over a new leaf and we will live better from this time on"?

Christ might have done that. If He had taken that course there are thousands of people whom He could have persuaded to do that; thousands whom He could persuade to say, "Well, it is too bad that we acted that way toward one another; it is not right, and I am sorry for it. And now let us just all leave that behind and turn over a new leaf and go on and do better." He could have got people to agree to that. But *could they have stuck to it?* No. For the wicked thing is there still that *made the division.* What caused the division? The enmity, their separation from God caused the separation from one another.

Then what in the world would have been the use of the Lord Himself trying to get men to agree to put away their differences without going to the root of the matter and getting rid of the enmity that caused the separation? Their separation from God had forced a separation among themselves. And the only way to destroy their separation from one another was of necessity to destroy their separation from God.

And this He did by abolishing the enmity. And we ministers can get a lesson from this, when churches call us to try to settle difficulties. We have nothing at all to do with settling difficulties between men as such. We are to get the difficulty between *God* and *man* settled and when that is done, all other separations will be ended.

It is true, the Jews in their separation from God had built up extra separations between themselves and the Gentiles. It is true that Christ wanted to put all those separations out of the way and He did do that. But the only way that He did it and the only way that He could do it was to destroy the thing that separated between them and God. All the separations between them and the Gentiles would be gone, when the separation, the enmity, between them and God was gone.

Oh, the blessed news that the enmity is abolished! It is abolished; thank the Lord. There is therefore now no need whatever of our having any friendship with the world. No need of our having any lack of obedience to the law of God. No need of any failure to be subject to God, for Jesus Christ has taken the enmity out of the way. He has abolished it, destroyed it. He has destroyed the wicked thing in which lies friendship with the world, in which lies lack of subject to God and failure to be subject to His law. It is gone; *in Christ* it is gone. Not outside of Christ. *In Christ* it is gone, abolished, annihilated. Thank the Lord. This is freedom indeed.

That has always been good news, of course. But to me now, in view of the situation which God has shown us as we are now placed in the world, this blessed news has come to me in the last few days as though I had never heard it before. It has come to me bringing such joy, such genuine Christian delight, that – well, it seems to me I am just as happy as a Christian.

Oh, the blessed fact that God says that thing which separates us from God, which joins us to the world and which does all the mischief, is abolished *in Him, who is our Peace*. Let us take the glad news tonight, rejoice in it all the night and all the day, that God may lead us on further and further into the green pastures and by the still waters of His glorious kingdom into which He has translated us. "Fear not, for behold I bring you good tidings of great joy which shall be to all people. For unto you [unto *me* I know] is born this day in the city of David, a Saviour, which is Christ the Lord." Thank the Lord.

Sermon 12

February 18, 1895

THE same text that closed the study last night will be our study for several lessons yet to come. Therefore, if any part of the text should be passed over and you think it has not been explained yet or has not been noticed even, just bear in mind that we are not nearly done with the text yet and each part will come in in its place.

Ephesians 2:13-18:

> But now, in Christ Jesus, ye who sometime were far off are made nigh by the blood of Christ. For he is our peace, who hath made both one, and hath broken down the middle wall of partition between us; having abolished in his flesh the enmity… for to make in himself of twain one new man, so making peace.

That is, He did it to make peace. Peace is made and only by this means. And it is all "in himself." And He made this peace, "*that* he might reconcile both [Jew and Gentile] unto God in one body by the cross, having slain the enmity thereby."

The text says "thereby."

The margin says, "having slain the enmity *in himself*"; the German says, "having put to death the enmity through himself"; "and came and preached peace to you which were afar off and to them that were nigh. For through him we both have access by one Spirit unto the Father."

I would mention again, as I did last night briefly, that it is the separation, the enmity, that existed between Jew and Gentile that is considered here. It is true that the destruction of that separation and enmity is considered, the taking away of it is studied and explained, and also the means by which it is taken away and the destroying of it is told. But as we mentioned last night, Christ did not spend any time trying to get the Jew and the Gentile, as of themselves, reconciled among themselves. He did not begin by trying to get them to agree to put away their differences, turn over a new leaf and try to do better, and forget the past and let bygones be bygones. He did not spend two minutes on that, and if He had spent ten thousand years, it would have done no good, because this separation, this enmity, that was between them was only the consequence, the fruit, of *the enmity* that existed *between them* and God.

Therefore, in order effectually to destroy the whole evil tree and its fruit as it stood between these, He destroyed the *root* of the whole thing by abolishing the enmity between them and God. And having done so "he came and announced the glad tidings – *peace to you* who were afar off and to those near." Greek.

Thirteenth verse: Therefore, "Now, *in Christ Jesus,* ye who sometime were far off are made nigh by the blood of Christ. For he is our peace who hath made both one." It is true that He made both Jew and Gentile one, but He first made *another* one, in order that these two, "both Jew and Gentile," might be one and before they could be made one.

Therefore, the "both" in this verse, that are made one, are not the "both" of verse 18. In verse 14 the two, the "both" are *God* and *man*; who is separated from God whether he be near or far off.

Therefore, first, He is our peace who hath made both *God* and *man* ONE and hath broken down the middle wall of partition between God and man, having abolished in His flesh *the enmity;* that is, the enmity which is in man against God, which is not subject to the law of God, neither indeed can be. This He did in order that He *in Himself* of TWO should make ONE *new man,* so making peace.

The new man is not made of two men who are at outs, but is made *of God* and *the man.* In the beginning man was made "in the image of God." And that signifies a good deal more than the shape of God. One looking upon him would be caused to think of God. He reflected the image of God; God was suggested to whoever looked upon the man. *God* and *the man* were *one.* And God and the man would have always remained one too, had not the man hearkened to Satan and received his mind which is enmity against God. This mind that is enmity against God, when received by the man, separated him from God. Now they were *two* and not one. And being *separated* from God and *in* sin, *God cannot come to him Himself, for the man cannot bear the unveiled glory of His presence.* "Our God is a consuming fire" to sin, and so for God to meet a man in that man's self or alone would be only to consume him.

Men in sin cannot meet God alone and exist.

This is shown in Rev. 6:13-17. The great day when the heaven departs as a scroll when it is rolled together and the face of God is seen by all the wicked ones upon the earth, then "the kings of the earth, and the great men, and the rich men, and the chief captains, and the mighty men, and every bond man, and every free man, hid themselves in the dens and in the rocks of the mountains and said to the mountains and rocks, Fall on us and hide us from the face of Him that sitteth on the throne and from the wrath of the Lamb, for the great day of His wrath is come; and who shall be able to stand?" A man who is in sin, a man in and of himself, meeting God, would rather have a mountain upon him than to be where the unveiled glory of God would shine upon him.

Therefore, in order that God might reach man, and be joined to him once more; in order that God might be revealed to man once more, and that man might be once more in the place which God made him for, *Jesus gave Himself,* and God appeared in Him with His glory so veiled by human flesh that man, sinful man, can look upon Him and live. In Christ man can meet God and live, because in Christ the glory of God is so veiled, so modified, that sinful man is not consumed. All of God is in Christ, for "in him dwelleth all the fullness of the godhead bodily." When Jesus came to bring man once more to God, He veiled this bright consuming glory so that now men can look upon God as He is in all His glory in Jesus Christ and live. Whereas, out of Christ, in Himself, alone, *no man* can see God and live. In Christ, out of Himself, no man can see God and *not* live. In Christ, to see God is to live, for in Him is life and the life is the light of men.

Thus God and man, by the enmity, were separate, but Christ comes between and in Him the man and God meet, and when God and the man meet in Christ, then those two – "both" – are *one*, and *there* is *the new man*. And "so," and only *so,* peace is made. So that in Christ, God and man are made as one; consequently, Christ is the at-one-ment between God and the man. A-t-o-n-e-m-e-n-t, making at one. Consequently, join the syllables together and He is the *atonement*. Oh, the Lord Jesus gave Himself and *in Himself* abolished the enmity to make *in Himself* of *two* – God and the man – *one new man,* so making peace.

Now we come to the other "both" in verse 16: "That he might reconcile *both* [both Jew and Gentile] unto *God in one body."* But what body is it in which He, Christ, reconciles "both" into God? His own, of course. His own, in which the at-one-ment is made. "Having slain the enmity thereby and came and preached peace to you which were afar off" to the Gentile, "and to them that were nigh," that is, the Jews.

The Jews were nigh "for their fathers' sakes." As in themselves, on their own merit, the Jews were separated from God and were just as far off as the Gentiles. But God had made promises to their fathers and they were beloved for the fathers' sakes. And they had the advantage, for to them pertained "the adoption, and the glory, and the covenants, and the giving of the law, and the service of God, and the promises." In this sense, and for this cause they were nigh. And He preached peace to them *that were nigh;* they needed peace preached to them.

Thus "through him we both have access by one Spirit unto the Father."

Now let us follow this expression, that the enmity is destroyed in Himself.

"Having abolished *in his flesh* the enmity" – having slain the enmity *in Himself. In Himself* of two, so making peace. It is all *in Himself.* No man can have the benefit of it except *in Him.* If there be those in the audience to whom this seems obscure and who would say, "I cannot see that" and would stand off and look at it as though it were something you would try to get hold of from without, I would say to such, You will never get it in that way. That is not the way it is done. It is *in Him* that it is done, not outside of Him. In Him only can it be known, not outside of Him at all. Surrender to Him, yield to Him, sink self in Him, then it will be all plain enough. Only *in Him* it is done, and only *in Him* can it be known. We are to study now how it was done in Him. And knowing this, we shall know how it is done for every one of us in Him.

First of all, I would call especial attention to that expression "in Him." This expression is not used in the Scriptures and I shall never expect to use in any such sense as that it is in Him as in a receptacle or a reservoir to which we are to go and take out what we may need and put it upon us or apply it to ourselves. No, no, no! That is not it. It can never be gotten in that way. It is not there as in a receptacle to which we are to go and take out what we would have of Him and enjoy it and apply it to ourselves and say, "Now I have got it."

No, it is *in Him,* and we ourselves are to be in Him, in order to have it. We are to sink ourselves *in Him.* Our self is to be lost *in Him.* Then He *has us.* Only *in Him* it is. We find it *only* in Him. And even when we would get it in Him, it is only by being ourselves overwhelmed *in Him. Never* are we to think of going to get it there and take it *out of Him* and use it ourselves. Therefore, where the Scriptures use the term "in Him," it means only that to all. All is *in Him* and we get it by being ourselves *in Him.*

Many people make a mistake here. They say, "Oh, yes, I believe on Him. I know it is in Him and I get it *from* Him." And they propose to take it *from* Him and apply it to themselves. Then soon they become quite well satisfied that *they* are righteous; *they* are holy, and they get so far along at last that in their estimation it is a settled fact that *they* are perfect and just *cannot* sin and are even beyond temptation. Such a view is certain to bring only such result, because it is *out of* Him. And it is *themselves* who are doing it.

But that is not the way. That is self still, because it is out of Christ. And "without Me," that is, outside of Him, "ye can do nothing," because ye are nothing. *In Him* it is and only in Him. And only as *we* are *in Him* can we have it or profit by it at all. The Scriptures will make that all plain. I thought best to set down this explanation so that in the studies that are to come of what is done *in Him* and what is given is *in Him,* we shall not make the mistake of thinking we are to find it in Him and take it out. No. We are to go to Him for it. There is where it is, and when we go to Him we are to enter into Him by faith and the Spirit of God and there remain and ever "be found in Him." Philippians 3:9.

Turn to the book of Hebrews now and we will study the first two chapters for the rest of this present lesson.

The question now is, How did Christ abolish this enmity "in His flesh" "in Himself"? I will first state the argument in both chapters in order that we may cover the two chapters in the short time we shall have.

In these two chapters the one great thought is the *contrast between Christ and the angels.* I do not say that is all there is in the two chapters, but that is the one thought that is above everything else.

In the first chapter and up to the fifth verse of the second chapter is the first contrast; in the second chapter from the fifth verse to the end of the chapter is the second contrast.

In the first chapter and up to the fifth verse of the second is the contrast between Christ and the angels, *with Christ as far above the angels* as God is, because He is God. In the second chapter, from the fifth verse onwards, is the contrast between Christ and the angels, but with Christ as far below the angels as man is below the angels, because Christ become man.

There is the outline of the two chapters. That is the statement of the case. Let us read the chapter:

> God, who at sundry times and in divers manners spake in time past unto the fathers by the prophets hath in these last days spoken unto us by his Son whom he hath appointed heir of all things, by whom also he made the worlds; who being the brightness of his glory and the express image of his person and upholding all things by the word of his power.

Or, as the German reads, "Holding up all things by his powerful word." That gives another turn to it; not simply the word of His power, but He carries all things, holds them up, by His powerful word. And we might pause a moment upon that one statement. How many things are held up by His word? All things. The world? Yes. The sun? Yes. All the starry heavens? Yes. Does the word that made them still hold them up? Yes. Can we be numbered among the "all things?" Assuredly so. Will He hold you up by His powerful word? That is the only way that He holds anything up.

Were you ever uneasy any time in your life, when you arose in the morning with the sun, for fear that the sun would drop out of place before noon or before sundown? Oh, no. Were you ever uneasy when you arose with the sun for fear that *you* yourself *as a Christian* would slip out of place before sundown? You know you have been. Why were you not as uneasy as to whether the sun would drop out of place before sundown, fearing that that might slip out of place and fall as you were that you yourself would fall? Oh, of course *no one* ever thinks of any such anxious question as to why the sun does not fall. It is always there and will stay there.

But it is perfectly fair for the Christian to ask, Why is it that the sun does not slip out of his place? And the answer is, The "powerful word" of Jesus Christ holds the sun there and causes him to go on in his course. And *that same power* is to hold up *the believer in Jesus.* That same word is to hold up the believer in Jesus and the believer in Jesus is to expect it to do so, just as certainly as it holds up the sun or the moon. That same powerful word is to hold up the Christian in the Christian's course, precisely the same as it holds the sun in his course. The Christian who will put his confidence upon that word that is to hold him up, as he puts his confidence in that word that holds up the sun will find that that word *will* hold him up as it holds up the sun.

If you think of this scripture tomorrow morning when you arise, you will think that God is holding up the sun. You will not wonder at it either; you will expect Him to do that and will not be watching uneasily to see whether the sun will slip out of its place. No. You will simply go about your work with your mind upon the work and leave the holding up of the sun altogether to God, to whom it belongs. Also tomorrow morning when you arise with the sun, just expect that same powerful word to hold you up as it does the sun. Leave this part to God too, and go about your work with all your might and put all your mind upon your work. Let God attend to that which belongs to Him, and give your mind to that which He has given you to do. And thus serve God "with *all* the mind." We cannot keep ourselves from falling. We cannot hold ourselves up. And He has not given us that task to do.

This is not contradicting the text that says, "Let Him that thinketh He standeth take heed lest He fall" because in this way the man is relying upon God to hold him up and does not depend upon his own efforts. And he who constantly bears in mind that God is holding him up and that he *must* be held up is not going to be boasting of his ability to stand. If I had to be carried in here this evening, perfectly helpless and two or three of the brethren should have to stand here and hold me up, it would not be very becoming in me to say, "See how I can stand." I would not be standing. I could not stand. Just the moment they should release their hold, I would fall.

It is precisely so with the Christian. The word of God says of the Christian, "To his own master he standeth or falleth. Yea, *he shall be holden up; for God is able to make him stand.*" Rom. 14:4. And the man whom God is holding up, who is trusting in God *to* hold him up, and knows that it is God alone who is making him stand – it is impossible for that man to begin to say, "I am standing now, and therefore there is no danger of my falling." Is there any danger of a man's falling while God holds him up? Of course not. It is only when he takes himself out of the Lord's hand and begins to try to hold himself up and then boasts that he can stand, it is then that there is not only danger but the thing is done. He has already fallen. He takes himself out of God's hand and he is bound to fall.

Now continuing in Hebrews 1:

> When he had by himself purged our sins, sat down on the right hand of the Majesty on high.

When did He sit down on the right hand of God? How long ago? Away back yonder, when He arose from the dead and went to heaven – nearly nineteen hundred years ago. But notice, He *had* purged our sins before He sat down there. "When He *had*"

– past tense – "by himself purged our sins, sat down." Are you glad of this? Are you glad that He purged your sins so long ago as that? *In Him* it is. *In Him* we find it. Let us thank Him it is so. The Word says so.

> Being made so much better than the angels as he hath by inheritance obtained a more excellent name than they. For unto which of the angels said he at any time, Thou art my Son, this day have I begotten thee? And again, I will be to him a Father, and he shall be to me a Son? And again, when he bringeth in the first-begotten into the world, he saith, And let all the angels of God worship him. And of the angels, he saith, Who maketh his angels spirits, and his ministers a flame of fire. But unto the Son he saith, Thy throne, O God, is for ever and ever.

What is His name? What does the Father call Him? God. "Thy throne, *O God*." Then that is His name. How did He get it? Fourth verse: "As He hath *by inheritance* obtained a more excellent *name* than the angels." You and I have a name that we have by inheritance. We may have four or five names, but we have only one name that we got by inheritance. And that is our Father's name. And that name we have just as soon as we exist and just because we exist. By the very fact of our existence we have that name; it belongs to us by nature.

The Lord Jesus "hath by inheritance" obtained this name of "God." Then that name belongs to Him just because He exists. It belongs to Him by nature. What nature is His, then? Precisely the nature of God. And God is His name, because that is what He is. He was not something else and then named that to make Him that, but He *was* that and was called God because He is God.

> A scepter of righteousness is the scepter of thy kingdom. Thou hast loved righteousness and hated iniquity; therefore, God, even thy God, hath anointed thee with the oil of gladness above thy fellows.

The Father still speaking, says:

> And, thou, Lord, in the beginning hast laid the foundation of the earth; and the heavens are the works of thine hands. They shall perish, but thou remainest: and they all shall wax old as doth a garment; and as a vesture shalt thou fold them up, and they shall be changed: but thou art the same."

No change with Him. Notice the connection in these words: "They shall *perish;*" "thou *remainest;*' they shall *be changed;* thou art *the same.*" When these perish and pass away there is no passing away to Him – Thou remainest. When these are folded up and changed, there is no change in Him, – Thou art the same.

> And thy years shall not fail. But to which of the angels said he at any time, Sit on my right hand, until I make thine enemies thy footstool? Are they not all ministering spirits, sent forth to minister for them who shall be heirs of salvation? Therefore, we ought to give

> the more earnest heed to the things which we have heard, lest at any time we should let them slip. For if the word spoken by angels was steadfast and every transgression and disobedience received a just recompense of reward; how shall we escape, if we neglect so great salvation; which at the first began to be spoken by the Lord, and was confirmed unto us by them that heard him; God also bearing them witness, both with signs and wonders, and with divers miracles, and gifts of the Holy Ghost, according to his own will?

There is the contrast between Christ and the angels so far. And where is Christ in the contrast? Where God is, with the angels worshiping Him. And if an angel's word was steadfast and received a just recompense of reward when it was disregarded, how shall we escape if we neglect the word of Him who is higher than the angels? How shall we escape if we neglect the word of God spoken by Himself?

Now turn to the other contrast. Hebrews 2:5:

> For unto the angels hath he not put in subjection the world to come, whereof we speak.

There are those two worlds of which we spoke last night. God said, I will put enmity between man and Satan. And that gives man a chance to choose which world. We have chosen the world to come. Unto the angels hath He not put in subjection that world either; that is the thing He is talking about. The world to come which we have chosen is not put in subjection to the angels.

> But one in a certain place testified, saying, What is man that thou art mindful of him? or the son of man, that thou visitest him?

Now what is the purpose, what is the force, of putting the word "but" in there? He has not put it in subjection to the angels, but He has said of man so and so. Does that suggest that He has put it in subjection to man? What do you think? Look at it again. "Unto the angels hath he not put in subjection the world to come, whereof we speak; *but*" – What part of speech is "but"? A conjunction. A conjunction joins two parts of a sentence. But this is a peculiar kind of conjunction, a disjunctive conjunction. A juncture is a joining, conjunct is to join together; disjunct is to separate. Then here is a word that both joins and separates. It is a *con*junction in that it joins the clauses; it is a *dis*junctive in that it separates the thoughts that are in the two sentences or clauses as the case may be.

Many people say, "I believe the Bible, but"; "Yes, I believe the Lord forgives sins, but"; "Yes, I confessed my sins, but." That "but" disjoins them from everything that they have said; it shows that they do not believe at all what they have said. What are the two things, then, that are separated by this "but" in Hebrews 2:6? First, who are the two persons who are separated by the "but"? One is the angels and the other is man. He has not put in subjection to the angels the world to come, but has put it in subjection to somebody and that somebody is *man*. Let us study it for that blessed truth.

> But one in a certain place testified, saying, What is man that thou art mindful of him? or the Son of man, that thou visitest him? Thou madest him a little lower than the angels; thou crownedst him with glory and honor and didst set him over the works of thy hands: thou hast put all things in subjection under his feet. For in that he put all in subjection under him, he left nothing that is not put under him. But now we see not yet all things put under him. But we see Jesus.

Where do we see Jesus? "We see Jesus, who was made a little lower than the angels." There is the contrast again between Christ and the angels. In the other contrast we saw Jesus higher than the angels; here we see Him lower than the angels. Why? Because man was made lower than the angels and by sin went still lower even. Now "we see certainly as it is true that as Jesus was where God is, so certainly He has come to where man is.

There is another thought we want to put right with that. He who was with God *where* God is, is with man *where* man is. And He who was with God *as* God is, is with man *as* man is. And He who was *one with God* as God is, is *one with man* as man is. And so certainly as *His* was *the nature of God* yonder, so certainly His is *the nature of man* here.

Let us read this blessed fact now in the Scriptures, and that will close the lesson for tonight. Tenth verse:

> For it became him for whom are all things, and by whom are all things, in bringing many sons unto glory, to make the captain of their salvation perfect through sufferings. For both he that sanctifieth and they who are sanctified are all *of one*.

Christ sanctifies, and it is men who are sanctified, and how many are there of them? One. It was Christ and God in heaven, and how many were there of them? One in nature. How is He with man on the earth and how many are of them? One, "all of one."

> For which cause he is not ashamed to call them brethren, saying, I will declare the name unto my brethren, in the midst of the church will I sing praise unto thee.

That time is coming soon, when Christ in the midst of the church will lead the singing. Remember, this is Christ speaking in these quotations. "And again, I will put my trust in him." This is Christ speaking – through the Psalms, too.

> And again, behold I and the children which God hath given me. Forasmuch then as the children are partakers of flesh and blood, he also likewise took part of the same; that through death he might destroy him that had the power of death, that is, the devil; and deliver them, who through fear of death were all their lifetime subject to bondage. For verily he took not on him the nature of angels; but he took on him the seed of Abraham. Wherefore in all things it behooved him to be made like unto his brethren.

He who was one of God has become one of man. We will follow the thought further tomorrow night.

Sermon 13

February 19, 1895

THE particular thought which will be the subject of our study at this time is that which is found in the 11th verse, second chapter of Hebrews: "Both he that sanctifieth and they who are sanctified are all of one." It is men of this world, sinful men, whom Christ sanctifies – He is the Sanctifier. And He and these are all *of* one.

In this part of the chapter you will remember we are studying man. In the first chapter, as we have seen, there is shown the contrast between Christ and the angels with Christ above the angels *as God*. In the second chapter the contrast is between Christ and the angels with Christ below the angels. God has not put in subjection to the angels the world to come whereof we speak. He has put it in subjection *to man* and *Christ* is the man. Therefore, Christ became man; He takes the place of man; He was born as man is born. In His human nature Christ came from the man from whom we all have come, so that the expression in this verse, "all of one," is the same as "all from one – as all coming forth from one. One man is the source and head of all our human nature. And the genealogy of Christ, as one of us, runs to Adam. Luke 3:38.

It is true that all men and all things are from God, but the thought in this chapter is man, and Christ as man. We are the sons of the first man, and so is Christ according to the flesh. We are now studying Christ in His human nature. The first chapter of Hebrews is Christ in His divine nature. The second chapter is Christ in human nature. The thought in these two chapters is clearly akin to that in the second chapter of Philippians, vers 5-8:

> Let this mind be in you which was also in Christ Jesus: who, being in the form of God, thought it not robbery to be equal with God: but made himself of no reputation, and took upon him the form of a servant, and was made in the likeness of men: and being found in fashion as a man, he humbled himself, and became obedient unto death, even the death of the cross.

In that passage Christ in the two forms is set forth. First, being in the form of God, He took the form of man. In Hebrews, first two chapters, it is *not* the *form but* the *nature.*

I repeat:

In the second chapter of Philippians we have Christ in the two *forms* – the form of God and the form of man. In Hebrews, first and second chapters, we have Christ in the two *natures,* the nature of God and the nature of man. You may have something in the form of man that would not be of the nature of man. You can have a piece of stone in the form of man, but it is not the nature of man. Jesus Christ took the *form* of man, that is true, and He did more; He took the *nature* of man.

Let us read now the fourteenth verse of the second chapter of Hebrews. "Forasmuch then as the children [the children of Adam, the human race] are partakers of flesh and blood, He also Himself likewise took part of the same". "Likewise means in this wise, in this way, in a way like this which is spoken of. Therefore, Christ took flesh and blood *in a way like* we take it. But how did we take flesh and blood? – By birth and clear from Adam too. He took flesh and blood *by birth* also and clear from Adam too. For it is written: He is the seed of David according to the flesh. Romans 1:3. While David calls Him Lord, He also is David's son. Matt. 22:42-45. His genealogy is traced to David, but it does not stop there. It goes to Abraham, because He is the seed of Abraham. He took on Him the seed of Abraham, as in the sixteenth verse of this second chapter of Hebrews. Nor does His genealogy stop with Abraham; it goes to Adam. Luke 3:38. Therefore He which sanctifieth among men and they who are sanctified among men are *all of one.* All coming from one man according to the flesh, are all of one. Thus on the human side, Christ's nature is precisely our nature.

Let us look at the other side again for an illustration of this oneness, that we may see the force of this expression that He and we are all of one.

On the other side, however, as in the first chapter of Hebrews, He is of *the nature of God.* The name God which He bears belongs to Him by the very fact of His existence; it belongs to Him by inheritance. As that name belongs to Him entirely because He exists and as certainly as He exists and as it belongs to Him by nature, it is certain that His nature is the nature of God.

Also, in the first chapter of John, first verse, it is written: "In the beginning was the Word, and the Word was with God. That word "with" does not express the reality of the thought as well as another. The German puts a word in there that defines the Greek closer than ours does. That says, "In the beginning was the Word, and the Word was *bei* God" literally, "The Word was *of* God." And that is true. The Greek word conveys the same idea as that my right arm is of me, of my body. The Greek therefore is literally; In the beginning "the word was God."

This simply illustrates *on that side* the fact as to what He is *on this side.* For as on the divine side, He was of God, of the nature of God, and was really God, so on the human side He is of man and of the nature of man and really man.

Look at the fourteenth verse of the first chapter of John. "And the Word was made flesh and dwelt among us." That tells the same story that we are reading here in the first two chapters of Hebrews. "In the beginning was the Word, and the Word was of God, and the Word was God." "And the Word was made flesh, and dwelt among us" – flesh and blood as ours is.

Now what kind of flesh is it? What kind of flesh alone is it that this world knows? Just such flesh as you and I have. This world does not know any other flesh of man and has not known any other since the necessity for Christs coming was created. Therefore, as this world knows only such flesh as we have, as it is now, it is certainly true that when the Word was made flesh," He was made just as flesh as ours is. It cannot be otherwise.

Again: What kind of flesh is our flesh, as it is in itself? Let us turn to the eighth chapter of Romans and read whether Christ's human nature meets ours and is as ours in that respect wherein ours is sinful flesh. Romans 8:3: "What the law could not do in that it was weak through the flesh, God sending his own Son" did.

There was something that the law could not do, and that God, sending His own Son, did. But why was it that the law could not do what it desired and what was required? It was weak through the flesh. The trouble was in the flesh. It was this that caused the law to fail of its purpose concerning man. Then God sent Christ to do what the law could not do. And the law having failed of its purpose because of the flesh and not because of any lack in itself, God must send Him to help the flesh and not to help the law. If the law had been in itself too weak to do what it was intended to do, then the thing for Him to have done to help the matter out would be to remedy the law. But the trouble was with the flesh, and therefore He must remedy the flesh.

It is true that the argument nowadays, springing up from that enmity that is against God and is not subject to the law of God, neither indeed can be, is that the law could not do what was intended and God sent His Son to weaken the law, so that the flesh could answer the demands of the law. But if I am weak and you are strong and I need help, it does not help me any to make you as weak as I am; I am as weak and helpless as before. There is no help at all in all that. But when I am weak and you are strong and you can bring to me your strength, that helps me. So the law was strong enough, but its purpose could not be accomplished through the weakness of the flesh. Therefore, God, to supply the need, must bring strength to weak flesh. He sent Christ to supply the need and therefore Christ must so arrange it that strength may be brought to our flesh itself which we have today, that the purpose of the law may be met in our flesh. So it is written: "God sending his own Son in the likeness of sinful flesh," in order "that the righteousness of the law might be fulfilled in us, who walk not after the flesh, but after the Spirit."

Now do not get a wrong idea of that word "likeness." It is not the shape; it is not the photograph; it is not the likeness in the sense of an image, but it is likeness in the sense of being like indeed. The word likeness here is not the thought that is in the second chapter of Philippians, where it is shape, the form, or likeness as to form, but here in the book of Hebrews it is likeness *in nature,* likeness to the flesh as it is in itself, God sending His own Son in that which is just like sinful flesh. And in order to be just like sinful flesh, it would have to be sinful flesh; in order to be made flesh at all, as it is in this world, He would have to be just such flesh as it is in this world, just such as we have and that is sinful flesh. This is what is said in the words "likeness of sinful flesh."

This is shown in the ninth and tenth verses of Hebrews 2, also: "We see Jesus, who was made a little lower than the angels" – not only as man was made lower than the angels when He was created.

Man was sinless when God made him a little lower than the angels. That was sinless flesh. But man fell from that place and condition and became sinful flesh.

Now we see Jesus, who was made a little lower than the angels, but not as man was made when he was first made a little lower than the angels, but as man is since he sinned and became still lower than the angels. That is where we see Jesus. Let us read and see: We see Jesus who was made a little lower than the angels. What for? "For the *suffering* of *death*." Then Christ's being made as much lower than the angels as man is, is as much lower than the angels as man is since he sinned and became subject to death. We see Him "crowned with glory and honor; that he by the grace of God should taste death for every man. For it became him [it was appropriate for him], for whom are all things and by whom are all things in bringing many sons unto glory, to make the captain of their salvation perfect through sufferings."

Therefore, as He became subject to suffering and death, this demonstrates strongly enough that the point lower than the angels at which Christ came to stand; where He does stand and where "we see him," is the point to which man came when he, in sin, stepped still lower than where God made him – even then a little lower than the angels.

Again: the sixteenth verse: "Verily he took not on him the nature of angels, but he took on him the seed of Abraham." He took not on Him the nature of angels, but He took on Him the nature of Abraham. But the nature of Abraham and of the seed of Abraham is only human nature.

Again: "Wherefore in all things it behooved him to be made like unto his brethren." In how many things? All things. Then in His human nature there is not a particle of difference between Him and you.

Let us read the scripture. Let us study this closely. I want to see that we shall stand by it. Let us read it over: "Are all of one." He took part of flesh and blood in the same way that we take part of flesh and blood. He took not the nature of angels but the seed, the nature, of Abraham. *Wherefore* – for these reasons – it behooved Him, what is behooved?

It was the proper thing for Him to do – it became Him, it was appropriate. It behooved Him to be made in all things like unto His brethren. Who are His brethren, though? The human race. "All of one," and for this cause He is not ashamed to call them brethren. Because we are *all of one,* He is not ashamed to call you and me brethren. Wherefore in all things it behooved Him to be made like unto His brethren."

Well, then, in His human nature, when He was upon the earth, was He in any wise different from what you are in your human nature tonight? [A few in the congregation responded, "NO"] I wish we had heard everybody in the house say, "No," with a loud voice. You are too timid altogether. The word of God says that, and we are to say, That is so, because there is salvation in just that one thing. No, it is not enough to say it that way: *the* salvation of God for human beings lies in just that one thing. We are not to be timid about it at all. There our salvation lies, and until we get there we are not sure of our salvation. That is where it is. "In all things it behooved him to be made like unto his brethren." What for? – O, "that he might be a merciful and faithful high priest in things pertaining to God, to make reconciliation for the sins of the people. For in that He Himself hath suffered being tempted, He is able to succor them that are tempted." Then don't you see that our salvation lies just there? Do you not see that it is right there where Christ comes to us? He came to us just where we are tempted and was made like us just where we are tempted, and there is the point where we meet Him – the living Saviour against the power of temptation.

Now the fourteenth verse of the fourth chapter of Hebrews:

> Seeing then that we have a great high priest that is passed into the heavens, Jesus, the Son of God, let us hold fast our profession. For we have not a high priest which cannot be touched with the feeling of our infirmities; but was in all points tempted like as we are.

He could not have been tempted in all points like as I am if He were not in all points like as I am to start with. Therefore, it behooved Him to be made in all points like me, if He is going to help me where I need help. I know that right there is where I need it. And oh, I know it is right there where I get it. Thank the Lord! There is where Christ stands and there is my help.

"We have not a high priest which cannot be touched" – two negatives there; have *not* a high priest which can*not* be touched. Then what do we have on the affirmative side? We have a high priest who *can* be touched with the feeling of our infirmities – my infirmities, your infirmities, our infirmities. Does He feel my infirmities? Yes. Does He feel your infirmities? Yes. What is an infirmity? Weakness, wavering, weakness – that is expressive enough. We have many of them. All of us have many of them. We feel our weaknesses. Thank the Lord, there is One who feels them also – yea, not only feels them but is touched with the feeling of them.

There is more in that word "touched" than simply that He is reached with the feeling of our weaknesses and feels as we feel. He feels as we feel, that is true, but beyond that He is "touched"; that is, He is tenderly affected; His sympathy is stirred. He is touched to tenderness and affected to sympathy and He helps us. This is what is said in the words, "touched with the feeling of our infirmities." Thank the Lord for such a Saviour!

But I say again, He cannot be tempted in all points like as I am unless He was in all points like I am to start with. He could not feel as I do unless He is where I am and *as* I am. In other words, He could not be tempted in all points as I am and feel as I feel unless He was just *myself* over again. The word of God says: "In all points like as we are."

Let us study this further.

There are things that will tempt you strongly that will draw hard on you, that are no more to me than a zephyr in a summer day. Something will draw hard on me, even to my overthrowing, that would not affect you at all. What strongly tempts one may not affect another. Then, in order to help me, Jesus must be where He can feel what I feel and be tempted in all points where I could be tempted with any power at all. What strongly tempts one may not affect another. Then, in order to help me, Jesus must be where He can feel what I feel and be tempted in all points where I could be tempted with any power at all. But as things that tempt me may not affect you at all and things that affect you may not affect me, Christ has to stand where you and I both are, so as to meet all the temptations of both. He must feel all those which you meet that do not affect me and also all those which I meet that do not affect you. He has to take the place of both of us. That is so.

Then there is the other man. There are things that tempt him to his overthrow that do not affect you or me either. Then Jesus had to take all the feelings and nature of *myself,* of *yourself,* and of *the other man* also, so that He could be tempted in all points like as I am and in all points like as you are and in all points like as the other man is. But when *you* and *I* and *the other man* are taken in Him, how many does that embrace? That takes the whole human race.

And this is exactly the truth. Christ was in *the place* and He had *the nature* of the whole human race. And in Him meet all the weaknesses of mankind, so that every man on earth who can be tempted at all finds in Jesus Christ power against that temptation. For every soul there is in Jesus Christ victory against all temptation and relief from the power of it. That is the truth.

Let us look at it from another side. There is one in the world – Satan, the god of this world – who is interested in seeing that we are tempted just as much as possible, but he does not have to employ much of his time nor very much of his power in temptation to get us to yield.

That same one was here and he was particularly interested in getting Jesus to yield to temptation. He tried Jesus upon every point upon which he would ever have to try me to get me to sin, and he tried in vain. He utterly failed to get Jesus to consent to sin in any single point upon which I can ever be tempted.

He also tried Jesus upon every point upon which he has ever tried you or ever can try you to get you to sin, and he utterly failed there too. That takes you and me both then, and Jesus has conquered in all points for both you and me.

But when he tried Jesus upon all the points that he has tried upon both you and me and failed there, as he did completely fail, he had to try Him more than that yet. He had to try Him upon all the points upon which he has tried the other man to get him to yield. Satan did this also and also there completely failed.

Thus Satan had to try, and he did try, Jesus upon all the points that he ever had to try me upon and upon all the points that he ever had to try you upon and also upon all the points that he would have to try the other man upon. Consequently, he had to try Jesus upon every point upon which it is possible for a temptation to rise in any man of the human race.

Satan is the author of all temptation, and he had to try Jesus in all points upon which he ever had to try any man. He also had to try Jesus upon every point upon which it is possible for Satan himself to raise a temptation. And in all he failed all the time. Thank the Lord!

More than that: Satan not only had to try Jesus upon all the points where he has ever had to try me, but he had to try Jesus with a good deal more power than he ever had to exert upon me. He never had to try very hard nor use very much of his power in temptation to get me to yield. But taking the same points upon which Satan has ever tried me in which he got me to sin or would ever have to try to get me to sin, he had to try Jesus on those same points a good deal harder than he ever did to get me to sin. He had to try Him with all the power of temptation that he possibly knows – that is, the devil I mean – and failed. Thank the Lord! So in Christ I am free.

He had to try Jesus in all points where he ever tempted or ever can tempt you and he had to try Him with all the power that he knows, *and he failed again.* Thank the Lord! So you are free in Christ. He had also to try Jesus upon every point that affects *the other man* with all his Satanic power also, and *still he failed.* Thank the Lord! And in Christ the other man is free.

Therefore, he had to try Jesus upon every point that ever the human could be tried upon and failed. He had to try Jesus with all the knowledge that he has and all the cunning that he knows and failed. And he had to try Jesus with *all his might* upon each particular point, *and still he failed.*

Then there is a threefold – yes, *a complete* – failure on the devil's part all around. In the presence of Christ, Satan is absolutely conquered, and in Christ we are conquerors of Satan. Jesus said, "The prince of this world cometh, and hath nothing in me." In Christ, then, we escape him. In Christ we meet in Satan a completely conquered and a completely exhausted enemy.

This is not to say that we have no more fighting to do. But it is to say and to say emphatically and joyfully that *in Christ* we fight the fight of *victory*. Out of Christ, we fight – but it is all defeat. In Him our victory is complete, as well as in all things in Him *we* are complete. But, O do not forget the expression: It is *in Him!*

Then, as Satan has exhausted all the temptations that he knows or possibly can know and has exhausted all his power in the temptation too, what is he? In the presence of Christ, what is he? Powerless. And when he finds us in Christ and then would reach us and harass us, what is he? Powerless. Praise and magnify the Lord!

Let us rejoice in this, for in Him we are victors; in Him we are free; in Him Satan is powerless toward us. Let us be thankful for that. In Him we are complete.

Sermon 14

February 21, 1895

YOU will remember the point that was made in one of Brother Prescott's lessons, when he called attention to the book of Ruth [Read Bulletin, p. 189].

Who was the redeemer in the book of Ruth? The nearest of kin. Boaz could not come in as redeemer until it was found that the one who was nearer than he could not perform the office of redeemer. The redeemer must be not only one who was near of kin, but he must be the *nearest* among those who were near, and therefore Boaz could not step into the place of redeemer until, by another's stepping out of the place, he became really the nearest. Now that is the precise point that is made in the second chapter of Hebrews.

In Ruth, you remember Naomi's husband had died, the inheritance had fallen into the hands of others, and when she came back from Moab, it had to be redeemed. No one but the nearest of kin could do it.

This is the story also in the second of Hebrews. Here is the man Adam, who had an inheritance – the earth – and he lost it and he himself was brought into bondage. In the gospel in Leviticus it is preached that if one had lost his inheritance, himself and his inheritance could be redeemed, but only the nearest of kin could redeem. Lev. 25:25, 26, 47-49. Upon earth here is a man, Adam, who lost his inheritance and himself, and you and I were in it all, and we need a redeemer. But only He who is nearest in blood relationship can perform the office of redeemer. Jesus Christ is nearer than a brother, nearer than anyone. He is a brother, but He is nearest among the brethren, nearest of kin, actually. Not only one with us but He is one of us and one with us by being one of us.

And the one lesson that we are studying still and the leading thought is how entirely Jesus is ourselves. We found in the preceding lesson that He is altogether ourselves. In all points of temptation, wherever we are tempted, He was ourselves right there; in all the points in which it is possible for me to be tempted, He, as I, stood right there, against all the knowledge and ingenuity of Satan to tempt me, Jesus, myself, stood right there and met it. Against all the power of Satan put forth in the temptation upon me, Jesus stood as myself and overcame.

So also with you and so with the other man, and thus comprehending the whole human race, He stands in every point wherever anyone of the human race can be tempted as in Himself or from Himself.

In all this, He is ourselves and in Him we are complete against the power of temptation. In Him we are overcomers, because He, as we, overcame. "Be of good cheer; I have overcome the world."

And in noticing the other evening how He became one of us, we found that it was by birth from the flesh. He is "the seed of David according to the flesh." He took not the nature of angels but the nature of the seed of Abraham, and His genealogy goes to Adam.

Now every man is tempted, you know, "when he is drawn away of his own lust and enticed." James 1:14. That is the definition of "temptation."

There is not a single drawing toward sin, there is not a single tendency to sin, in you and me that was not in Adam when he stepped out of the garden. All the iniquity and all the sin that have come into the world came from that, and came from him as he was there. It did not all appear in him; it did not all manifest itself in him in open action, but it has manifested itself in open action *in* those who have come from him.

Thus all the tendencies to sin that have appeared or that are in me came to me from Adam, and all that are in you came from Adam, and all that are in the other man came from Adam. So all the tendencies to sin that are in the human race came from Adam. But Jesus Christ felt in these temptations; He was tempted upon all these points in the flesh which He derived from David, from Abraham, and from Adam. In His genealogy are a number of characters set forth as they were lived in the men, and they were not righteous. Manasseh is there, who did worse than any other king ever in Judah and caused Judah to do worse than the heathen. Solomon is there with the description of his character in the Bible just as it is. David is there. Rahab is there. Judah is there. Jacob is there. All are there just as they were. Now Jesus came according to the flesh at the end of that line of mankind. And there is such a thing as heredity. You and I have traits of character or cut of feature that have come to us from away back – perhaps not from our own father, perhaps not from a grandfather, but from a great-grandfather away back in the years. And this is referred to in the law of God:

> Visiting the iniquity of the fathers upon the children unto the third and fourth generation of them that hate me; and showing mercy unto thousands of them that love me and keep my commandments.

That "like produces like" is a good law, a righteous law. It is a law of God, and though the law be transgressed, it still does the same.

Transgression of the law does not change the law, whether it be moral or physical. The law works when it is transgressed, through the evil that is incurred, just as it would have worked in righteousness always if no evil had ever been incurred. If man had remained righteous always, as God made him, his descent would have been in the right line. When the law was transgressed, the descent followed on the wrong line, and the law worked in the crooked way, by its being perverted.

It is a good law which says that everything shall have a tendency to go toward the center of the earth. We could not get along in the world without that law. It is that which holds us upon the earth and enables us to walk and move about upon it. And yet if there be a break between us and the earth, if our feet slip out from under us or if we be on a high station, a pinnacle, and it breaks and the straight connection with the earth is broken between us and it, why, the law works and it brings us down with a terrible jolt, you know. Well, the same law that enables us to live and move and walk around upon the earth as comfortably as we do, which works so beneficially while we act in harmony with it, that law continues to work when we get out of harmony with it and it works as directly as before – *but it hurts.*

Now that is simply an illustration of this law of human nature. If man had remained where God put him and as He put him, the law would have worked directly and easily; since man has got out of harmony with it, it still works directly, but it hurts. Now that law of heredity reached from Adam to the flesh of Jesus Christ as certainly as it reaches from Adam to the flesh of any of the rest of us, for He was one of us. In Him there were things that reached Him from Adam; in Him there were things that reached Him from David, from Manasseh, from the genealogy away back from the beginning until His birth.

Thus in the flesh of Jesus Christ – not in Himself, but in His flesh – our flesh which He took in the human nature – there were just the same tendencies to sin that are in you and me. And when He was tempted, it was the "drawing away of these desires that were in the flesh." These tendencies to sin that were in His flesh drew upon Him and sought to entice Him, to consent to the wrong. But by the love of God and by His trust in God, He received the power and the strength and the grace to say, "No," to all of it and put it all under foot. And thus being in the likeness of sinful flesh He condemned sin in the flesh.

All the tendencies to sin that are in me were in Him, and not one of them was ever allowed to appear in Him. All the tendencies to sin that are in you were in Him, and not one of them was ever allowed to appear – every one was put under foot and kept there. All the tendencies to sin that are in the other man were in Him, and not one of them was ever allowed to appear. That is simply saying that all the tendencies to sin that are in human flesh were in His human flesh, and not one of them was ever allowed to appear; He conquered them all. And in Him we all have victory over them all.

Many of these tendencies to sin that are in us have appeared in action, and have become sins committed, have become sins in the open. There is a difference between a tendency to sin and the open appearing of that sin in the actions. There are tendencies to sin in us that have not yet appeared, but multitudes have appeared. Now all the tendencies that have not appeared, He conquered. What of the sins that have actually appeared? "The Lord hath laid on Him the iniquity of us all" (Isa. 53:6) "Who his own self bare our sins in his own body on the tree." 1 Peter 2:24. Thus it is plain that all the tendencies to sin that are in us and have not appeared and all the sins which have appeared were laid upon Him. It is terrible. It is true. But, O, joy! In that terrible truth lies the completeness of our salvation.

Note another view:

Those sins which we have committed, we ourselves felt the guilt of them and were conscious of condemnation because of them. These were all imputed to Him. They were all laid upon Him. Now a question: Did He feel the guilt of the sins that were imputed to Him? Was He conscious of the condemnation of the sins – our sins – that were laid upon Him? He never was conscious of sins that He committed, for He did not commit any. That is true. But our sins were laid upon Him and we were guilty. Did He realize the guilt of these sins? Was He conscious of condemnation because of these sins?

We will look at that in such a way that every soul in the house shall say, "Yes." I will say that another way: We will look at it in such a way that every soul in the house will either say "Yes" or may say "Yes" if he will, because there may be some in the house who have not had the experience that I will bring for the illustration, but many have it, and then they can say, "Yes." All others who have had the experience will say "Yes" at once.

God imputes righteousness, the righteousness of Christ, unto the believing sinner. Here is a man who has never known anything in his life but sin, never anything but the guilt of sin, never anything but the condemnation of sin. That man believes on Jesus Christ, and God imputes to that man the righteousness of Christ. Then that man who never committed a particle of righteousness in his life is conscious of righteousness. Something has entered his life that was never there before. He is conscious of it, and he is conscious of the joy of it and the freedom of it.

Now God imputed our sins to Jesus Christ as certainly as He imputes His righteousness to us. But when He imputes righteousness to us who are nothing but sinners, we realize it and are conscious of it and conscious of the joy of it. Therefore, when He imputed our sins to *Jesus,* He was conscious of the guilt of them and the condemnation of them, just as certainly as the believing sinner is conscious of the righteousness of Christ and the peace and joy of it that is imputed to him – that is, that is laid upon him.

In all this also, Jesus was precisely ourselves. Or in all points He was truly made like unto us. In all points of temptation, He was ourselves. He was one of us in the flesh; He was ourselves, and thus He was ourselves in temptation. And in points in guilt and condemnation He was precisely ourselves, because it was our sins, our guilt and our condemnation that were laid upon Him.

Now another thing upon what we have said: "our sins" – how many of them? All were laid upon Him, and He carried the guilt and the condemnation of them all, and also answered for them, paid for them, atoned for them. Then in Him we are free from every sin that we have ever committed. That is the truth. Let us be glad of it and praise God with everlasting joy.

He took all the sins which we have committed; He answered for them and took them away from us forever and all the tendencies to sin which have not appeared in actual sins – these He put forever under foot. Thus He sweeps the whole board and we are free and complete in Him.

O, He is a complete Saviour. He is a Saviour from sins committed and the Conqueror of the tendencies to commit sins. In Him we have the victory. We are no more responsible for these tendencies being in us that we are responsible for the sun shining, but every man on earth is responsible for these things appearing in open action in him, because Jesus Christ has made provision against their ever appearing in open action. Before we learned of Christ, many of them had appeared in open action. The Lord hath laid upon Him all these and He has taken them away. Since we learned of Christ, these tendencies which have not appeared He condemned as sin in the flesh. And shall He who believes in Jesus allow that which Christ condemned in the flesh to rule over Him in the flesh? This is the victory that belongs to the believer in Jesus.

It is true that, although a man may have all this in Jesus, he cannot profit by it without himself being a believer in Jesus. Take the man who does not believe in Jesus at all tonight. Has not Christ made all the provision for him that He has for Elijah, who is in heaven tonight? And if this man wants to have Christ for his Saviour, if he wants provision made for all his sins and salvation from all of them, does Christ have to do anything now in order to provide for this man's sins or to save him from them? No. That is all done. He made all that provision for every man when He was in the flesh and every man who believes in Him receives this without there being any need of any part of it being done over again. He "made one sacrifice for sins forever." And having by Himself purged us from our sins, He sat down on the right hand of the Majesty on high. Thus it is all in Him and every believer in Him possesses it all in Him and in Him is complete. It is in Him and that is the blessedness of it. "In Him dwelleth all the fullness of the godhead bodily." And God gives His eternal Spirit and us eternal life – eternity in which to live – in order that that eternal Spirit may reveal to us and make known to us the eternal depths of the salvation that we have in Him whose goings forth have been from the days of eternity.

Now let us look at it in another way. Turn to Romans 5:12:

> Wherefore, as by one man sin entered into the world, and death by sin; and so death passed upon all men, for that all have sinned.

Now, leaving out the verses in parenthesis for the moment, and reading them afterward, read the eighteenth verse:

> Therefore, as by the offense of one [that man that sinned] judgment came upon all men to condemnation; even so by the righteousness of one [that Man that did not sin] the free gift came upon all men unto justification of life. For as by one man's disobedience [that man that sinned] many were made sinners, so by the obedience of one [that Man that did not sin] shall many be made righteous.

Now read the parenthesis:

> For until the law sin was in the world: but sin is not imputed when there is no law. Nevertheless, death reigned from Adam to Moses, even over them that had not sinned after the similitude of Adam's transgression, who is the figure of him that was to come.

Adam, then, was the figure of Him that was to come. That one to come is Christ. Adam was the figure of Him. Wherein was Adam the figure of Him? In his righteousness? No. For he did not keep it. In his sin? No. For Christ did not sin. Wherein, then, was Adam the figure of Christ? In this: That all that were in the world were included in Adam, and all that are in the world are included in Christ. In other words: Adam in his sin reached all the world; Jesus Christ, the second Adam, in His righteousness touches all humanity. That is where Adam is the figure of Him that was to come. So read on:

> But not as the offense, so also is the free gift: for if through the offense of one many be dead, much more the grace of God and the gift by grace, which is by one man, Jesus Christ, hath abounded unto many.

There are two men, then, whom we are studying: That one man by whom sin entered; that one man by whom righteousness entered.

> And not as it was by one that sinned, so is the gift: for the judgment was by one to condemnation but the free gift is of many offenses unto justification. For if by one man's offense death reigned by one [that is, by the first Adam]; much more they which receive abundance of grace and of the gift of righteousness shall reign in life by one, Jesus Christ [the second Adam].

Read another text in connection with this before we touch the particular study of it. 1 Cor. 15:45-49:

> So it is written, The first man Adam was made a living soul; the last Adam was made a quickening spirit. Howbeit that was not first which is spiritual, but that which is natural; and afterward that which is spiritual. The first man is of the earth, earthy: the second man is the Lord from heaven. As is the earthy, such are they also that are earthy: and as is the heavenly, such are they also that are heavenly. And as we have borne the image of the earthy, we shall also bear the image of the heavenly."

The first Adam touched all of us; what he did included all of us. If he had remained true to God, that would have included all of us. And when he fell away from God, that included us and took us also. Whatever he should have done embraced us, and what he did made us what we are.

Now, here is another Adam. Does He touch as many as the first Adam did? That is the question. That is what we are studying now. Does the second Adam touch as many as did the first Adam? And the answer is that it is certainly true that what the second Adam did embraces all that were embraced in what the first Adam did. What He should have done, what He could have done, would embrace all.

Suppose Christ had yielded to temptation and had sinned. Would that have meant anything to us? It would have meant everything to us. The first Adam's sin meant all this to us; sin on the part of the second Adam would have meant all this to us.

The first Adam's righteousness would have meant all to us and the second Adam's righteousness means all to as many as believe. That is correct in a certain sense, but not in the sense in which we are studying it now. We are now studying from the side of the Adams. We will look at it from our side presently.

The question is, Does the second Adam's righteousness embrace as many as does the first Adam's sin? Look closely. Without our consent at all, without our having anything to do with it, we were all included in the first Adam; we were there. All the human race were in the first Adam. What that first Adam – what that first man, did meant us; it involved us. That which the first Adam did brought us into sin, and the end of sin is death, and that touches every one of us and involves every one of us.

Jesus Christ, the second man, took our sinful nature. He touched us "in all points." He became we and died the death. And so in Him and by that every man that has ever lived upon the earth and was involved in the first Adam is involve in this and will live again. There will be a resurrection of the dead, both of the just and of the unjust. Every soul shall live again by the second Adam from the death that came by the first Adam.

"Well," says one, "we are involved in other sins besides that one." Not without our choice. When God said, "I will put enmity between thee and the woman and between thy seed and her seed," He set every man free to choose which master he would serve, and since that, every man that has sinned in this world has done it because he chose to. "If our gospel be hid, it is hid to them that are lost: in whom the god of this world hath blinded the minds of them which believe not," – not them who had no chance to believe; the god of this world blinds no man until he has shut his eyes of faith. When he shuts his eyes of faith, then Satan will see that they are kept shut as long as possible.

I read the text again: "If our gospel," – the everlasting gospel, the gospel of Jesus Christ which is Christ in you the hope of glory, from the days of the first Adam's sin until now – "if our gospel be hid, it is hid to them that are lost." It is hid to them "in whom the god of this world hath blinded the minds." And why did he blind the minds? Because they "believe not."

Abraham, a heathen, born a heathen, as all the rest of us are, and raised a heathen, grew up in a family of heathens, worshiping idols and the heavenly hosts. He turned from it all unto God and opened his eyes of faith and used them, and Satan never had a chance to blind his eyes. And Abraham, a heathen, thus turning from among heathens unto God and finding God in Jesus Christ in the fullness of hope – that is one reason why God has set him before all the world. He is an example of what every heathen on this earth may find. He is a God-set-forth example of how every heathen is without excuse if he does not find God in Jesus Christ, by the everlasting gospel. Abraham is set before all nations in witness of the fact that every heathen is responsible in his own way if he does not find what Abraham found.

Therefore, just as far as the first Adam reaches man, so far the second Adam reaches man. The first Adam brought man under the condemnation of sin, even unto death; the second Adam's righteousness undoes that and makes every man live again. As soon as Adam sinned, God gave him a second chance and set him free to choose which master he would have. Since that time every man is free to choose which way he will go; therefore, he is responsible for his own individual sins. And when Jesus Christ has set us all free from the sin and the death which came upon us from the first Adam, that freedom is for every man, and every man can have it for the choosing.

The Lord will not compel any one to take it. He compels no one to sin and He compels no one to be righteous. Everyone sins upon his own choice. The Scriptures demonstrate it. And every one can be made perfectly righteous at his choice. And the Scriptures demonstrate this. No man will die the second death who has not chosen sin rather than righteousness, death rather than life. In Jesus Christ there is furnished in completeness all that man needs or ever can have in righteousness, and all there is for any man to do is to choose Christ and then it is his.

So then as the first Adam was We, the second Adam is We. In all points He is as weak as are we. Read two texts: He says of *us*, "Without me ye can *do nothing*." Of *Himself* He says: "Of mine own self I can do nothing."

These two texts are all we want now. They tell the whole story. To be without Christ is to be without God, and there the man can do nothing. He is utterly helpless of himself and in himself. That is where the man is who is without God.

Jesus Christ says: "Of mine own self I can do nothing." Then that shows that the Lord Jesus put Himself in this world, in the flesh, in His human nature, precisely where the man is in this world who is without God. He put Himself precisely where lost man is. He left out His divine self and became we. And there, helpless as we are without God,

He ran the risk of getting back to where God is and bringing us with Him. It was a fearful risk, but, glory to God, He won. The thing was accomplished, and in Him we are saved.

When He stood where we are, He said, "I will put my trust in Him" and that trust was never disappointed. In response to that trust the Father dwelt in Him and with Him and kept Him from sinning. Who was He? We. And thus the Lord Jesus has brought to every man in this world divine faith. That is the faith of the Lord Jesus. That is saving faith. Faith is not something that comes from ourselves with which we believe upon Him, but it is that something with which He believed – the faith which He exercised, which He brings to us, and which becomes ours and works in us – the gift of God. That is what the word means, "Here are they that keep the commandments of God and the faith of Jesus." They keep the faith of Jesus because it is that divine faith which Jesus exercised Himself.

He being we brought to us that divine faith which saves the soul – that divine faith by which we can say with Him, "I will put my trust in Him." And in so putting our trust in Him, that trust today will never be disappointed anymore than it was then. God responded then to the trust and dwelt with Him. God will respond today to that trust in us and will dwell with us.

God dwelt with Him and He was ourselves. Therefore, His name is Emmanuel, God with us. Not God with Him. God was with Him before the world was; He could have remained there and not come here at all and still God could have remained with Him and His name could have been God with Him. He could have come into this world as He was in heaven and His name could still have been God with Him. But that never could have been God with us. But what we needed was God with us. God with Him does not help us, unless He is we. But that is the blessedness of it. He who was one of God became one of us; He who was God became we, in order that God with Him should be God with us. O, that is His name! That is His name! Rejoice in that name forevermore – God with us!

Sermon 15

February 22, 1895

We are still studying the name of Christ, which is "God with us." And as stated before, He could not be God with us without becoming ourselves, because it is not Himself that is manifest in the world. We do not see Jesus in this world, as He was in heaven; He did not come into this world as He was in heaven, nor was that personality manifested in the world which was in heaven before He came. He emptied Himself and became ourselves. Then putting His trust in God, God dwelt with Him. And He being ourselves and God being with Him, He is "God with us." That is His name.

If He had come into the world as He was in heaven, being God, manifesting Himself as He was there and God being with Him, His name would not have been "God with us," for He would not then have been ourselves. But He emptied Himself. He Himself was not manifested in the world. For it is written: "No man knoweth the Son but the Father" – not simply no man, but no one. No one knoweth the Son but the Father. "Neither knoweth any man the Father, save the Son and he to whomsoever the Son will reveal Him." It is not written, No man knoweth the Son but the Father and He to whom the Father will reveal Him. No. No man knoweth the Son at all, but the Father. And the Father does not reveal the Son in the world, but the Son reveals the Father. Christ is not the revelation of Himself. He is the revelation of the Father to the world and in the world and to men.

Therefore, He says, "No man knoweth the Father but the Son and he to whomsoever the Son will reveal the Father."

So it is the Father that is revealed in the world and revealed to us and revealed in us in Christ. This is the one thing that we are studying all the time. This is the center around which everything else circles. And Christ having taken our human nature in all things in the flesh and so having become ourselves, when we read of Him and the Father's dealings with Him, we are reading of ourselves and of the Father's dealings with us. What God did to Him was to us; what God did for Him was for us. And therefore, again it is written: "He hath made Him to be sin for us, who knew no sin; that we might be made the righteousness of God in Him." 2 Cor. 5:21.

In all points it behooved Him to be made like unto His brethren, and He is our brother in the nearest blood relationship. We are now to study another phase of this great subject: First in the Psalms – Christ in the Psalms – that we may see how entirely the Psalms mean Christ and that the one whose experience is recorded there is Christ.

It is impossible to touch the whole 150 Psalms in detail in one lesson or in a dozen lessons; yet in a sense we can touch the whole 150 by so touching a few as to show the one great secret of the whole number and that secret is Christ. We shall take some of the Psalms of which God Himself has made the application to Christ so that there can be no possible doubt that that Psalm refers to Christ. Then when we read these Psalms, we know that we are reading of Jesus Christ and of God's dealings with Him – He too being ourselves all the time, weak as we are, sinful as are we in the flesh, made to be sinners just as we are, all our guilt and our sins being laid upon Him and He feeling the guilt and the condemnation of it in all things as ourselves.

Take the fortieth Psalm, which refers to Christ at His coming into the world. Turn to the fortieth Psalm and the tenth of Hebrews both at once. Beginning with Psalm 40:6: "Sacrifice and offering thou didst not desire; mine ears hast thou opened." The margin reads, "Mine ears hast thou digged." The secret of the reference there is to that passage in the twenty-first chapter of Exodus, 1-6, where if a man be a Hebrew servant, he shall serve his master a certain number of years and the year of release he shall go out free. But if he says: "I love my master, my wife and my children; I will not go out free," then the master shall bring him to the doorpost and bore his ear through with an awl, and he shall be his servant forever. That hole bored through his ear with an awl was an outward sign that that man's ears were always opened to the word of the master, ready to obey.

Now as Christ came into the world as man, He said to the Father: "Sacrifice and offering thou didst not desire; mine ears hast thou opened." Mine ears are opened to thy word, ready for thy commands; I will not go out; I love my Master and my children. I will not go out. I am thy servant forever.

"Burnt offering and sin offering has thou not required. Then said I, Lo, I come: in the volume of the book it is written of me, I delight to do thy will, O my God."

Now see Hebrews 10:5-9:

> Wherefore, when he cometh into the world, he saith, Sacrifice and offering thou wouldst not, but a body hast thou prepared me; in burnt offerings and sacrifices for sin thou hast had no pleasure. Then said I, Lo, I come (in the volume of the book it is written of me) to do thy will, O God. Above when he said, Sacrifice and offering and burnt offerings and offering for sin thou wouldest not, neither hadst pleasure therein; which are offered by the law; then said he, Lo, I come to do thy will, O God. He taketh away the first, that he may establish the second.

There is the Lord's application of the fortieth Psalm to Christ, and He said this when He came into the world. Let us read on, then, in the fortieth Psalm:

> I delight to do thy will, O my God: yea thy law is within my heart. I have preached righteousness in the great congregation: lo, I have not refrained my lips, O Lord, thou knowest. I have not hid thy righteousness within my heart; I have declared thy faithfulness and thy salvation: I have not concealed thy lovingkindness and thy truth from the great congregation. Withhold not thou thy tender mercies from me, O Lord: let thy loving kindness and thy truth continually preserve me. For innumerable evils have compassed me about [Who? Christ.]; mine iniquities have taken hold upon me, so that I am not able to look up; they are more than the hairs of mine head: therefore, my heart faileth me.

Who? Christ. Where did He get iniquity? Oh, "the Lord hath laid upon Him the iniquity of us all."

Were they not more than the hairs of His head? And when He would look at Himself and consider Himself, where would He appear in His own sight? Oh, "my heart faileth me," because of the enormity of the guilt and the condemnation of the sin – our sins that were laid upon Him.

But in His divine faith and trust in the Father, He continues:

> Be pleased, O Lord, to deliver me: O Lord, make haste to help me. Let them be ashamed and confounded together that seek after my soul to destroy it; let them be driven backward and put to shame that wish me evil. Let them be desolate for a reward of their shame that say unto me, Aha, aha. [Didn't they say that to Him on the cross?] Let all those that seek thee rejoice and be glad in thee; let such as love thy salvation say continually, The Lord be magnified.

Who said so? He who was conscious of iniquities in such number that they were more than the hairs of His head. He who was so bowed down and so burdened with these – He was praising and rejoicing in the Lord!

> But I am poor and needy; yet the Lord thinketh upon me: thou art my help and deliverer; make no tarrying O my God.

Now turn to the first verse of the fortieth Psalm:

> I waited patiently for the Lord; and he inclined unto me, and heard my cry.

Who? Christ, and He was ourselves. Shall we, then, say the word: "*I* waited patiently for the Lord, and He inclined unto *me* and heard *my* cry?" Assuredly. What, laden with sin as I am? sinner as I am? sinful flesh as I have? How do I know that He hears my cry? Ah, He has demonstrated it for a whole lifetime in my nearest of kin. He has demonstrated it in my flesh that He inclines – leans over – to listen to my cry. O, there are times, you know, when our sins seem to be so mountain high. We are so discouraged by them. And Satan is right there ready to say, "Yes, you ought to be discouraged by them. There is no use of your praying to the Lord; He will not have anything to do with such as you are. You are too bad." And we begin to think that the Lord will not hear our prayers at all. Away with such thoughts! Not only will He hear but He is listening to hear. Remember the statement in Malachi, "The Lord *hearkened* and heard." To hearken is to listen, then the Lord is listening to hear the prayers of people laden with sin.

But there are times in our discouragement when the waters go over our souls, when we can hardly muster up the courage of faith to speak our prayers aloud. O, at such times as that, if they are too faint in our faith to reach Him as He listens, then He leans over and listens; He inclines His ear and hears. That is the Lord. That is the Father of our Lord Jesus Christ, the Lover and Saviour of sinners. Then if He should lead you and me through the deep waters and they go over our souls as they did over His, O, we can wait patiently for the Lord. He will incline unto us. He will lean over and hear our cry!

> He brought me up also out of a horrible pit, out of the miry clay, and set my feet upon a rock and established my goings. And he hath put a new song in my mouth, even praise unto our God: many shall see it and fear and shall trust in the Lord. [Who said so? Jesus.] Blessed is that man that maketh the Lord his trust and respecteth not the proud nor such as turn aside to lies.

Now turn to the twenty-second Psalm. There is so much in that that is familiar to everybody, that all know where it applies. First verse:

> My God, my God, why hast thou forsaken me? [Who said so? Jesus on the cross.] Why art thou so far from helping me and from the words of my roaring? O my God, I cry in the daytime but thou hearest not: and in the night season, and am not silent. But thou art holy, O thou that inhabitest the praises of Israel. Our fathers trusted in thee [He came in the line of the fathers.] They trusted, and thou didst deliver them. They cried unto thee, and were delivered: they trusted in thee and were not confounded. But I am a worm and no man; a reproach of man and despised of the people. All they that see me laugh me to scorn: they shoot out the lip, they shake the head, saying, He trusted on the Lord that he would deliver him, let him deliver him, seeing he delighted in him.

You know that is the record of His crucifixion; this is the crucifixion Psalm.

> But thou art he that took me out of the womb: thou didst make me hope when I was upon my mother's breasts. I was cast upon thee from the womb: thou art my God from my mother's belly. Be not far from me; for trouble is near; for there is none to help. Many bulls have compassed me; strong bulls of Bashan have beset me round. They gaped upon me with their mouths, as a ravening and a roaring lion. I am poured out like water, and all my bones are out of joint: my heart is like wax; it is melted in the midst of my bowels. My strength is dried up like a potsherd, and my tongue cleaveth to my jaws; and thou hast brought me into the dust of death. For dogs have compassed me: the assembly of the wicked have enclosed me: they pierced my hands and my feet. I may tell all my bones:

> they look and stare upon me. They part my garments among them; and cast lots upon my vesture [Here is his experience on the cross.] But be not thou far from me, O Lord: O my strength, haste thee to help me. Deliver my soul from the sword; my darling [Margin, "my only one." Septuagint, "my only begotten."] from the power of the dog. Save me from the lion's mouth: for thou hast heard me from the horns of the unicorns. I will declare thy name unto my brethren: in the midst of the congregation will I praise thee. Ye that fear the Lord, praise him; all ye the seed of Jacob, glorify him; and fear him, all ye the seed of Israel. For he hath not despised nor abhorred the affliction of the afflicted; neither hath he hid his face from him: but when he cried unto him, he heard.

Who says so? Who says that from the cry of the afflicted one, from the sinner who is burdened and laden with sin, more than the hairs of His head? Who says that God the Father will not turn away from such a one? Christ says so. And He knows it. Who says that the Father will not hide His face from such as I, and such as you? Christ says so, and He has demonstrated it; for is He not now alive and in glory at the right hand of God? And in that it is demonstrated before the universe that God will not hide His face from the man whose iniquities are gone over His head and are more than the hairs of His head. Then be of good cheer; be of good courage. He is our salvation; He has wrought it out. He has demonstrated to all men that God is Saviour of sinner.

> My praise shall be of thee in the great congregation; I will pay my vows before them that fear him.

Will you?

Now note: Who was He when He was saying this? He was ourselves. Then who shall it be that is saying it still? Will it not count now for us in Him, as well as it did eighteen hundred years ago for us in Him? It counted for us then in Him because He was ourselves, and now in Him is it not the same thing?

Now the last two verses of the twenty-second Psalm:

> A seed shall serve him; it shall be accounted to the Lord for a generation. They shall come and shall declare his righteousness unto a people that shall be born, that he hath done this.

The twenty-third Psalm comes next after the twenty-second.

"The Lord is my shepherd." Whose? Christ's. The twenty-second is the crucifixion hymn, the crucifixion Psalm. Where is the twenty-third, then?

Let us see:

> The Lord is my shepherd; I shall not want. He maketh me to lie down in green pastures; he leadeth me beside the still waters. He restoreth my soul: he leadeth me in the paths of righteousness.

Who? Me, a sinner? one laden with sins? Will He lead me in the paths of righteousness? Yes. How do you know? He did it once. In Christ He led me in the paths of righteousness once, for His name's sake, a whole lifetime. Therefore, I know that in Christ He will lead me, a sinful man, again and ever in the paths of righteousness for His name's sake. That is faith.

Taking these words as we have heard in Brother Prescott's lesson this evening, as being themselves the salvation of God which comes to us, they themselves will work in us the salvation of God itself. That is where Christ got it. When He put Himself where we are, where did He get salvation? He did not save Himself. That was the taunt, "He saved others; Himself He cannot save. . . Let Him now come down from the cross and we will believe on Him." He could have done it. But if He had saved Himself, it would have ruined us. We would have been lost if He had saved Himself. O, but He saves us! Then what saved Him? This word of salvation saved Him when He was ourselves, and it saves us when we are in Him. He leads me in the paths of righteousness for His name's sake – *me, me!* And this in order that every one on the earth can say *in Him,* "He leadeth me."

"Yea, though I walk through the valley of the shadow of death." Where was He in the twenty-second Psalm? On the cross, facing death. The twenty-third Psalm comes right in there, in proper order, you see, as He steps into the dark valley. "Though I walk through the valley of the shadow of death, I will fear no evil: for thou art with me; thy rod and thy staff they comfort me." Who? Christ and *in Him* ourselves, and we know it because God did it once for us in Him. And in Him it is done still for us.

"Thou preparest a table before me in the presence of mine enemies: thou anointest my head with oil; my cup runneth over. Surely goodness and mercy shall follow me all the days of my life." Who? Me. Thank the Lord! How do I know? Because they did follow me once in Him. Goodness and mercy did follow me from birth unto the grave once in this world in Him, and as long as I am in Him, they follow me still. "Surely goodness and mercy shall follow me all the days of my life: and I will dwell in the house of the Lord forever." How do I know? Ah, because that in Him it has been done once for me. It has been demonstrated before the universe that it is so, and I take it and am glad.

Then the twenty-fourth Psalm comes right on after the twenty-third. The twenty-second is the crucifixion psalm; the twenty-third takes Him through the valley of the shadow of death; and the twenty-fourth is the ascension psalm.

> Lift up your heads, O ye gates; and be ye lifted up, ye everlasting doors; and the King of glory shall come in. Who is this King of glory? The Lord strong and mighty, the Lord mighty in battle. Lift up your heads, O ye gates; even lift them up, ye everlasting doors; and the King of glory shall come in.

He did it once for me in Him; in Him it is done still for me; and in Him *I* shall dwell in the house of the Lord forever.

This is all only illustrative of the truth as to Christ in the Psalms. Look at the sixty-ninth Psalm and we shall see this further. Indeed, where can we look in the Psalms without seeing it? That is the question. Where in the Psalms can we look and not see it? I will read a verse or two in the sixty-ninth Psalm, though, that you may see that this is exactly applicable there.

Fourth verse:

"They that hate me without a cause are more than the hairs of mine head." The scripture was fulfilled, "They hate me without a cause," you remember.

Seventh verse:

"For thy sake I have borne reproach; shame hath covered my face. I am become a stranger unto my brethren, and an alien unto my mother's children. For the zeal of thine house hath eaten me up." "And his disciples remembered that it was written, The zeal of thine house hath eaten me up." "The reproaches of them that reproached thee fell on me." Paul writes in Romans 15:3 "For even Christ pleased not himself; but, as it is written, The reproaches of them that reproached thee fell on me."

Now Psalm 69:20, 21:

> Reproach hath broken my heart; and I am full of heaviness: and I looked for some to take pity, but there was none: and for comforters, but I found none. They gave me also gall for my meat; and in my thirst they gave me vinegar to drink.

Then that psalm applies to Christ.

Look at the first verse: "Save me, O, God; for the waters are come in unto my soul. I sink in the deep mire, where there is no standing; I am come into deep waters, where the floods overflow me. I am weary of my crying: my throat is dried: mine eyes fail while I wait for my God." Then follows, "They that hate me without a cause." etc. Then the fifth verse: "O God, thou knowest my foolishness and my sins are not hid from thee." Whose sins? Christ's – the righteous one, who knew no sin, *made* to bear sin for us! Our sins were upon Him; the guilt and the condemnation of these were not hid from God.

O, it was a terrible thing, that He should undo Himself and become ourselves in all things in order that we might be saved – running the risk, the fearful risk, of losing all – risking all to save all. But what were we of ourselves? From head to foot nothing but a body of sin. Yet He risked all to save us, it is true. But we were nothing. True, but in His love and in His pity He did it. Thank the Lord that He had the royal courage to do it. And He won it. And we are saved in Him.

We read here His confession of sin. This was He as ourselves and in our place, confessing our sins and we needed that also. He was baptized in our behalf, because no baptism on our part could be perfect so as to be accepted in righteousness. "It must be perfect to be accepted." No man's confession of sin can, in itself, ever be so perfect as to be accepted of God in righteousness, because man is imperfect. But "it must be perfect to be accepted."

Where then, shall perfection of confession be found? Ah! In Him my confession of sin is perfect; for He made the confession. How many times when persons have made confession as thoroughly as they know how, Satan gets the advantage of them by the suggestion: 'You have not properly confessed your sin. You have not confessed hard enough to get forgiveness. O, of course you have confessed, but you have not done it hard enough. God cannot forgive you on such a confession as that'.

Hold the word of God up before Him and tell Him: There is One who is perfect; He bore my sins and He has made the confession, and when He shows me the sin, I confess it according to my power and ability and as God reveals it to me and *in Him* and by virtue of His confession, mine is accepted in righteousness. His confession is perfect in every respect and God accepts mine *in Him*.

Then in Him we have exemption from Satan's discouragement as to whether we have confessed our sins hard enough, sought them out faithfully enough or repented enough. In Christ we have repentance; in Him we have confession; in Him we have perfection, and in Him we are complete. O, He is the Saviour!

Weak as we; sinful as we – simply ourselves – He went through this world and never sinned. He was sinful as we, weak as we, helpless as we, helpless as the man is who is without God, yet by His trust in God, God so visited Him, so abode with Him, so strengthened Him, that, instead of sin ever being manifested, the righteousness of God was always manifested.

But who was He? He was ourselves. Then God has demonstrated once in the world and to the universe that He will so come to me and you and so live with us as we are in the world today and will cause His grace and His power to so abide with us that, in spite of all our sinfulness, in spite of all our weaknesses, the righteousness and the holy influence of God will be manifested to men instead of ourselves and our sinfulness.

The mystery of God is not God manifest in sinless flesh. There is mystery about God being manifest in sinless flesh; that is natural enough. Is not God Himself sinless? Is there then any room for wonder that God could manifest Himself through or in sinless flesh? Is there any mystery as to God's manifesting His power and His righteous glory through Gabriel or through the bright seraphim or the cherubim? No. That is natural enough. But the wonder is that God can do that through and in *sinful* flesh. That is the mystery of God. God manifest in *sinful* flesh.

In Jesus Christ as He was in sinful flesh, God has demonstrated before the universe that He can so take possession of sinful flesh as to manifest His own presence, His power, and His glory, instead of sin manifesting itself. And all that the Son asks of any man in order to accomplish this in him is that the man will let the Lord have him as the Lord Jesus did.

Jesus said, "I will put my trust in Him."

And in that trust Christ brought to every one the divine faith by which we can put our trust in Him. And when we do so separate from the world and put our sole trust in Him, then God will so take us and so use us that our sinful selves shall not appear to influence or affect anybody, but God will manifest His righteous self, His glory, before men, in spite of all ourselves and our sinfulness. That is the truth. And that is *the mystery of God,* "Christ in you, the hope of glory." God manifest in sinful flesh.

Upon this point, also, Satan discourages many. To the believing sinner Satan says: You are too sinful to count yourself a Christian. God cannot have anything to do with you. Look at yourself. You know you are good for nothing.

Satan has discouraged us thousands of times with that kind of argument.

But God has wrought out an argument that puts this plea of Satan all to shame, for Jesus came and became ourselves – sinful as we are, laden with the sins of the world – far more sins than there are upon me. And in Him, laden with ten thousand times more sins than ever were upon me, God has demonstrated that with one so sinful as that, He will come and live a whole lifetime and manifest Himself and His righteousness in spite of all the sinfulness and in spite of the devil. God laid help upon One who is mighty, and that help reaches us. Thank the Lord.

Brethren, that does me good. For I know that if ever anything good is to be manifested in this world where I am, it must come from some source besides myself. That is settled. But, O! the blessedness of it is, God has demonstrated that He will manifest His righteous self instead of my sinful self when I let Him have me. I cannot manifest righteousness of myself; I cannot manifest His righteousness in myself. No. I let Him have me, absolutely, overwhelmingly. Then He attends to that. He has demonstrated it so. He has demonstrated a whole lifetime what God is when He is joined with me in sinful flesh. He can do it again as certainly as He can have me.

Will you let Him have you? O, does it call for too full a surrender? No. It is becoming. How full a surrender did He make? He surrendered all Himself. Christ gave up Himself, emptied Himself. The French translation is, "He annihilated Himself." He undid Himself and sank Himself in us in order that God, instead of ourselves and His righteousness, instead of our sinfulness, might be manifested in us in our sinful flesh. Then let us respond and sink ourselves in Him, that God may still be manifest in sinful flesh.

Now using that statement that is sometimes used in a jocular way about the man – I use it reverently, and it is a good illustration; it is a right illustration – who said: "I and my wife are one, and I am the one."

Christ and the man are one, and the question always is, Which shall be the one? Christ has allied Himself with every man on the earth, but multitudes say, "Yes, that is all right enough, but I am the one." Many arrogantly refuse all, exclaiming: "I am the one; I am enough." But the Christian, the believer, yielding to Jesus Christ, says, "Yes, thank the Lord! He and I are one and He is the one."

Christ has allied Himself with every human being, on His own part; and if every human being in the world tonight should drop everything and say, "Yes, that is a fact; He and I are one, and He is the one," every soul would be saved tonight, and Christ would appear in every soul tomorrow.

Now brethren there is another thing that comes in here in our own practical experience. Christ has allied Himself to every human being. Then when He said, "Inasmuch as ye have done it [or not done it] unto one of the least of these my brethren; ye have done it [or not done it] unto me," how widespread is that truth? Suppose one comes to my door as a tramp; suppose He be ill dressed and perhaps has not had a good chance to wash Himself as clean as He ought to be. Who is allied to Him? Jesus. Who has invested His all in that man? The Lord Jesus. Then as I treat that man, who is affected? The Lord Jesus, to be sure.

Shall I treat that man according to the estimate of Christ's investment or according to my opinions, as the world looks upon the man? That is the question.

Suppose here is a man that does not believe in Jesus – a worldly man, a drinking man, a swearing man – and he comes to me in some way – he may come to my door for something to eat or I may meet him as he is walking by the way. Suppose that out of respect to Christ I treat that man as Christ's purchase, as the one in whom Christ has invested all, and suppose that man never believes in Jesus at all and dies an infidel and perishes in perdition, how does Christ look upon that which I did toward the man? In the judgment, if I shall stand on the right hand, will He say anything about that which I did? O, He will say, "I was ahungered, and ye gave me meat: I was thirsty, and ye gave me drink: naked and ye clothed me: I was sick and ye visited me." Why, Lord, I know nothing about that. When did I ever see you hungry and fed you? or sick and helped you? or naked and clothed you? I know nothing about this. Oh, "Inasmuch as ye have done it unto one of the least of these my brethren, ye have done it unto me."

But suppose a man comes and says, "I am hungry; I would like something to eat." And I respond: "What are you drifting around the country for like this – an able-bodied man, as you are? Why don't you go to work?" "Well, I can't find work." "O well, *I* get plenty of work; *I* can find work; *I* have not got out of work yet. I think work is not exactly what you want. I don't have anything for such folks as you are." I do not give him anything, and he goes off.

In that day we shall all stand before the throne and I find myself standing on the left hand and I say: "Why, Lord, Lord, I believe on you; don't you know, I believed the truth? I believed in the Third Angel's Message; indeed, I was a preacher and preached in the Tabernacle in Battle Creek. I did much for the cause. In thy name I did many wonderful things." But the answer is "I was ahungered and you gave me no meat: I was thirsty and ye gave me no drink: naked and ye clothed me not: sick and in prison and ye visited me not." I wonderingly inquire, "When did I ever see you hungry or in need or sick? I thought you were in heaven, glorified with all your trials past, and I wanted to get up here to see you. I did not suppose you were on earth where I could ever see you hungry or sick." He replies: "I came to your door one morning and asked for something to eat, after having been almost shelterless through the night": I answer, "You? No. I never saw you there." Well, He might point to such and such a time when a man did come to my door in just such a condition as that. But I say. "O, do you mean that man? surely that was not you." He answers finally; "Inasmuch as ye did it not to one of the least of these, ye did it not to me. Depart from me. I never knew you."

Whether a man gives Christ the credit for what He has invested in Him or not, as a believer in Jesus I must give to Christ the credit for what He has invested in that man. It is not a question whether that man gives Him credit for what He has invested in Him. It is a question whether those professing to believe in His name will give Him credit. That is where the great lack comes in the profession of Christianity too many times, as well as in those who deny Him and make no pretension to His name. It is not astonishing that a man who does not believe in Christ at all should give Christ no credit for His investment in Him, but here am I, a professor of Jesus. It is astonishing that I should not give Christ the credit for the investment that He has made in that man.

In the fifty-eighth of Isaiah the Lord describes the fast that He has chosen. It is, "That thou hide not thyself from thine own flesh." Who is our own flesh? Jesus Christ is. And Jesus Christ, as He has allied Himself to that man, is my flesh. See "that thou hide not thyself from thine own flesh." This is the fast that the Lord has chosen: Feed the hungry, relieve the oppressed, judge the fatherless, plea for the widow and spread abroad the good of His name and the charity of His goodness everywhere. He has allied Himself to human flesh, and in doing it to these, we are doing it to Him. That is Christianity.

Sermon 16

February 24, 1895

Turn to the fifty-eighth chapter of Isaiah. Let us read a portion of that chapter to begin with this evening, as connecting with the close of the lesson we had last night:

> Cry aloud, spare not, lift up thy voice like a trumpet and show my people their transgression and the house of Jacob their sins. Yet they seek me daily and delight to know my ways as a nation that did righteousness and forsook not the ordinance of their God.

Just as though they were in harmony with all the ordinances of the Lord.

> They ask of me the ordinances of justice; they take delight in approaching to God. Wherefore have we fasted, say they, and thou seest not? wherefore have we afflicted our soul and thou takest no knowledge? [Here is the answer.] Behold, in the day of your fast ye find pleasure and exact all your labors. Behold, ye fast for strife and debate and to smite with the fist of wickedness: ye shall not fast as ye do this day, to make your voice to be heard on high. Is it such a fast that I have chosen?

The text asks, "Is it . . . a day for a man to afflict his soul?" The margin is the better reading: "Is it . . . for a man to afflict his soul for a day?"

A man proposes to fast; he goes without victuals, perhaps from breakfast to supper – and afflicts his soul by thus going hungry and calls that a fast. He has afflicted his soul for a day.

> Is it such a fast that I have chosen? for a man to afflict his soul for a day? Is it to bow down his head as a bulrush and to spread sackcloth and ashes under him? wilt thou call this a fast and an acceptable day to the Lord?

Here is the fast that the Lord has appointed:

> Is not this the fast that I have chosen? to loose the bands of wickedness, to undo the heavy burdens, and to let the oppressed go free and that ye break every yoke? Is it not to deal thy bread to the hungry and that thou bring the poor that are cast out to thy house? when thou seest the naked, that thou cover him and that thou hide not thyself from thine own flesh?

That is the point at which the lesson closed last night.

That is the fast that God has chosen for His people; that is an acceptable fast unto the Lord. But that fast never can be observed until those who would observe it have come to the place where they shall see Jesus Christ allied, as He is, to every soul on this earth and shall treat him according to the alliance that Christ has made with him. When we reach that place – and we reach it in Jesus Christ, for it is there – then that will be the fast that we will observe right along.

I have a sentence here that I will read. I found it in a Testimony the other day:

> Search heaven and earth and there is no truth revealed more powerful than that which is manifested in mercy to the very ones who need your sympathy and aid in breaking the yoke and setting free the oppressed. Here the truth is lived, the truth is obeyed, the truth is taught, as it is in Jesus.

So, then, in manifesting mercy to those who need sympathy, in manifesting aid in breaking the yoke, and setting free the oppressed, – *in that* the truth is lived, the truth is obeyed; in that the truth is taught, as it is in Jesus. Assuredly. Does not that bring us right where Jesus is? Is not that Jesus Himself? The very thing that we are studying is that Christ has allied Himself with every soul on the earth. He has linked Himself with every human being, with every one in sinful flesh, and we are not to hide ourselves from Him who is our flesh. And when we who profess the name of Christ shall respect Him in every man with whom He has allied Himself, there will be just one grand Christian Help Band wherever Seventh-day Adventists are found. Then Christian Help work will be going on everywhere and all the time, for that is Christianity itself.

Now I have not a thing to say against the organization of Christian Help Bands that have been organized, but it is too bad that they had to be organized out of so few Seventh-day Adventists. That is all the trouble. Why should it be that only a portion of the church should be ready to engage in Christian Help work or compose a Christian Help Band? What is our profession in the world? We profess the name of Christ, which in the nature of things, demands that we respect the investment that He has made in every human soul and that we minister to all in need.

On the other hand, the organization of Christian Help Bands or any other kind of bands to do this thing from the side of mere duty, urging ourselves on to do it and pledging ourselves to do it without seeing Jesus Christ in it and without this connection with Christ and this love for Him that sees His interests in all human beings and ministers to Him as He is linked to all men – that will miss it also. Other kinds of Christian work will go along with that, but this is the greatest. "Search heaven and earth and there is no truth revealed more powerful" in Christian work and in teaching the truth as it is in Jesus. In heaven and earth there is nothing like it.

Just in this time, when such a fast as that is needed everywhere and among us especially, how blessed a thing it is that the Lord brings us right to that point and reveals the whole subject to us, giving us the Spirit and the secret that will do the whole of it in Christ's name, for His sake, with His Spirit, and to every man, because every soul is the purchase of Christ. Wherever we meet a human being, Christ has allied Himself with that man. Whoever He is, the Lord is interested in Him; He has invested all that He has in that man.

This truth draws us to the point where we shall always be doing everything possible to put forth the attractions of Christ, the graces of Christ and the goodness of Christ to men who know Him not but in whom He has invested all so that they may be drawn to where they, too, will respect the goodness of Christ and the wondrous investment that He has made in them.

If you are doing it for the man's sake or for your own credit, you may be taken in, of course. But if you do it as unto Christ and because of Christ's interest in the man, it is literally impossible for you ever to be "taken in, for Christ ever liveth and doth not forget. "Give to Him that asketh thee, and from him that would borrow of thee turn not thou away."

Here is the principle: It is to Christ that we are doing it. And as stated in the previous lesson, though the man may despise Christ and never believe on Him as long as the world lasts and may sink into perdition at the last, Christ in that great day when I stand on His right hand yonder will not have forgotten it. And in remembrance of it He will then say: "Inasmuch as ye have done it unto one of the least of these my brethren, ye have done it unto me."

You remember the place where He says:

"Whosoever shall give to drink unto one of these little ones a cup of cold water only in the name of a disciple, verily I say unto you, he shall in no wise lose his reward." Matt. 10:42. And this being so, when done only in the name of a disciple, how much more when it is done always in the name of the Lord Himself! "For God is not unrighteous to forget your work and labor of love which ye have showed toward His name in that ye have ministered to the saints and do minister." Heb. 6:10. Do you minister? That is the question.

This is the true fellowship of man, the true brotherhood of man. A great deal is said nowadays about "the fatherhood of God and the brotherhood of man." But it is just the brotherhood of such men as they approve all the time. If you belong to our order, then that is the brotherhood of man, but if you do not, we have nothing to do with you. Even churches also act the same way: If you belong to our church, then that is the brotherhood of man, but if you do not belong to our church, why, we have no particular interest in you, as we have nothing to do, properly, with caring for those who are outside of our church. This is our brotherhood of man.

All this is not the brotherhood of man at all. The true fatherhood of God and brotherhood of man is the brotherhood of man in Jesus Christ. It is to see Jesus Christ as He has allied Himself to every man, and as He has invested all He has in every man. He has broken down the middle wall of partition. In His flesh, which was our flesh, He has broken down the middle wall of partition that was between us, for to make in Himself of twain one new man, so making peace indeed. And in Him there is neither Greek nor Jew, black nor white, barbarian, Cythian, bond, nor free; nothing of the kind. All are one in Christ Jesus, and there is no respect of persons with God.

In Jesus Christ alone is the fatherhood of God and the brotherhood of man, and in Jesus Christ we find the brotherhood of man only when we find Christ the Brother of every man.

It is written, "For which cause He is not ashamed to call them brethren."

Not ashamed to call who brethren? Every one that is of flesh and blood – Christ is not ashamed to call him brother. He is not ashamed to go and take him by the hand, even though his breath does smell of liquor and say, "Come with me, and let us go a better way." That is the brotherhood of man.

It has been Satan's work always to get men to think that God is far away as possible. But it is the Lord's everlasting effort to get men to find out that He is as near to every one as possible. So it is written: He is not far from every one of us.

The great trouble with heathenism was to think that God was so far away – not only far away but full of wrath at them all, and only waiting to get a chance to pick them up and savagely shake them and plunge them into perdition. So viewing Him, they made offerings to get Him in a good humor and to keep Him from hurting them. But He was not far from every one of them all the time. "Not far." That is near – so near that all they had to do was to "feel after him." Although they were blind and in the dark too, all they had to do was to feel after Him and they would "find him." Acts 17:21-28.

Then the papacy came in, the very incarnation of that enmity between man and God. This incarnation of evil entered under the name of Christianity, and it again puts God and Christ so far away that nobody can come near to them. Everybody else comes in before God.

Then in addition to all this, He is so far away that Mary and her mother and her father – and then all the rest of the Catholic saints clear down to Joan of Arc and Christopher Columbus pretty soon – all these have to come in between God and men so as to make such a connection that all can be sure that they are noticed by Him.

But this is all of Satan's invention. Christ is not so far away as that. He is not far enough away to get a single relation in between Him and me or between Him and you. And this is just where God wants us to view Him – so near that it is impossible for anything or anybody to get between. But to how many people has He come so near? He is not far from every one of us, even the heathen.

The incarnation of that enmity that is against God and that separates between man and God – the papacy built up this, and now here is this same thought that we mentioned a moment ago, the false idea that He is so holy that it would be entirely unbecoming in Him to come near to us and be possessed of such a nature as we have – sinful, depraved, fallen human nature. Therefore, Mary must be born immaculate, perfect, sinless, and higher than the cherubim and seraphim and then Christ must be so born of her as to take His human nature in absolute sinlessness from her. But that puts Him farther away from us than the cherubim and the seraphim are and in a sinless nature.

But if He comes no nearer to us than in a sinless nature, that is a long way off, because I need somebody that is nearer to me than that. I need someone to help me who knows something about sinful nature, for that is the nature that I have, and such the Lord did take. He became one of us. Thus, you see, this is present truth in every respect, now that the papacy is taking possession of the world and the image of it is going on in the wrong way, forgetting all that God is in Jesus Christ and all that Christ is in the world – having the form of godliness without the reality, without the power. In this day is it not just the thing that is needed in the world, that God should proclaim the real merits of Jesus Christ once more and His holiness?

It is true He is holy; He is altogether holy. But His holiness is not that kind that makes Him afraid to be in company with people who are not holy for fear He will get His holiness spoiled. Anybody who has such a kind of holiness that they cannot be found in the company – in the name of Jesus Christ – of people who are fallen and lost and degraded, without spoiling it would better get rid of it as quickly as possible and get the right kind, because that kind of holiness is not worth having. It is already spoiled.

[*Question:* What about the reputation? The Christian has no reputation. He has character. The Christian asks no questions about reputation. Character, character is all that the Christian cares for and that the character of God, revealed in Jesus Christ.]

But there is a great amount of just that kind of holiness among professed Christians in these days – indeed, I am not sure that it is all outside of the Seventh-day Adventist denomination.

It is that kind of "holiness" which leads many to be ready to exclaim if a brother or sister – a sister especially – should go among the fallen, unfortunate ones and begin to work for them and sympathize with them and help them up: "O, well, if you are going with such people as that, I cannot associate with you any more. Indeed, I am not sure that

I want to belong to the church any more, if you are going to work for such people and bring them into the church."

The answer to all such expressions as those is: Very good. If you do not want to belong to the church with such people as that, you would better get out of the church as quickly as possible, for very soon the church of Jesus Christ is going to have just that kind of people in it. "The publicans and the harlots go into the kingdom before you."

The church of Jesus Christ, in a little while, is going to be so molded upon the grace of Jesus Christ and so filled with His holy character that its members will not be afraid to go, as did He, to the lowest depths to pick up the fallen. They will have such measure of the holiness of Jesus Christ that they will not be afraid of becoming defiled by going *in His name,* down to the lowest.

But that kind of holiness which says: "Come not near to me, for I am holier than thou" – stand aloof or you will defile my holy garments – O, that is the holiness of the devil! Away with it!

God's holiness is pure, that is true; it is such holiness that sin cannot bear the presence of it. It is holiness of such transcendent purity and power as to be a consuming fire to sin.

Its consuming power upon sin is because of its wondrous purity, and therefore because of the wondrous purity, and the power of that wondrous purity of the holiness of God in Jesus Christ, He longs to come in contact with those who are laden with sins, who are permeated through and through with sins in order that this holiness, finding an entrance, shall consume the sin and save the soul. That is Christ's holiness.

It is one of the most blessed truths in the Bible, that our God is a consuming fire because of His holiness. For then in Jesus Christ we meet Him whose holiness is a consuming fire to sin, and that is the pledge of our salvation in perfection from every stain of sin. The brightness, the glory, the all-consuming purity of that holiness will take every vestige of sin and sinfulness out of the man who will meet God in Jesus Christ.

Thus in His true holiness, Christ could come and did come to sinful men in sinful flesh, where sinful men are. Thus in Christ and in Christ alone is found the brotherhood of man. All indeed are one in Christ Jesus our Lord.

Some have found and all may find in the Testimonies the statement that Christ has not "like *passions*" as we have. The statement is there; every one may find it there, of course.

Now there will be no difficulty in any of these studies from beginning to end. If you will stick precisely to what is said and not go beyond what is said nor put into it what is not said, whether it be touching Church and State, separation from the world or this of Christ in our flesh. Stick strictly to what is said. Do not go to drawing curious conclusions. Some have drawn the conclusion some time ago – and you can see what a fearful conclusion it is – that "Christ became ourselves; He is our flesh. Therefore, *I am Christ.*" They say Christ forgave sins; *I* can forgive sins; He wrought miracles; *I* must work miracles. That is a fearful argument. There are no two ways about that.

Christ became ourselves, in our place, weak as we, and in all points like as we are, in order that He might be that forever and never that we should be Himself. No. It is God who is to be manifested always and not ourselves. In order that this might be, Christ emptied Himself and took ourselves in order that God Himself might come to us, appear in us, and be revealed in us and through us in all things. It is always God and never ourselves. That which ruined us at the start was the exaltation of ourselves, the setting forth of ourselves and the putting of ourselves above God. In order that we might get rid of our wicked selves, Christ emptied His righteous self and stood in the place of our wicked selves and crucified ourselves, putting ourselves under foot always, in order that God might be all in all. How much? All. All in how many? All. It was done that God might be all that there is in me and all there is in you and all there is in Christ. Assuredly that is what this was done for. We are not to exalt ourselves. Christ is to increase. I am to decrease. He is to live. I am to die. He is to be exalted. I am to be emptied.

Sermon 17

February 25, 1895

Now as to Christ's not having "like passions" with us: In the Scriptures all the way through He is like us and with us according to the flesh. He is the seed of David according to the flesh. He was made in the likeness of sinful flesh. Don't go too far. He was made in the likeness of sinful flesh, not in the likeness of sinful mind. Do not drag His mind into it. His flesh was our flesh, but the mind was "the mind of Christ Jesus."

Therefore it is written: "Let this mind be in you which was also in Christ Jesus." If He had taken our mind, how, then, could we ever have been exhorted to "let this mind be in you which was also in Christ Jesus?" It would have been so already. But what kind of mind is ours? O, it is corrupted with sin also. Look at ourselves in the second chapter of Ephesians, beginning with the first verse and reading to the third, but the third verse is the one that has this particular point in it:

Now I refer you also to page 191 of the Bulletin, to the lessons we studied on the destruction of that enmity.

We studied there where the enmity came from, you remember – how it got into this world – the ground is covered in this that I have just read. Adam had the mind of Jesus Christ in the garden; he had the divine mind – the divine and the human were united, sinlessly. Satan came in and offered his inducements through the appetite, through the flesh. Adam and Eve forsook the mind of Jesus Christ, the mind of God that was in them, and accepted the suggestions and the leadings of this other mind. Thus they were enslaved to that and so are we all. Now Jesus Christ comes into the world, taking our flesh, and in His sufferings and temptations in the wilderness He fights the battle upon the point of appetite.

Where Adam and Eve failed and where sin entered He fought the battle over and victory was won and righteousness entered. He having fasted forty days and forty nights – perfectly helpless, human as ourselves, hungry as we – there came to Him the temptation, "If thou be the Son of God, command that these stones be made bread." He answered, "It is written, Man shall not live by bread alone, but by every word that proceedeth out of the mouth of God."

Then Satan took another turn. He argued: You are trusting in the word of God, are you? All right. Here the word of God says: "He shall give his angels charge concerning thee: and in their hands they shall bear thee up, lest at any time thou dash thy foot against a stone." Now you are trusting in the word of God: you jump off here, for it is written, "He shall give his angels charge concerning thee." Jesus answered again: "It is written again, Thou shalt not tempt the Lord thy God."

Then Satan took Jesus upon an exceeding high mountain and showed Him all the glory of them too – the glory, the honor, the dignity – he showed Him all that. And there at that moment there was stirred up all the ambition that ever appeared in Napoleon or Caesar or Alexander or all of them put together. But from Jesus still the answer is: "It is written, Thou shalt worship the Lord thy God, and Him only shalt thou serve."

Then the devil departed from Him for a season, and angels came and ministered unto Him. There was the power of Satan conquered in man on the point of appetite – just where that power was gained over man. This man at the first had the mind of God; he forsook it and took the mind of Satan. In Jesus Christ the mind of God is brought back once more to the sons of men, and Satan is conquered. Therefore, it is gloriously true, as the word reads in Dr. Young's translation and in the German, as it does in the Greek: "We know that the Son of God is come and has given us a mind."

Read the last words of 1 Cor. 2:16: "We have the mind of Christ." Put the two transactions together. The German and the Danish and also the Greek are alike. Put the two together: "We know that the Son of God is come and has given us a mind" and "*We have the mind of Christ.*" Thank the Lord!

Read in Romans now. I will read from the Greek, beginning with the twenty-fourth verse of the seventh chapter. You remember from the tenth to the twenty-fourth verses is that contest: The good I would do, I do not; and the evil I hate, that I do. I find then a law, that, when I would do good, evil is present with me. I see another law in my members, warring against the law of my mind and bringing me into captivity to the law of sin which is in my members. There the flesh has control and draws the mind after it, fulfilling the desires of the flesh and of the mind. Now.

> O wretched man that I am! Who shall deliver me from the body of this death? I thank God through Jesus Christ our Lord. So then I myself with the mind indeed serve the law of God [or rather serve God's law, literally here]; but with the flesh, sin's law. There is then now no condemnation to those in Christ Jesus who walk not according to flesh but according to Spirit. For the law of the Spirit of life in Christ Jesus set me free from the law of sin and of death. For the law being powerless, in that it was weak through the flesh, God having sent his own son in likeness of flesh of sin, and for sin, condemned sin in the flesh, that the requirement of the law should be fulfilled in us, who not according to flesh walk, but according to Spirit. For they that according to flesh are, the things of the flesh mind; and they according to Spirit, the things of the Spirit. For the mind of the flesh is death; but the

> mind of the Spirit [that is, the Spirit's mind; the one is the flesh's mind, and the other is the Spirit's mind], life and peace. Because the mind of the flesh is enmity toward God: for to the law of God it is not subject; for neither can it be; and they that in flesh are, God please cannot [that is, cannot please God]. But ye are not in flesh, but in spirit, if indeed the Spirit of God dwells in you; but if any one the Spirit of Christ has not, he is not of him: but if Christ be in you, the body is dead, on account of sin, but the Spirit life [is] on account of righteousness.
>
> You hath he quickened, who were dead in trespasses and sins; wherein in time past ye walked according to the course of this world, according to the prince of the power of the air, the spirit that now worketh in the children of disobedience: among whom also we all had our conversation [our manner of walk] in times past in the lusts of our flesh, fulfilling the desires of the flesh and of the mind.

Our minds have consented to sin. We have felt the enticements of the flesh and our minds yielded, our minds consented and did the wills and the desires of the flesh, fulfilling the desires of the flesh and of the mind. The flesh leads and our minds have followed, and with the flesh the law of sin is served. When the mind can lead, the law of God is served. But as our minds have surrendered, yielded to sin, they have themselves become sinful and weak and are led away by the power of sin in the flesh.

Now the flesh of Jesus Christ was our flesh and in it was all that is in our flesh – all the tendencies to sin that are in our flesh were in His flesh, drawing upon Him to get Him to consent to sin. Suppose He had consented to sin with His mind – what then? Then His mind would have been corrupted and then He would have become of like passions with us. But in that case He Himself would have been a sinner; He would have been entirely enslaved and we all would have been lost – everything would have perished.

I will read now from the new *Life of Christ*, advance copy, upon this very point:

> It is true that Christ at one time said of himself, "The prince of this world cometh, and hath nothing in me." John 14:30. Satan finds in human hearts some point where he can gain a foothold; some sinful desire is cherished, by means of which his temptations assert their power.

Where does he start the temptation? In the flesh. Satan reaches the mind through the flesh; God reaches the flesh through the mind. Satan controls the mind through the flesh. Through this means – through the lusts of the flesh, the lusts of the eyes, the pride of life, and through ambition for the world and the honor and respect of men – through these things Satan draws upon us, upon our minds to get us to yield. Our minds respond and we cherish that thing. By this means his temptations assert their power. Then we have sinned. But until that drawing of our flesh is cherished, there is no sin. There is temptation, but not sin. Every man is tempted when he is drawn away thus and enticed, and when lust has conceived, when that desire is cherished, then it brings forth sin, and sin when it is finished bringeth forth death.

Read farther now:

> Some sinful desire [with us] is cherished, by means of which his temptations assert their power. But he could find nothing in the Son of God that would enable him to gain the victory. Jesus did not consent to sin. Not even by a thought could he be brought to yield to the power of temptation.

Thus you see that where the victory comes, where the battlefield is, is right upon the line between the flesh and the mind. The battle is fought in the realm of the thoughts. The battle against the flesh, I mean, is fought altogether and the victory won in the realm of the thoughts. Therefore, Jesus Christ came in just such flesh as ours but with a mind that held its integrity against every temptation, against every inducement to sin – a mind that never consented to sin – no, never in the least conceivable shadow of a thought.

And by that means He has brought that divine man to every man on earth. Therefore, every man for the choosing and by choosing can have that divine mind that conquers sin in the flesh. Dr. Young's translation of 1 John 5:20 is: "Ye know that the Son of God has come, and hath given us a mind." The German says the same thing exactly and the Greek too – "has given us a mind." To be sure he has. That is what He came for. We had the carnal mind, the mind that followed Satan and yielded to the flesh. What was it that enslaved Eve's mind? O, she saw that the tree was good for food. It was not good for any such thing. The appetite, the lusts of the flesh, the desires of the flesh, led her off. She took of the tree and did eat. The appetite led, and enslaved the mind – that is, the mind of the flesh, and that is enmity against God; it comes from Satan. In Jesus Christ it is destroyed by the divine mind which He brought into the flesh. By this divine mind He put the enmity underfoot and kept it there. By this He condemned sin in the flesh. So there is our victory. In Him is our victory, and it is all in having that mind which was in Him.

O, it is all told in the beginning. There came in this enmity, and Satan took man captive and enslaved the mind. God says, "I will put enmity between thee and the woman and between thy seed and her seed." Who was her seed? Christ. "It [her seed] shall bruise thy head and thou shalt bruise his" *head?* No, sir. No, sir. "Thou shalt bruise his heel." All that Satan could do with Christ was to entice the flesh, to lay temptations before the flesh. He could not affect the mind of Christ. But Christ reaches the mind of Satan, where the enmity lies and where it exists and He destroys that wicked thing. It is all told there in the story in Genesis.

The blessedness of it is, Satan can only deal with the flesh. He can stir up the desires of the flesh, but the mind of Christ stands there and says, No, no. The law of God is to be served and the body of flesh must come under.

We shall have to follow this thought further. But even only so far there is blessing, there is joy, there is *salvation* in it for every soul. Therefore "let this mind be in you, which was also in Christ Jesus." That conquers sin in the sinful flesh. By His promise we are made partakers of the divine nature. Divinity and humanity are united once more when the divine mind of Jesus Christ by His divine faith abides in human flesh. Let them be united in you and be glad and rejoice forevermore in it.

Thus you see the mind which we have is the flesh's mind. It is controlled by the flesh and it came to us from whom? Satan. Therefore, it is enmity against God. And that mind of Satan is the mind of self, always self, in the place of God. Now Christ came to bring to us another mind than that. While we have Satan's mind, the flesh ruling, we serve the law of sin. God can reveal to us His law and we can consent that that is good and desire to fulfill it and make resolutions to do so and sign bargains and make contracts even, "but I see another law in my members [in my flesh], warring against the law of my mind [against that desire, that wish of my mind, that delights in the law of God], and bringing me into captivity to the law of sin which is in my members. O wretched man that I am!" But Christ comes and brings another mind – the Spirit's mind – to us and gives us that. He gives us a mind and we have His mind by His Holy Spirit. Then and therefore with the mind – the Spirit's mind, the mind of Christ which He hath given us – the law of God is served. Thank the Lord.

So see the difference. In the seventh of Romans there is described the man in whom the flesh rules and leads the mind astray, against the will of the man even. In the ninth chapter of 1 Corinthians, verses 26, 27, is described the man in whom the mind has control. This is the Christian. The mind has control of the body and the body is under, and he keeps it under. Therefore it is written in another place (Rom. 12:2):

> Be not conformed to this world: but be ye transformed by the renewing of your mind.

And the Greek word is the same word exactly as that: "If any man be in Christ, he is a *new creation,*" he is a new creature – not an old man changed over, but a new – made one. So this is not an old mind made over but a new – created mind. That is the mind of Christ wrought in us by the Spirit of God, giving us the mind of Christ and so making an entirely new mind in us and for us.

This is shown in Romans, eighth chapter: "They that are after the flesh do mind the things of the flesh," because they do the works of the flesh, the mind follows sin that way. "But they that after the Spirit [mind], the things of the Spirit." And "if any man have not the Spirit of Christ, he is none of his."

That which brings to us the mind of Jesus Christ is the Holy Ghost. Indeed, the Spirit of God brings Jesus Christ Himself to us. By the Holy Ghost the real presence of Christ is with us and dwells in us. Can He bring Christ to us without bringing the mind of Christ to us? Assuredly not. So then in the nature of things there is the mind of Christ which He came into the world to give us.

Now see how this follows further, and what it cost to do that, and how it was done. This mind of the flesh is the minding of self. It is enmity against God and is controlled through the flesh. Jesus Christ came into this flesh Himself – the glorious One – He who made the worlds, the Word of God – was made flesh Himself and He was our flesh. And He, that divine One who was in heaven was in our sinful flesh. Yet that divine One, when in sinful flesh never manifested a particle of His divine self in resisting the temptations that were in that flesh but emptied Himself.

We are here studying the same subject that we have been studying these three or four years, but God is leading us further along in the study of it, and I am glad. We have been studying for three or four years, "Let this mind be in you which was also in Christ Jesus," who emptied Himself. That mind must be in us in order for us to be emptied, for we cannot of ourselves empty ourselves. Nothing but divinity can do that. That is an infinite thing. Can the mind of Satan empty itself of self? No. Can the mind that is in us, that minding of self, empty itself of self? No. Self cannot do it. Jesus Christ, the divine One, the infinite One, came in His divine person in this same flesh of ours and never allowed His divine power, His personal self, to be manifested at all in resisting these temptations and enticements and drawings of the flesh.

What was it, then, that conquered sin there and kept Him from sinning? It was the power of God the Father that kept Him. Now where does that touch us? Here. We cannot empty ourselves, but His divine mind comes into us and by that divine power we can empty ourselves of our wicked selves and then by that divine power the mind of Jesus Christ, of God the Father, comes to us and keeps us from the power of temptation. Thus Christ, emptying His divine self, His righteous self, brings to us the power by which we are emptied of our wicked selves. And this is how He abolished in His flesh the enmity and made it possible for the enmity to be destroyed in you and me.

Do you see that? I know it takes close thinking, and I know too that when you have thought upon that and have got it clearly, then the mind cannot go any further. There we come face to face with the mystery of God itself, and human, finite intellect must stop and say, That is holy ground. That is beyond my measure. I can go no further. I surrender to God.

[*Question:* Did not Christ depend on God to keep Him? *Answer:* Yes, that is what I am saying. That is the point.]

Christ depended in the Father all the time. Christ Himself, who made the worlds, was all the time in that sinful flesh of mine and yours which He took. He who made the worlds was there in His divine presence all the time, but never did He allow Himself to appear at all or to do anything at all that was done. That was kept back, and when these temptations come upon Him, He could have annihilated them all with the assertion – in righteousness of His divine self. But if He had done so, it would have ruined us.

To have asserted Himself, to have allowed Himself to appear, even in righteousness, *would have ruined us,* because we who are only wicked never would have had anything before us then but the manifestation of self. Set before men who are only wicked, manifestation of self, even in divine righteousness, as an example to be followed and you simply make men that much more confirmed in selfishness and the wickedness of selfishness. Therefore, in order that we in our wicked selves might be delivered from our wicked selves, the divine One, the holy One, kept under, surrendered, emptied all the manifestation of His righteous self. And that does accomplish it. He accomplished it by keeping Himself back all the time and leaving everything entirely to the Father to hold Him against these temptations. He was Conqueror through the grace and power of the Father, which came to Him upon His trust and upon His emptying Himself of self.

There is where you and I are now. There is where it comes to you and me. We are tempted, we are tried, and there is always room for us to assert ourselves and we undertake to make things move. There are suggestions which rise that such and such things are "too much for even a Christian to bear," and that "Christian humility is not intended to go as far as that." Some one strikes you on the cheek or breaks your wagon or tools or he may stone your tent or meetinghouse. Satan suggests, "Now you send those fellows up. You take the law to them. Christians are not to bear such things as that in the world; that is not fair." You answer Him: "That is so. There is no use of that. We will teach those fellows a lesson."

Yes, and perhaps you do. But what is that? That is *self*-defense. That is *self*-replying. No. Keep back that wicked self. Let God attend to the matter. "Vengeance is mine; I will repay, saith the Lord." That is what Jesus Christ did. He was spit upon; He was taunted; He was struck upon the face; His hair was pulled; a crown of thorns was put upon His head and in mockery the knee was bowed, with "Hail King of the Jews." They blindfolded Him and then struck Him and cried: "Prophesy, who is it that smote thee?" All that was put upon Him. And in His human nature He bore all that, because His divine self was kept back.

Was there any suggestion to Him, suppose you, to drive back that riotous crowd? to let loose one manifestation of His divinity and sweep away the whole wicked company? Satan was there to suggest it to Him, if nothing else. What did He do? He stood defenseless as the Lamb of God. There was no assertion of His divine self, no sign of it – only the man standing there, leaving all to God to do whatsoever He pleased.

He said to Pilate: "Thou couldst have no power at all against me, except it were given thee from above." That is the faith of Jesus. And that is what the prophecy means when it says, "Here are they that keep the commandments of God, and the faith of Jesus." We are to have that divine faith of Jesus Christ, which comes to us in the gift of the mind which He gives. That mind which He gives to me will exercise in me the same faith it exercised in Him. So we keep the faith of Jesus.

So then there was He, by that self-surrender keeping back His righteous self and refusing ever to allow it to appear under the most grievous temptations – and the Spirit of Prophecy tells us that what was brought upon Him there in the night of His betrayal were the very things that were the hardest for human nature to submit to. But He, by the keeping back of His divine self, *caused human nature to submit to it* by the power of the Father, who kept Him from sinning. And by that means He brings us to that same divine mind, that same divine power, that when we shall be taunted, when we shall be stricken upon the face, when we shall be spit upon, when we shall be persecuted as He was – as shortly we shall be – that divine mind which was in Him being given to us will keep back our natural selves, our sinful selves and we will leave all to God. Then the Father will keep us now in Him, as He kept us then in Him. That is our victory and there is how He destroyed the enmity for us. And *in Him* it is destroyed in us. Thank the Lord!

I will read a portion now from the "Spirit of Prophecy" that will help in the understanding of the subject.

First from an article published in the *Review and Herald* of July 5, 1887. It is so good that I will read a few passages to go into the Bulletin with this lesson so that all can have it and so that all may know for certain that the steps we have taken in this study are exactly correct:

> The apostle would call our attention from ourselves to the Author of our salvation. He presents before us his two natures, human and divine. Here is the description of the divine: "Who, being in the form of God, thought it not robbery to be equal with God." He was the "brightness of his glory and the express image of his person."
>
> Now of the human: He "was made in the likeness of men: and being found in fashion as a man, he humbled himself, and became obedient unto death." He voluntarily assumed human nature. It was his own act, and by his own consent. He clothed his divinity with humanity. He was all the while as God, but he did not appear as God. He veiled the demonstrations of Deity, which had commanded the homage and called forth the admiration of the universe of God. He was God while upon earth, but he divested himself of the form of God and in its stead took the form and fashion of man. He walked the earth as a man. For our sakes he became poor, that we through his poverty might become rich. He laid aside his glory and his majesty. He was God, but the glories of the form of God he for a while relinquished. Though he walked among men in poverty, scattering his blessings wherever he went, at his word legions of angels would surround their Redeemer and do him homage.

When Peter, at the time of Christ's betrayal, resisted the officers and took the sword and raised it and cut off an ear of the servant of the high priest, Jesus said, Put up your sword. Don't you know that I could call twelve legions of angels?

> But he walked on the earth unrecognized, unconfessed with but few exceptions by his creatures. The atmosphere was polluted with sin and with curses instead of the anthems of praise. His lot was poverty and humiliation. As he passed to and fro on his mission of mercy to relieve the sick, to lift up the oppressed, scarce a solitary voice called him blessed, and the greatest of the nation passed him by with disdain.
>
> Contrast this with the riches of glory, the wealth of praise pouring forth from immortal tongues, the millions of rich voices in the universe of God in anthems of adoration. But he humbled himself, and took mortality upon him. As a member of the human family he was mortal, but as God he was the fountain of life to the world. He could, in his divine person, ever have withstood the advances of death and refused to come under its dominion, but he voluntarily laid down his life, that in doing so he might give life, and bring immortality to light. He bore the sins of the world and endured the penalty which rolled like a mountain upon his divine soul. He yielded up his life a sacrifice, that man might not eternally die. He died, not by being compelled to die, but by his own free will.

That is self-sacrifice; that is self-emptying.

> This was humility. The whole treasure of heaven was poured out in one gift to save fallen man. He brought into his human nature all the life-giving energies that human beings will need and must receive.

And He brings it into my human nature yet, to your human nature, at our choice, by the Spirit of God bringing to us His divine presence and emptying us of ourselves and causing God to appear instead of self.

> Wondrous combination of man and God! He might have helped his human nature to stand the inroads of disease by pouring from his divine nature vitality and undecaying vigor to the human. But he humbled himself to man's nature. He did this that the Scripture might be fulfilled. And the plan was entered into by the Son of God, knowing all the steps in his humiliation that he must descend to make an expiation for the sins of a condemned, groaning world. What humility was this! It amazed angels. The tongue can never describe it; the imagination can never take it in.

But we can take in the blessed *fact* and enjoy the benefit of that to all eternity and God will give us eternity in which to take in the rest.

"The eternal Word consented to be made flesh. God became man." He became man; what am I? A man. What are you? A man. He became ourselves and God with Him is God with us.

"But He stepped still lower." What, still lower than that yet? Yes, sir.

"The man," that is Christ, "must humble himself *as a man*." Because we need to humble ourselves, He not only humbled Himself as God, but when He became man, He humbled Himself as a man, so that we might humble ourselves to God.

He emptied Himself as God and became man, and then *as man* He humbled Himself that we might humble ourselves. And all that we might be saved! In it is salvation. Shall we not take it and enjoy it day and night and be ever just as thankful as a Christian?

> But he stepped still lower. The man must humble himself as a man to bear insult, reproach, shameful accusations, and abuse. There seemed to be no safe place for him in his own territory. He had to flee from place to place for his life. He was betrayed by one of his disciples; he was denied by one of his most zealous followers. He was mocked; he was crowned with a crown of thorns. He was scourged. He was forced to bear the burden of the cross. He was not insensible to this contempt and ignominy. He submitted, but O, he felt the bitterness as no other being could feel it! He was pure, holy, and undefiled, yet arraigned as a criminal. The adorable Redeemer stepped down from the high exaltation. Step by step he humbled himself to die, but what a death! It was the most shameful, the most cruel – the death on the cross as a malefactor. He did not die as a hero in the eyes of the world, loaded with honors, as men die in battle. He died a condemned criminal, suspended between the heavens and the earth – died a lingering death of shame, exposed to the revilings and tauntings of a debased, crime-loaded, profligate multitude. "All they that see me laugh me to scorn: they shoot out the lip, they shake the head." Ps. 22:7. He was numbered with the transgressors and his kinsmen according to the flesh disowned him. His mother beheld his humiliation and he was forced to see the sword pierce her heart. He endured the cross, despised the shame. He made it of small account in consideration of the results he was working out in behalf of not only the inhabitants of this speck of a world, but the whole universe – every world which God had created.
>
> Christ was to die as man's substitute. Man was a criminal under sentence of death for transgression of the law of God as a traitor, a rebel; hence a substitute for man must die as a malefactor, because he stood in the place of the traitors, with all their treasured sins upon his divine soul. It was not enough that Jesus should die in order to meet the demands of the broken law; but he died a shameful death. The prophet gives to the world his words: "I hid not my face from shame and spitting!"
>
> In consideration of this, can men have one particle of self-exaltation? As they trace down the life and humiliation and sufferings of Christ, can they lift their proud heads as though they were to bear no shame, no trials, no humiliation? I say to the followers of Christ, Look to Calvary and blush for shame at your self-important ideas. All this humiliation of the Majesty of heaven was for guilty, condemned man. He went lower and lower in his humiliation, until there were no lower depths he could reach in order to lift up man from his moral defilement.

How low down were we then when, in order to lift us up from moral defilement He had to go step by step lower and lower until there were no lower depths He could reach? Think of it and see how low we were! All this was for you who are striving for the supremacy, striving for human praise, for human exaltation – you who are afraid you will not receive all that praise, all that deference from human minds, that you think is your due! Is this Christ like?

> Let this mind be in you which was also in Christ Jesus. He died to make an atonement, and to be a pattern for every one who would be his disciple. Shall selfishness come into your hearts? and shall those who set not before them the pattern, Jesus, extol your merits? You have none, except as they come through Jesus Christ. Shall pride be harbored after you have seen Deity humbling himself, and then as man debasing himself, until as man there were no lower depths to which he could descend? Be astonished, O, ye heavens, and be amazed, O ye inhabitants of the earth, that such returns should be made to your Lord.
>
> What contempt, what wickedness, what formality, what pride, what efforts made to lift up man and glorify himself, when the Lord of glory humbled himself, agonized, and died the shameful death on the cross in our behalf.
>
> Who is learning the meekness and lowliness of the pattern? Who is striving earnestly to master self? Who is lifting his cross and following Jesus? Who is wrestling against self-conceit? Who is setting himself in good earnest and with all his energies to overcome Satanic envyings, jealousies, evil-surmisings, and lasciviousness, cleansing the soul-temple from all defilements, and opening the door of the heart for Jesus to come it? Would that these words might have that impression on the mind that all who read them might cultivate the grace of humility, be self-denying, more disposed to esteem others better than themselves, having the mind and spirit of Christ to bear one another's burdens. O, that we might write deeply on our hearts, as we contemplate the great condescension and humiliation to which the Son of God descended, that we might be partakers of the divine nature.

Now I read a few lines from the advance pages of the new *Life of Christ*.

> In order to carry out the great work of redemption, the Redeemer must take the place of fallen man. Burdened with the sins of the world, he must go over the ground where Adam stumbled. He must take up the work just where Adam failed, and endure a test of the same character, but infinitely more severe than that which had vanquished him. It is impossible for man fully to comprehend Satan's temptations to our Saviour. Every enticement to evil which men find so difficult to resist, was brought to bear upon the Son of God in as much greater degree as his character was superior to that of fallen man.
>
> When Adam was assailed by the tempter, he was without the taint of sin. He stood before God in the strength of perfect manhood, all the organs and faculties of his being fully developed and harmoniously balanced; and he was surrounded with things of beauty, and communed daily with the holy angels. What a contrast to this perfect being did the second Adam present, as he entered the desolate wilderness to cope with Satan. For four thousand years the race had been decreasing in size and physical strength, and deteriorating in moral worth; and in order to elevate fallen man, Christ must reach him where he stood. He assumed human nature, bearing the infirmities and degeneracy of the race. He humiliated himself to the lowest depths of human woe, that he might sympathize with man and rescue him from the degradation into which sin had plunged him.
>
> "For it became him for whom are all things, and by whom are all things, in bringing many sons unto glory, to make the Captain of their salvation perfect through sufferings." Heb. 2:10. "And being made perfect, he became the author of eternal salvation unto all

them that obey him." Heb. 5:9. "Wherefore in all things it behooved him to be made like unto his brethren, that he might be a merciful and faithful high priest in things pertaining to God to make reconciliation for the sins of the people. For in that he himself hath suffered being tempted, he is able to succor them that are tempted." Heb. 2:17, 18. "We have not a high priest which cannot be touched with the feeling of our infirmities; but was in all points tempted like as we are, yet without sin." Heb. 4:15.

It is true that Christ at one time said of himself, "The prince of this world cometh, and hath nothing in me." John 14:30. Satan finds in human hearts some point where he can gain a foothold; some sinful desire is cherished, by means of which his temptations assert their power. But he could find nothing in the Son of God that would enable him to gain the victory. Jesus did not consent to sin. Not even by a thought could he be brought to the power of Satan's temptations. Yet it is written of Christ that he was tempted in all points like as we are. Many hold that from the nature of Christ is was impossible for Satan's temptations to weaken or overthrow him. Then Christ could not have been placed in Adam's position, to go over the ground where Adam stumbled and fell; he could not have gained the victory that Adam failed to gain. Unless he was placed in a position as trying as that in which Adam stood, he could not redeem Adam's failure. If man has in any sense a more trying conflict to endure than had Christ, then Christ is not able to succor him when tempted. Christ took humanity with all its liabilities. He took the nature of man with the possibility of yielding to temptation, and he relied upon divine power to keep him.

The union of the divine with the human is one of the most mysterious, as well as the most precious, truths of the plan of redemption. It is of this that Paul speaks when he says, "Without controversy great is the mystery of godliness: God was manifest in the flesh." 1 Tim. 3:16. While it is impossible for finite minds fully to grasp this great truth or fathom its significance, we may learn from it lessons of vital importance to us in our struggles against temptation. Christ came to the world to bring divine power to humanity, to make man a partaker of the divine nature.

You see, we are on firm ground all the way, so that when it is said that He took our flesh but still was not a partaker of our passions, it is all straight; it is all correct, because His divine mind never consented to sin. And that mind is brought *to us* by the Holy Spirit that is freely given unto us.

"We know that the Son of God has come, and hath given us a mind" and "we have the mind of Christ." "Let this mind be in you, which was also in Christ Jesus."

Sermon 18

February 25, 1895

We will begin our study this evening with Rom. 7:25: "With the mind I myself serve the law of God." I repeat the expression that I made in the previous lesson – that it is in the realm of the thoughts where the law of God is served, where the contention against sin is carried on and the victory won.

The lust of the flesh, the lust of the eye, and the pride of life – these tendencies to sin that are in the flesh, drawing upon us – in this is the temptation. But temptation is not sin. Not until the desire is cherished is there sin. But as soon as the desire is cherished, as soon as we consent to it and receive it into the mind and hold it there, then there is sin; and whether that desire is carried out in action or not, the sin is committed. In the mind, in fact, we have already enjoyed the desire. In consenting to it we have already done the thing so far as the mind itself goes. All that can come after that is simply the sensual part, the sense of enjoying the satisfaction of the flesh.

This is shown in the Saviour's words in Matt. 5:27,28:

> Ye have heard that it was said by them of old time, Thou shalt not commit adultery: but I say unto you that whosoever looketh on a woman to lust after her hath committed adultery with her already in his heart.

Therefore, the only place where the Lord could bring help and deliverance to us, is right in the place where the thoughts are, at the very root of the thing that is sin, the very point where the sin is conceived and where it begins.

Consequently, when tempted and tried as He was – when He was spit upon, when they struck Him in the face and on the head in the trial in Jerusalem and in all His public ministry when the Pharisees, the Sadducees, the scribes, and the priests in their iniquity and hypocrisy, *which He knew,* were all doing everything they could to irritate Him and get Him stirred up – when He was constantly tried thus, His hand was never raised to return the blow. He never had to check any such motion, because not even the *impulse* to make any such motion was ever allowed. Yet He had our human nature in which such impulses are so natural. Why then did not these motions manifest themselves in our human nature in Him?

For the reason that He was so surrendered to the will of the Father that the power of God through the Holy Spirit so worked against the flesh and fought the battle right in the field of the thoughts, never, in the subtlest form of the thought was there allowed any such thing to conceive. So that under all these insults and grievous trials He was just as calm, our human nature in Him was just as calm, as it was when the Holy Spirit in the form of a dove overshadowed Him on the banks of the Jordan.

Now "*let this mind be in you.*" It is not enough for a Christian to become all stirred up and say a few spiteful words or raise the hand in resentment and *then* say to Himself, "O, I am a Christian; I must not say this or do that." No. We are to be so submitted to the power of God and to the influence of the Spirit of God that our thoughts shall be so completely controlled that the victory shall be won already and not even the impulse be allowed. Then we shall be Christians everywhere and all the time under all circumstances and against all influences. But until we do reach that point, we are not sure that we shall show a Christian spirit under all circumstances and at all times and against all insults.

As stated in the previous lesson, the things that were heaped upon Christ and which He bore were the very things that were the hardest for human nature to bear. And we, before we get through with the cause in which we are engaged are going to have to meet these very things that are hardest for human nature to bear, and unless we have the battle won already and are Christians indeed, we are not sure that we shall show the Christian spirit in these times when it is most needed. In fact, the time when the Christian spirit is most needed is all the time.

Now in Jesus the Lord has brought to us just the power that will give us into the hand of God and cause us to be so submitted to Him that He shall so fully control every thought that we shall be Christians all the time and everywhere, "bringing into captivity every thought to the obedience of Christ."

"The kingdom of God is within you."

Christ dwells within us and He is the King. The law of God is written upon the heart and that is the law of the kingdom. Where the King and the law of the kingdom are, there is the kingdom. In the inmost recesses, the secret chamber of the heart, at the very root, the fountain of the thought – there Christ sets up His throne; there the law of God is written by the Spirit; there the King asserts His authority and sets forth the principles of His government and allegiance to that is Christianity. Thus at the very citadel of the soul, the very citadel of the thoughts, the very place, the only place, where sin can enter – there God sets up His throne; there He establishes His kingdom; there He puts His law, and the power to cause the authority of the law to be recognized and the principles of the law to be carried out in the life, and the result is peace only and all the time. That is the very thing that Christ hath brought to us, and which comes to us in the mind of Christ.

Let us look at that a little further. When Christ had our human nature, He was there in His divine self but didn't manifest any of His divine self in that place. What did He do with His divine self in our flesh when He became ourselves? His divine self was always kept back – emptied – in order that our evil, satanic selves might be kept back – emptied. Now in the flesh He Himself did nothing. He says: "Of mine own self I can do nothing." He was there all the time. His own divine self, who made the heavens, was there all the time. But from beginning to end He Himself did nothing. Himself was kept back; He was emptied. Who, then did that which was done in Him? The Father that dwelleth in Me, "He doeth the works, He speaks the worlds" – Then who was it that opposed the power of temptation in Him in our flesh? The Father. It was the Father who kept Him from sinning. He was "kept by the power of God" as we are to be "kept by the power of God." 1 Peter 1:5.

He was our sinful selves *in the flesh,* and here were all these tendencies to sin being stirred up in His flesh to get Him to consent to sin. But He Himself did not keep Himself from sinning. To have done so would have been Himself manifesting Himself against the power of Satan, and this would have destroyed the plan of salvation, even though He had not sinned. And though at the cross the words were said in mockery, they were literally true: "He saved others; *Himself* He cannot save." Therefore, He kept Himself entirely out. He emptied Himself, and by His keeping Himself back, that gave the Father an opportunity to come in and work against the sinful flesh and save Him and save us *in Him.*

Sinners are separated from God, and God wants to come back to the very place from which sin has driven Him in human flesh. He could not come to us, in ourselves, for we could not bear His presence. Therefore, Christ came in our flesh and the Father dwelt with Him. He could bear the presence of God in its fullness, and so God could dwell with Him in His fullness and this could bring the fullness of God to us in our flesh.

Christ came in that sinful flesh but did not do anything of Himself against the temptation and the power of sin in the flesh. He emptied Himself and the Father worked in human flesh against the power of sin and kept Him from sinning.

Now it is written of the Christian: "Ye are kept by the power of God through faith." That is done in Christ. We yield to Christ; Christ abides in us, giving us His mind. That mind of Christ enables our wicked self to be in the background. The mind of Christ – "let this mind be in you which was also in Christ Jesus" – puts our wicked selves beneath and keeps ourselves back and keeps us from asserting ourselves, for any manifestation of ourself is of itself sin. When the mind of Christ puts ourselves beneath, that gives the Father a chance to work with us and keep us from sinning. And thus God "worketh in you, both to will and to do of his good pleasure." Thus it is always the Father and Christ and ourselves. It is the Father manifested in us through Christ, and *in Christ.*

The mind of Christ empties us of our sinful selves and keeps us from asserting ourselves in order that God, the Father, may join Himself to us and work against the power of sin and keep us from sinning. Thus Christ "is our peace, who hath made both [God and us] one, and hath broken down the middle wall of partition between us; having abolished in his flesh the enmity . . . for to make in himself of twain one new man, so making peace." So it is always the Father and Christ and we; we, the sinners; God the sinless; Christ joining the sinless One to the sinful one and in Himself abolishing the enmity, emptying self in us, in order that God and we may be one, and thus make one new man, so making peace. And thus the peace of God which passeth all understanding shall keep your hearts and minds through, or in, Jesus Christ.

Is it not a most blessed thing that the Lord Jesus has done that for us and so takes up His abode in us and so settles that question that there can be no more doubt that the Father will keep us from sinning than there is that He has kept Him from sinning already? No more doubt; because when Christ is there, He is there for the purpose of emptying self in us. And when ourselves are gone, will it be any very great difficulty for the Father to manifest Himself? When ourselves are kept from asserting ourselves there will be no difficulty for God to assert Himself in our flesh. That is the mystery of God: "Christ in you, the hope of glory." God manifest in the flesh. It is not simply Christ manifest in the flesh; it is God manifest in the flesh. For when Jesus came in the world Himself, it was not Christ manifest in the flesh; it was God manifest in the flesh, for "he that hath seen me, hath seen the Father."

Christ emptied Himself in order that God might be manifest in the flesh, in sinful flesh, and when He comes to us and dwells in us, upon our choice, bringing to us that divine mind of His which is the mind that empties self wherever it goes, wherever it can find an entrance, wherever it can find any place to act, the mind of Christ is the emptying of self, is the abolishing of self, the destruction of self, the annihilation of self. Therefore, when by our choice that divine mind comes to us, the result is as certain that ourselves will be emptied as that the mind dwells in us. And as soon as that is done, God works fully and manifests Himself, in sinful flesh though it be. And that is victory. That is triumph.

And thus with the mind we serve the law of God. The law is manifested, it is fulfilled, its principles shine *in the life,* because the life is the character of God manifest in human flesh, sinful flesh, through Jesus Christ. It seems to me that that thought ought to raise every one of us above all the power of Satan and of sin. It will do that as certainly as we surrender to that divine mind and let it abide in us as it abode in Him. It will do it.

Indeed, the word to us all the time is, "Arise, shine."

But we cannot raise ourselves; it is the truth and the power of God that is to raise us. But is not here the direct truth that will raise a man? Yes, sir; it will raise Him from the dead, as we shall find before we get done with this. But this thought was necessary to be followed through, that we may see how complete the victory is and how certain we are of it as surely as we surrender to Christ and accept that mind that was in Him. And thus always bear in mind that the battle is fought against sin in the realm of the thoughts and that the Victor, the Warrior, that has fought the battle there and won the victory there in every conceivable kind of contest – that same blessed One comes and sets up His throne at the citadel of the very imagination of the thought, the very root of the thought of the heart of the believing sinner. He sets up His throne there and plants the principles of His law there and reigns there. Thus it is that as sin hath reigned unto death, even so now in this way might grace reign. Did sin reign? Certainly. Did it reign with power? Assuredly. It reigned. It ruled. Well, as that has reigned, even so grace shall reign. Is grace, then, to reign as certainly, as powerfully in fact, as ever sin did? Much more, much more fully, much more abundantly, much more gloriously. Just as certainly as ever sin did reign in us, so certainly when we are in Jesus Christ the grace of God is to reign much more abundantly, "That as sin hath reigned unto death, even so might grace reign through righteousness unto eternal life by Jesus Christ our Lord." That being so, we can go on in victory unto perfection.

From that height – for it is proper to call it a height – to which this truth raises us, we can go on enjoying, reading with gratitude, what we have in Him and receiving it in the fullness of the soul. But unless we have the Lord to take us to that height and seat us there and put us where He has possession of the citadel so that we are certain where He is and in that where we are, all these other things are vague, indefinite, and seem to be beyond us – sometimes almost within our reach and we long to get where we can really have hold on them and know the reality of them, but yet they are always just a little beyond our reach and we are unsatisfied. But when we surrender fully, completely, absolutely, with no reservation, letting the whole world and all there is of it, go, then we receive that divine mind of His by the Spirit of God that gives to Him possession of that citadel, that lifts us to that height where all these other things are not simply within *reach* – O, no, they are *in the heart* and are a rejoicing in the life! We then *in Him* have them in possession and we know it and the joy of it is just what Peter said, "unspeakable and full of glory."

So then, as the Lord has lifted us to this height, and will hold us there, now let us go ahead and read and receive, as we read, what we have in Him. Begin with Romans 6:6.

That is the scripture that comes most directly in connection with this particular thought that we have studied so far this evening. "Knowing this." – Knowing what? "Knowing this, that our old man is crucified with him." Good! In Jesus Christ, in His flesh, was not human nature, sinful flesh, crucified? Whose? Who was He? He was man; He was ourselves. Then whose sinful flesh, whose human nature, was crucified on the cross of Jesus Christ? – Mine. Therefore, as certainly as I have that blessed truth settled in my heart and mind, that Jesus Christ was man, human nature, sinful nature, and that He was myself in the flesh – as certainly as I have that, it follows just as certainly as that He was crucified on the cross, so was I. My human nature, myself there, was crucified there. Therefore, I can say with absolute truth and the certainty and confidence of faith, "I am crucified with Christ." It is so.

We hear people so many times say, "I want self to be crucified." Well, we turn and read the text to them, "Knowing this, that our old man *is* crucified." And they respond: "Well, I wish it were so." Turn to the next text and read, "*I* am crucified with Christ." It says *I* am. Who is? Are you? Still they answer, I don't see that I am. I wish it were so, but I cannot see how I am crucified and I cannot see how reading that there and saying that that is so will make it so." But the word of God says so and it is so because it says so and it would be true and everlastingly effectual if that were all there is to it. But in this case it is so *because it is so.* God does not speak that word to make it so in us; He speaks that word because it is so in us, in Christ.

In the first chapter of Hebrews you remember we had an illustration of this. God did not call Christ God to make Him God. No. He called Him God *because He was God.* If He had not been that, then for God to speak to Him the word of "God," and lay it upon Him, would have caused Him to be that, because that is the power of the word of God. But that is not it. That would be so if that were all there were to it, but it is so also in another way. He was God and when God called Him God, He did so because that is what He was. So in that double sense it is everlastingly so. It is so by "two immutable things."

Now it is the same way here. Our old man is crucified, yet when God sets forth His word that it is so, we accepting that word and surrendering to it, it is so to each one who accepts it because the word has the divine power in it to cause it to be so. And by that means it would be everlastingly so, even if that were all there is to it. But that is not all there is to it, because in Jesus Christ human nature has been crucified on the cross, actually, literally, and that is my human nature, that is *myself* in Him that was crucified there. And therefore God sets down the record of everyone who is in Christ, "He is crucified." So that by the two immutable things, by the double fact, it is so. Therefore, we can say with perfect freedom, – it is no boasting, it is not presumption in any sense; it is simply the confession of faith in Jesus Christ, "*I* am crucified with Christ." Is not He crucified? Then as certainly as I am with Him, am I not crucified with Him? The word of God says so. "Our old man is crucified with Him?" Very good. Let us thank the Lord that that is so.

What is the use, then, of our trying, longing, *to get* ourselves crucified, so that we can believe that we are accepted of God? Why, it is done, thank the Lord! In Him it is done. As certainly as the soul by faith sinks self in Jesus Christ and by that divine power which He has brought to us to do it, so certainly it is done as a divine fact.

And it is only the genuine expression of faith to tell, to acknowledge, that divine fact that "I am crucified with Christ." Jesus sunk His divine self in our human nature and altogether was crucified. When we sink ourselves in Him, it is so still, because in Him only is it done. It is all *in Him*. We call attention to the thought we had in the lesson a few evenings ago, that it is not in Him in the sense of His being a receptacle to which we can go and take it out and apply it to ourselves. No. But it is in Him in the sense that it is all there and when we are in Him, when we go into the receptacle, when we sink into Him, we have it all in Him as we are in Him.

Therefore, now let every soul of us say by the faith of Jesus Christ, "Knowing this, that our old man is crucified with Him." "I am crucified with Christ: nevertheless I live, yet not I, but Christ liveth in me." He is alive again. And because He lives, we live also. "Nevertheless I live; *yet not I,* but Christ liveth in me: and the life which I now live in the flesh I live by the faith" – *in* the Son of God? "the faith *of* the Son of God," – that divine faith which He brought to human nature and which He gives to you and to me. We "live by the faith of the Son of God who loved me, and gave himself for me." Gal. 2:20. O, He loved Me! When He gave Himself in all His glory and all His wondrous worth for me, who was nothing, is it much that I should give myself to Him?

But there is more of the verse.

Rom. 6:6 still: "Knowing this, that our old man is crucified with him, that the body of sin might be destroyed that henceforth we should not serve sin." Good! In Him we have the victory, victory from the service of sin. There is victory over the service of sin, in this knowing that we are crucified with Him.

Now I say that this blessed fact which we find in Him lifts us right to that place; yea, and the fact holds us in the place. That is so. There is a power in it. That is a fact. We will have occasion to see it more fully presently.

When He was crucified, what followed? When He was nailed to the cross, what came next? He died. Now read in this same chapter, eighth verse: "Now if we be dead with Christ" – well, what else can there be? As certainly as I am crucified with Him, I shall be dead with Him. Being crucified with Him, we shall be dead with Him.

Dead with Him? Do we know that? Look back at the fourth verse. When He had been crucified and had died, what followed? He was buried – the burial of the dead. And what of us? Now, "therefore, we are buried with him." Buried with Him! Were we crucified with Him? Did we die with Him? Have the Father and Christ wrought out in human nature the death of sinful self? Yes. Whose? Mine.

Then do you not see that all this is *a gift of faith* that is to be taken with everything else that God gives of faith? The death of the old man is in Christ, and in Him we have it and thank God for it. With Him the old man was crucified. With Him the old man died, and when He was buried, the old man was buried. My human, old, sinful self was crucified, died and was buried with Him. And with Him it is buried yet *when I am in Him.* Out of Him I have it not, of course. Every one that is outside of Him has none of this. In Him it is – in Him. And we receive it all by faith in Him.

We are simply studying now the fact that we have in Him, the facts which are given to us in Him and which are to be taken by faith. These are facts of faith.

We thank the Lord that all this is literal fact – that our old man is crucified, dead, and buried *with Him* and that in Him we have that gift. In Him we have the gift and the fact of the death of the old man – the death of the human, sinful nature and the burial of it. And when that old thing is crucified and dead and buried, then the next verse – the seventh: "He that is dead is freed from sin."

So then, knowing "that our old man is crucified with him" that henceforth we should not serve sin, we are free from the service of sin. Brethren I am satisfied it is just as much our place day by day *now* to thank God for freedom from the service of sin as it is to breathe. I say it over. I say it is just as much our place, our privilege and our right to claim *in Christ* – in Him only and as we believe in Him – and to thank God for freedom from the service of sin as it is to breathe the breath that we breathe as we get up in the morning.

How can I ever have the blessing and the benefit there is in that thing if I do not *take* the thing? If I am always hesitating and afraid that I am not free from the service of sin, how long will it take to get me free from the service of sin? That very hesitating, that very fear, is from doubt, is from unbelief, and is sin in itself. But in Him, when God has wrought out for us indeed freedom from the service of sin, we have the right to thank God for it and as certainly as we claim it and thank Him for it, we shall enjoy it. "He that is dead is freed from sin" (margin, "is justified from sin"). And it is in Him, and we have it as we are in Him by faith.

Let us therefore read the first verse of the sixth of Romans:

> What shall we say then? Shall we continue in sin that grace may abound? God forbid. How shall we that are dead to sin live any longer therein.

Can a man live on what he died of? No. Then when the man has died of sin, can he live in sin? can he live with sin? A man dies of delirium tremens or typhoid fever. Can he live on delirium tremens or typhoid fever, even if by a possibility he should be brought to live long enough to realize that he was there? The very thought of it would be death to him, because it killed him once. So it is with the man who dies of sin. The very appearance of it, the very bringing of it before him after that is death to him. If he has consciousness enough and life enough to realize that it is there, he will die of it again. He cannot live on what he died of.

But the great trouble with many people is that they do not get sick enough of sin to die. That is the difficulty. They get sick perhaps of some *particular* sin and they want to stop that and "want to die" to that and they think they have left that off. Then they get sick of some other particular sin that they think is not becoming to them – they cannot have the favor and the estimation of the people with that particular sin so manifest and they try to leave that off. But they do not get sick of sin – sin in itself, sin in the conception, sin in the abstract, whether it be in one particular way or another particular way. They do not get sick enough of sin itself to die to sin. When the man gets sick enough – not of sins but of *sin,* the very suggestion of sin, and the thought of sin – why you cannot get him to live in it any more. He cannot live in it; it killed him once. And he cannot live in what he died of.

We have constantly the opportunity to sin. Opportunities to sin are ever presented to us. Opportunities to sin and to live in it are presented day by day.

But it stands written: "Always bearing about in the body the dying of the Lord Jesus." "I die daily." As certainly as I have died to sin, the suggestion of sin is death to me. It is death to me *in Him*.

Therefore, this is put in the form of a surprised, astonished question, "How shall we, that are dead to sin, live any longer therein? Know ye not, that so many of us as were baptized into Jesus Christ were baptized into his death?" Baptism means baptism into His death.

> Therefore we are buried with him by baptism into death; that like as Christ was raised up from the dead by the glory of the Father, even so we also should walk in newness of life.

Turn to Colossians. There was the word you remember that we had in Brother Durland's lesson one day.

Col. 2:20:

> Wherefore if ye be dead with Christ from the rudiments of the world [the elements of the world, worldliness, and this thing that leads to the world – the enmity], why, as though living in the world, are ye subject to the world?

That is simply speaking of our deliverance from the service of sin. It is simply saying, in other words, what is said in Rom. 6:6, "Our old man is crucified with him, that the body of sin might be destroyed, that henceforth we should not serve sin." Why, as though living outside of Him are we still doing those same things? No, sir. Rom. 6:14, "For sin shall not have dominion over you."

The man who is delivered from the domination of sin is delivered from the service of sin. In Jesus Christ it is a fact, too.

So read on from Romans 6:6-14.

> Knowing this, that our old man is crucified with him, that the body of sin might be destroyed, that henceforth we should not serve sin. For he that is dead is freed from sin. Now if we be dead with Christ, we believe that we shall also live with him.

Is He alive? Yes. Thank the Lord! Who died? Jesus died, and we are dead with Him. And He is alive, and we who believe in Him are alive with Him. That, however, will come more fully afterward.

> Knowing that Christ being raised from the dead, dieth no more; death hath no more dominion over him. For in that he died, he died unto sin once: but in that he liveth, he liveth unto God.

Let us hold to this. Let us thank God this moment and henceforward, day by day, with every thought, "I am crucified with Him." As certainly as He is crucified, I am crucified; as certainly as He is dead, I am dead with Him; as certainly as He is buried, I was buried with Him; as certainly as He is risen, I am risen with Him, and henceforth I shall not serve sin. In Him we are free from the dominion of sin and from the service of sin. Thank the Lord for His unspeakable gift!

Sermon 19

February 27, 1895

We are to begin the comparison of Heb. 2:14, 15 with Rom. 6:11-14. Read first in Hebrews:

> Forasmuch then as the children are partakers of flesh and blood, he himself likewise took part of the same; that through death he might destroy him that had the power of death, that is, the devil; and deliver them, who through fear of death were all their lifetime subject to bondage.

That is what Christ did to deliver us. Now read in Romans:

> Likewise reckon ye also yourselves to be dead indeed unto sin, but alive unto God through Jesus Christ our Lord. Let not sin therefore reign in your mortal body, that ye should obey it in the lusts thereof. Neither yield ye your members as instruments of unrighteousness unto sin; but yield yourselves unto God, as those that are alive from the dead, and your members as instruments of righteousness unto God. For sin shall not have dominion over you.

Just as He also Himself likewise did that to deliver us, so we also ourselves likewise are to yield, in order to be delivered. And when we do so, we are delivered. He did that in order to deliver us, who all our lifetime were subject to bondage; we do that, and then we are free from the bondage and sin has no more dominion over us. Thus Rom. 6:11-14 is the response of faith in the individual, to Christ's action as in Heb. 2:14, 15.

But the Lord did more for Him than to raise Him from the dead, and He has done more for us in Him than to raise us from the dead.

He died. He was raised from the dead. We died with Him, and what then? Did we rise with Him? Have we a resurrection with Him? Have we life from the dead in Him? We are crucified with Him. We died with Him. We are buried with Him, *and He was raised from the dead.* Then what of us? We are risen with Him. But God did more for Him than to raise Him from the dead. God did more with Him than to raise Him from the dead. He raised Him, and also seated Him at His own right hand in heaven. What of us? Do we stop short? No, sir. Are we not in Him? As we are in Him while He was alive on the earth, as we are in Him on the cross, as we are in Him in death, as we are in Him in the resurrection, so we are in Him in the ascension and we are in Him at the right hand of God.

That would follow, anyway, from what we read last night, but let us read this itself in the Scriptures and see that it is certainly so. As we have followed God's working in Him so far, shall we follow it all the way? Last night and in the lessons before, we were glad to go with Him through temptation and gain the victory. We were glad last night with Him to go to the cross and find ourselves crucified there, so that we could say in genuine faith, "I am crucified with Christ." We were glad to go into the grave with Him, into death with Him, so that it can be a genuine reckoning of faith to reckon ourselves also to be dead indeed. We are glad of all that. Let us be glad also to come forth from death with Him, in order that we may live a new life as He. And when we have come forth with Him from the dead – for "if we be dead with Christ, we believe that we shall also live with Him" let us rise with Him as He is risen – not only from the dead, but to where He is. If God says so, if He proposes to carry us there and to carry the subject that far, shall we go? Assuredly, yes. Let us not think strange of it if He should; let us follow with Him there just as freely as we followed with Him against temptation and to the cross and into death.

Therefore take the second chapter of Ephesians, beginning with the fourth verse:

> God, who is rich in mercy, for his great love wherewith he loved us, even when we were dead in sins, hath quickened us together with Christ.

Quicken is to make alive, make us alive together with Christ.

Next verse:

"And hath raised us up together." Together with whom? Christ. "And made us sit together." With whom? Christ. Where? "Made us sit together in heavenly places in Christ Jesus." The word "places" is supplied there in our version. It is also supplied in Eph. 1:2; 1:20.

In the Greek it is *epouraniois,* and in the verbal translation is rendered "the heavenlies." God has given us life together with Him: God has raised us up together and made us sit together with Him, *wherever He sits.* Where then does He sit? "He was received up into heaven and sat on the right hand of the Majesty on high." Heb. 1:3. God "has raised us up together with him; and made us sit together with him," where He sits.

Now the German makes it plainer than our Authorized Version and plainer than this translation of the Greek even:

> Da wir tot waren in den Sunden, hat er uns saint Christo [that word *saint* means along with. And that is the Greek word literally. The Greek means "along with" "together" and "at the same time," and so the German words give it] – *hat er uns saint Christo lebendig gemacht* [made alive us along with Him]. . . *und hat uns saint ihm auferwecket* [along with

> Him *waked up*, and not simply waked up like a man that is asleep and gets his eyes open but still lies there but waked up in such a way that he gets up. So that we with Him are given life from the dead and he has waked us up in such a way that we get up and rise with Him.] *und saint ihm in das himmlische Wesen gesetzt, in Christo Jesu.*

I have drawn out the definition of that word *Wesen* in full here and it signifies essence, existence, being, manner of being, nature, character, disposition, air, demeanor, conduct; means of existence, property, estate, economy; existing arrangement, system, concern.

So He has made us sit with Christ in heaven; in the heavenly existence; in the heavenly essence; made us sit together with Him in the heavenly being; in the heavenly manner of being; in the heavenly nature; in the heavenly character; in the heavenly disposition; in the heavenly air; in the heavenly demeanor; in the heavenly conduct; He has made us sit together with Him in the heavenly means of existence – for "our life is hid with Christ in God," our means of existence is in heaven – "Give us this day our daily bread" – the heavenly means of existence, heavenly property, estate, economy, existing arrangement, the existing order of things. We belong to heaven, to the heavenly system altogether.

That is where God has put us in Christ. So then, as we, along with Him, in the heavenly existence, essence, air, disposition, and all, *are made to sit in Christ Jesus,* shall we sit there in Him?

In other words, shall we rise? What is the word? Arise, shine. Arise first and then shine. We cannot shine until we rise. But what will this truth do for us? Will it not raise us? How high? Do you not see that it takes us out of this world and puts us along with Jesus Christ in the heavenly kingdom? Is it not plain then that Jesus Christ has brought heaven to earth to Him who believes? Therefore, it is written, He "hath delivered us from the power of darkness and hath translated us into the kingdom of His dear Son." The kingdom of heaven is likened unto this so and so; the kingdom of heaven is like unto so and so; the kingdom of heaven is like unto so and so; the kingdom of heaven is nigh at hand. Well, what is that kingdom of heaven? He translates us into it – has translated us into it. Shall we reside there and enjoy its blessed atmosphere and enjoy the disposition, the air, all the system and manner of existence that belong there and belong to us there?

Now we cannot raise ourselves even to this height; we are to submit to the truth and it will raise us. Look at it again.

In the first chapter of Ephesians, beginning with the fifteenth verse:

> Wherefore I also, after I heard of your faith in the Lord Jesus and love unto all the saints, cease not to give thanks for you, making mention of you in my prayers [and this is the prayer]; that the God of our Lord Jesus Christ, the Father of glory, may give unto you the spirit of wisdom and revelation in the knowledge of him.

To how many? To whom? For how many is this prayer written? Will you take the prayer, then, yourself this evening? and accept the thing that is prayed for on your behalf? Whose word is it, anyway? Is it merely a prayer of a man? Is it not the word of God? Then is not the word of Jesus Christ by His Spirit expressing His will and His wish concerning us as to what we shall have? Let us accept it, then. It is His will.

Read on:

> The eyes of your understanding being enlightened; that ye may know what is the hope of his calling, and what the riches of the glory of his inheritance in the saints, and what is the exceeding greatness of his power to usward [toward us] who believe.

He wants us to know what is the exceeding greatness of His power toward us who believe. And the Greek word there is the word from which comes our *word* "dynamite."

> The exceeding greatness of His power to usward who believe, according to the working of His mighty power, which He wrought in Christ, when He raised Him from the dead, and set Him at His own right hand in the heavenly [existence, in heaven].

The German is, "Seated at his right in heaven."

Now that power of God raised up Jesus Christ and set Him at His right in heaven. Every soul of us will say that, but He wants you and me to know the working of that power in ourselves which raised up Christ and seated Him there. When we know the working of that power in us that raised up Christ and seated Him there, what will it do for us? It will raise us up and seat us there.

The second chapter of Colossians tells the same story, beginning with the twelfth verse:

> Buried with him in baptism, wherein also ye are risen with him through the faith of the operation of God, who hath raised him from the dead. And you, being dead in your sins and the uncircumcision of your flesh, hath he quickened [made alive] together with him, having forgiven you all trespasses; blotting out the handwriting of ordinances that was against us, which was contrary to us, and took it out of the way, nailing it to his cross.

Now the first verse of the third chapter:

> If ye then be risen with Christ, seek those things which are above, where Christ sitteth on the right hand of God.

Then every one that is risen is to seek the things that are above. Whereabouts above? How high above? As high above as the place where Christ sits. But how can I seek the things where Christ sits unless I am near enough there to look around and seek those things and put my mind upon them? It is all in that.

> If ye then be risen with Christ, seek those things which are above, where Christ sitteth on the right hand of God . . . for ye are dead, and your life is hid with Christ in God.

Shall we take that precisely as the Lord gives it, without any querying? I know it is wonderful; I know that to a good many it seems too good to be true, but there is nothing God does that is too good to be true, because God does it. If it were said of anybody else, it would be too good to be true, because they could not do it, but when God says anything, it is not too good to be true; it is good enough to be true, because He does it. therefore, brethren, let us rise, and that will separate us from the world; that will put us in the place where long ago the prophet was told to look a little higher, to see those who were in the right way. But, O, shall we not drop everything and die with Him and take the death that we have in Him and let that death that has been wrought in Him work in us? And then that life which has been wrought in Him, that power which has been wrought in Him, will do for us what it did for Him. That will take us out of Babylon; there will be none of Babylon's material about us at all. We will be so far from Babylon and all the Babylonish garments, that we will be seated at the right hand of God, clothed in heavenly apparel; and that is the only clothing that becomes the people now, for we are soon to enter in to the wedding supper, and the fine linen with which the bride and guests are clothed is the righteousness of the saints. But He supplies it all. We have it all in Him.

Let us look at this in another way. I am not particular to get away from this thought tonight, and it is good enough to dwell upon all the time we shall have this evening. Let us look at it from another side now. We have studied for several lessons the fact that He in human nature was ourselves, and He in us and we in Him met temptation and the power of Satan and conquered it all in this world, because God was with Him. God was dealing with Him. God was holding Him and keeping Him. He surrendered all and God kept Him. In Him we surrender all, and God keeps us. And the Lord's dealings with Him are the Lord's dealings with us, and that led to crucifixion; that is true – the crucifixion of His righteous, divine self, and in that it leads us to the crucifixion of our evil self, which separates from God. In Him is destroyed the enmity. So God went with Him and went with Him in human nature, all the way through this world, but God did not get done with His human nature in this world.

The Father was not done dealing with Christ in His human nature nor done dealing with human nature in Christ, when the Son had been nailed to the cross. He had something more to do with human nature than to take it only to the cross. He took it even unto death, but He did not stop there with human nature. He took it to the cross and into death, but He did not stop there. He did not leave it there. He brought forth human nature from the tomb, immortalized. He did all this, but He was not yet done with human nature, for He took that human nature which had been raised from the dead, immortalized, and He raised it up and set it at His own right hand, glorified with the fullness of the brightness of the glory of God – in heaven itself. So that God's mind concerning human nature, concerning you and me, is never met, never fulfilled, until He finds us at His own right hand, glorified.

There is revivifying power in that blessed truth. In Jesus Christ, the Father has set before the universe the thought of His mind concerning mankind. O, how much, how far, a man misses every purpose, every idea, of his existence, who is content with anything less than that which God has prepared for him! Brethren, do you not see that we have been content to stay too low down? that we have been content to have our minds too far from what God has for us? That is a fact. But now, as He comes and calls us into this, let us go where He will lead us. It is faith that does it; it is not presumption; it is the only right thing to do. Every one that does not do it will be left so far behind that he will perish in a little while. Here the heavenly Shepherd is leading us. He is leading us into green pastures and by the still waters – and by those still waters, too, that flow from the throne of God, the waters of life itself. Let us drink deep and live.

Now we can look at that yet farther. I will say again that the Lord, in order to show mankind what He has prepared for us, what His purpose is concerning each man, has set before us an example, so that everyone in the world can see God's purpose concerning himself and can see it fully worked out. God's purpose concerning us in this world is to keep us from sinning in spite of all the power of sin and Satan. His purpose concerning Himself and us in this world is that God shall be manifested in sinful flesh. That is, in His power He Himself shall be manifested instead of ourselves. It is, therefore, that our wicked self shall be crucified, shall be dead and buried, and that we shall be raised from that deadness in sin and uncircumcision of the flesh to newness of life in Jesus Christ and in God and seated at His right hand, glorified. That is the Lord's purpose concerning you and me.

Now let us read it: Rom. 8:28:

> And we know that all things work together for good to them that love God.

How do we know it? He not only says so but He has worked it out before our eyes; He has given a living demonstration of it. So He carries us right through that now.

"We know that all things work together for good to them that love God, to them who are the called according to his purpose." What purpose? Why, His eternal purpose concerning all creatures, concerning man with the rest, which He purposed in Christ Jesus our Lord. That purpose from eternity is purposed in Jesus Christ, and when we are in Jesus Christ that purpose embraces us. When we yield to Christ, sinking ourselves in Him, we become a part of that eternal purpose, and then just as certainly as God's purpose is to succeed, we shall be all right, for we are a part of His purpose. Then just as certainly as Satan can do nothing against God's purpose, so certainly He can do nothing against us, for we are in that purpose. Just as certainly, then, as all that Satan does, and all that the enemies of God's truth can do, working against God and His divine purpose, and at last all these things against us – so certainly as all this cannot defeat or cripple that eternal purpose, so certainly it cannot defeat or cripple us, because in Christ we are a fixture in that purpose. O, it is all in Him, and God has created us anew in Him.

Read on then. God tells us how we know that all things work together for good to those who are called according to God's purpose. "For" – what does that mean? It means the same here as "because"; that is, we know this because God has done something here to demonstrate it so that we can know it. What is this then by which we know it? We know it *because* "whom he did foreknow he also did predestinate to be conformed to the image of his Son." What is God's predestination, then? What is the design that He has fixed beforehand, that He has prepared beforehand for every man in the world? For He has foreknown all; He has called all. "Look unto me, and be ye saved, all the ends of the earth." Isa. 45:22.

What is the destiny that He has prepared beforehand for every one? O, it is that we should be conformed to the image of His Son. Where? While we are in this world, conformed to the image of His Son, as His Son was in this world. But He did not get done with His Son in this world; He took Him from this world. Then as certainly as His eternal purpose carried Christ beyond this world, that predestined purpose is concerning *us* beyond this world, and carries us beyond this world. And as certainly as His predestined purpose is that we shall be conformed to the image of Jesus Christ in this world, as He was in this world, so certain it is that we shall be conformed to the image of Jesus Christ in that other world, as He is in that other world.

God's eternal purpose prepared beforehand for every one of us, for you, for me, is that we shall be like Jesus Christ as He is, glorified, and at the right hand of God tonight. In Christ He has demonstrated this. In Christ, from birth to the heavenly throne, He has shown that that is His purpose concerning every man. Thus He has demonstrated before the universe that such is His great purpose for human beings.

God's ideal of a man is not as man stands in this world. Take the finest figure of a man who ever stood in this world – the tallest, the most symmetrical, the best educated, the finest in every respect, the fullest, completest man in himself – is that God's ideal of man? No. you remember that we found back in one of our lessons that God's ideal of a man is *God* and the *man* joined in that new man that is made in Christ Jesus by the destruction of the enmity. That new man that is made of the union of God and man is God's ideal man.

But yet take that man as he stands in this world, in the perfect symmetry of human perfection, and unite God with him so that only God is manifested in him, that is not yet God's full ideal of a man, for the man is still in this world. The ideal of God concerning that man is never met until that man stands at God's right hand in heaven glorified. O, He has prepared great things for us, and I propose to enjoy them! Yes, sir, I propose to open up and let the wondrous power work and enjoy it as I go.

Read on therefore. "Whom he did foreknow, he also did predestinate, to be conformed to the image of his Son, that he might be the first-born among many brethren." O, "He is not ashamed to call them brethren." "He that sanctifieth and they that are sanctified are all of one." "Moreover, whom he did predestinate, them he also called: and whom he called [those in whom that call meets its purpose and in whom the call is effective. He calls every soul, that is true on His part, but the call does not meet its purpose; only those who respond and meet the purpose of that call, in whom the call takes hold], them he also justified: and whom he justified [mark, not those who justify themselves, those whom he justified], them he also glorified."

Then do you not see that God's purpose concerning man is not fulfilled until man is glorified? Therefore, Jesus came into the world as we do. He took our human nature as we do, by birth. He went through this world in human nature – God dealing with human nature. He went to the cross and died – God dealing with human nature on the cross and in the grave and God raising Him and setting Him at the right hand of God, glorified – that is His eternal purpose. That is God's eternal predestination. That is the plan He has arranged and fixed for you. Will you let Him carry out the plan? We cannot do it. He must. But He has shown His ability to do it. He has proven that. Nobody can dispute that. He has proven His ability to take us and fulfill His purpose concerning human nature, concerning sinful flesh as it is in this world. And I am glad of it.

But see here: "Whom he called, them he also justified; and whom he justified," – What did He do next? He glorified them. Now a question: those whom He justifies He glorifies; He cannot glorify them until He has justified them. What means, then, this special message of justification that God has been sending these years to the church and to the world? It means that God is preparing to glorify His people. But we are glorified only at the coming of the Lord; therefore, this special message of justification which God has been sending us is to prepare us for glorification at the coming of the Lord. In this, God is giving to us the strongest sign that it is possible for Him to give, that the next thing is the coming of the Lord.

He will prepare us. We cannot prepare ourselves. We tried a long while to justify ourselves, to make ourselves just right, and thus get ready for the coming of the Lord. We have tried to do so well that we could approve ourselves and be satisfied and say, "Now I can meet the Lord." But we never were satisfied. No. It is not done that way. Whom He justified, them He glorified. Now since God justifies, it is His own work, and when He is ready for us to meet the Lord, it will be all right, because it is He Himself who prepares us to meet the Lord. Therefore, we trust in Him, we yield to Him, and take

His justification and, depending only on that, we shall be ready to meet the Lord Jesus whenever God chooses to send Him.

Thus He is preparing now to glorify us. Again I say, It is a fact that we have been content to live too far below the wondrous privileges that God has prepared for us. Let the precious truth raise us to where He wants us.

No master workman looks at a piece of work He is doing, as it is half finished, and criticizes that and begins to find fault with that. There may be faults about it, but it is not finished yet. And while He works on it to take away all the faults still He looks at it as it is in His finished purpose, in His own original plan, in His own mind.

It would be an awful thing if the wondrous Master Workman of all were to look at us as we are half finished and say, That is good for nothing. No, He doesn't do that. He looks at us as we are in His eternal purpose in Christ, and goes on with His wondrous work. You and I may look at it and say, "I don't see how the Lord is ever going to make a Christian out of me and make me fit for heaven or anything else." That may be so as we see it. And if He looked at us as we *look at ourselves* and if He were as poor a workman as we, that would be all there could be of it; we could never be of any worth. But He is not such a workman as we and therefore He does not look at us *as we see ourselves.* No. He looks at us as we are in His finished purpose. Although we may appear all rough, marred, and scarred now, as we are here and in ourselves, He sees us as we are *yonder* in Christ.

He is the Workman. And as we have confidence in Him, we will let Him carry on the work, and as He carries it on, we will look at it as He sees it. Has He not given us an example of His workmanship? God has set before us in Christ His complete workmanship in sinful flesh. In Christ He has completed it and set it there at His right hand. Now He says to us, "Look at that. That is what I am able to do with sinful flesh. Now you put your confidence in me and let me work and you watch and see what I am going to do. You trust my workmanship. Let me attend to the work and you trust me, and I will carry on the work." It is the Lord doing it all. It is not our task at all.

Now you can go outside of this Tabernacle and look up at that window (referring to the window at the back of the pulpit), and it looks like only a mess of melted glass thrown together, black and unsightly. But come inside and look from within, and you will see it as a beautiful piece of workmanship, and written there in clear texts: "Justified freely by his grace through the redemption that is in Christ Jesus"; the law of God written out in full and the words, "Here are they that keep the commandments of God and the faith of Jesus."

Likewise, you and I can look at ourselves as we too often do from the outside and all looks awry, dark, and ungainly, and appears as though it were only a tangled mass. God looks at it from the inside, as it is in Jesus. And when we are in Jesus and look through the light that God has given us, when we look from *the inside* as we are in

Jesus Christ we shall also see, written in clear texts by the Spirit of God, "Justified by faith, we have peace with God through our Lord Jesus Christ." We shall see the whole law of God written in the heart and shining in the life and the words, "Here are they that keep the commandments of God and the faith of Jesus." All this we shall see in the light of God as that light is reflected and shines in Jesus Christ.

Now I want you to know that this is certainly so. Way back in the Bulletin, bottom of page 182, we have this sentence, "I would that every soul who sees the evidences of the truth" – Do you see them, brethren? Are there not evidences enough here to save us? "I would that every soul who sees the evidences of the truth would accept Jesus Christ as his personal Saviour." Do you take Him now as your personal Saviour in the fullness in which He has revealed Himself where He is and ourselves in Him where He is? Do you? Then read this:

> Those who thus accept Christ are looked upon by God not as they are in Adam, but as they are in *Jesus Christ,* as the sons and daughters of God.

He looks at us as we are in Christ, for in Him He has perfected His plan concerning us. Are you glad of it? Let us take it in, brethren. O! it does my soul good day by day as the Lord opens up these things! It is just as good to me, as I long for it to be to you, so let us receive it in the fullness of that self-abandoned faith that Jesus Christ has brought to us. Let us take it and thank God for it day by day. Let the power of it work in us, raise us from the dead, and set us at God's right hand in the heavenly places in Jesus Christ, where He sits. Why should we not have a praise meeting for what God has done for us? It is Sabbath. Could we not enjoy it? What do you want to say?

[Here followed a praise-meeting, of which a Baptist minister who was present, seeing the large numbers praising God all at once, remarked: "Some might be ready to say that such a number of voices makes confusion. But with all speaking together the praises of the Lord, surely, the Lord and the angels see only perfect harmony, and so do we."]

Sermon 20

February 27, 1895

In John 17:4 the first clause of the verse is the words of Christ in that prayer for us all: "I have glorified thee on the earth." In the previous lesson we were brought to consider the purpose of God concerning man, even His eternal purpose and that that purpose is fulfilled before the whole universe in Jesus Christ in human flesh. The purpose of man's existence is to glorify God, and this has been shown before the universe in Jesus Christ, for God's eternal purpose concerning man was purposed in Christ and carried out in Christ for every man, since man sinned, and He says, "I have glorified thee on the earth." This shows that the purpose of God in man's creation is that man shall glorify Him. And what we shall study this evening is how we should glorify God, how God is glorified in man, and what it is to glorify God.

When we study Christ and see what He did and what God did in Him, we shall know what it is to glorify God. And in Him we find what is the purpose of our creation, what is the purpose of our existence, and in fact, what is the purpose of the creation and the existence of every intelligent creature in the universe.

We have seen in preceding lessons that God alone was manifested in Christ in the world. Christ Himself was not manifested; He was kept back. He was emptied and became ourselves on the human side and then God, and God alone, was manifested in Him. Then what is it to glorify God? It is to be in the place where God and God alone shall be manifested in the individual. And that is the purpose of the creation and the existence of every angel and of every man.

To glorify God, it is necessary for each one to be in the condition and in the position in which none but God shall be manifested, because that was the position of Jesus Christ. Therefore, He said, "The words that I speak unto you I speak not of myself" (John 14:10). "I came . . . not to do mine own will but the will of him that sent me" (John 6:38). "The Father that dwelleth in me, he doeth the works" (John 14:10). "I can of mine own self do nothing" (John 5:30). "No man can come to me, except the Father which hath sent me draw him" (John 6:44). "He that hath seen me hath seen the Father, and how sayest thou then, Show us the Father" (John 14:9)? "He that speaketh of himself seeketh his own glory, but he that seeketh his glory that sent him, the same is true and no unrighteousness is in him" (John 7:18).

Therefore, He said, "The words that I speak . . . I speak not of myself," because as in the other verse, he that speaks of himself, that is, from himself, seeks his own glory. But Christ was not seeking His own glory. He was seeking the glory of Him that sent Him; therefore, He said, "The words that I speak . . . I speak not of myself." In so doing, He sought the glory of Him that sent Him, and there stands the record that "he is true, and there is no unrighteousness in him."

He was so entirely emptied of Himself, so entirely was He from being manifested in any way, that no influence went forth from Him except the influence of the Father. This was so to such an extent that no man could come to Him except the Father drew that man to Him. That shows how completely He Himself was kept in the background, how completely He was emptied. It was done so thoroughly that no man could come to Him – that no man could feel any influence from Him or be drawn to Him, except from the Father Himself. The manifestation of the Father – that could draw any man to Christ.

That simply illustrates the one grand fact that we are studying just now – what it is to glorify God. It is to be so entirely emptied of self that nothing but God shall be manifested and no influence go forth from the individual but the influence of God – so emptied that everything, every word – all that is manifested – will be only of God and will tell only of the Father.

"I have glorified thee on the earth." When He was upon the earth, He was in our human, sinful flesh, and when He emptied Himself and kept Himself back, the Father so dwelt in Him and manifested Himself there, that all the works of the flesh were quenched, and the overshadowing glory of God, the character of God, the goodness of God, were manifested instead of anything of the human.

This is the same as we had in a previous lesson, that God manifest in the flesh, God manifest in sinful flesh, is the mystery of God – not God manifested in sin*less* flesh, but in sin*ful* flesh. That is to say, God will so dwell in our sinful flesh today that although that flesh be sinful, its sinfulness will not be felt or realized, nor cast any influence upon others, that God will so dwell yet in sinful flesh that in spite of all the sinfulness of sinful flesh, His influence, His glory, His righteousness, His character, shall be manifested wherever that person goes.

This was precisely the case with Jesus in the flesh. And so God has demonstrated to us all how we should glorify God. He has demonstrated to the universe how the universe is to glorify God – that is, that God and God alone shall be manifested in every intelligence in the universe. That was the intent of God from the beginning. That was His purpose, His eternal purpose, which He purposed in Christ Jesus our Lord.

We might read it now. We shall have occasion to refer to it afterward. We will read the text that tells it all in a word. Eph. 1:9, 10, "Having made known unto us the mystery of his will, according to his good pleasure which he hath purposed in himself."

What is that will which He hath purposed in Himself? He, being the eternal God, purposing this purpose in Himself, it being His own purpose – it is the same that is spoken of in another place as His "eternal purpose." What is God's eternal purpose which He purposed in Christ Jesus the Lord? Here it is: "That in the dispensation of the fullness of times he might gather together in one all things in Christ, both which are in heaven and which are on earth."

Look that over now, and think that God "might gather together in one all things in Christ." Who is the "one" into whom God gathers all things in Christ? That "one" is God. Who was in Christ? "God was in Christ." Nobody was manifested there but God. God dwelt in Christ. Now in Christ He is gathering "together in one all things," "both which are in heaven and which are on earth." Therefore, His purpose in the dispensation of the fullness of times is to gather together in Himself all things in Christ. Through Christ, by Christ, and in Christ, all things in heaven and earth are gathered together in the one God, so that God alone will be manifested throughout the whole universe, that when the dispensation of times is completed and God's eternal purpose stands before the universe completed, wherever you look, upon whomsoever you look, you will see God reflected. You will see the image of God reflected. And God will be "all in all." That is what we see in Jesus Christ. 2 Cor. 4:6:

> For God, who commanded the light to shine out of darkness hath shined in our hearts to give the light of the knowledge of the glory of God in the face of Jesus Christ.

We look into the face of Jesus Christ. What do we see? We see God. We see the Father. We do not see Christ reflected in the face of Jesus Christ. He emptied Himself, that God might be reflected, that God might shine forth to man, who could not bear His presence in His human flesh. Jesus Christ took man's flesh, which as a veil so modified the bright beams of the glory of God that we might look and live. We cannot look upon the unveiled face of God, not as much as the children of Israel might look upon the face of Moses. Therefore, Jesus gathers in Himself man's flesh and veils the bright, consuming glory of the Father, so that we, looking into His face, can see God reflected and can see and love Him as He is and thus have the life that is in Him.

This thought is noticed in 2 Cor. 3:18.

I will merely touch the verse for the present. We will have occasion to refer to it again before we are through with the lesson. "We all, with open face beholding as in a glass the glory of the Lord" – where do we behold the glory of the Lord? "In the face of Jesus Christ." But He says we behold it as in a mirror. What is a mirror for? A mirror gives no light of its own. A mirror reflects the light that shines upon it. We all, with open face, behold in the face of Jesus Christ, as in a glass, the glory of the Lord; therefore, Christ is the one through whom the Father is reflected to the whole universe.

He alone could reflect the Father in His fullness, because His goings forth have been from the days of eternity, and as it says in the eighth of Proverbs, "I was with him, as one brought up with him." He was one of God, equal with God and His nature is the nature of God. Therefore, one grand necessity that He alone should come to the world and save man was because the Father wanted to manifest Himself fully to the sons of men, and none in the universe could manifest the Father in His fullness except the only begotten Son, who is in the image of the Father. No creature could do it, because He is not great enough. Only He whose goings forth have been from the days of eternity could do it; consequently, He came and God dwelt in Him. How much? "All the fullness of the Godhead bodily" is reflected in Him. And this is not only to men on the earth, but it is that in the dispensation of the fullness of times He might gather together in one – in Christ – all things which are in heaven and which are on earth. In Christ God is manifested to the angels and reflected to men in the world in a way in which they cannot see God otherwise.

So, then, we have so much as to what it means to glorify God and as to how it is done. It is to be so emptied of self that God alone shall be manifested in His righteousness, His character, which is His glory. In Christ is shown the Father's purpose concerning us. All that was done in Christ was to show what will be done in us, for He was ourselves. Therefore, it is for us constantly to have before our minds the one great thought that we are to glorify God upon the earth.

In Him and by Him we find that divine mind which in Christ emptied His righteous self. By this divine mind, our unrighteousness is emptied, in order that God may be glorified in us and it may be true of us, "I have glorified thee on the earth."

Let us read those two verses in Corinthians now for our own sakes. A while ago we read them as from His side, "God, who commanded the light to shine out of darkness, hath shined in our hearts to give the light of the knowledge of the glory of God in the face of Jesus Christ." 2 Cor. 4:6. Look at ourselves now. What, first, has God done? Shined into our hearts. What for? "To give the light of the knowledge of the glory of God in the face of Jesus Christ." Don't you see, then, that God in Jesus Christ is manifesting, showing forth from the face of Christ His glory which, reflected in us, shines also to others? Therefore, "ye are the light of the world." We are the light of the world because the light of the glory of God, shining forth from Jesus Christ into our hearts, is reflected, shines forth, to others, that people seeing us, seeing our good works, may glorify God in the "day of visitation." "May glorify the Father, which is in heaven."

Study the process. There is the Father, dwelling in light which no man can approach unto, whom no man hath seen, nor can see, of such transcendent glory, of such all-consuming brightness of holiness, that no man could look upon Him and live. But the Father wants us to look upon Him and live. Therefore, the only begotten of the Father yielded Himself freely as the gift and became ourselves in human flesh that the

Father in Him might so veil His consuming glory and the rays of His brightness, that we might look and live. And when we look there and live, that bright, shining glory from the face of Jesus Christ shines into our hearts and is reflected to the world.

Now the last verse of the third chapter again, "We all, with open face beholding as in a glass the glory of the Lord, are changed into the same image." The image of whom? The image of Jesus Christ. We are "changed into the same image from glory to glory, even as by the Spirit of the Lord." Jesus Christ reflected the image of God; we, changed into the same image, shall reflect the image of God.

The German gives another reading, more emphatic, even, than ours here. I will read it in English. "But now is reflected in us all the glory of the Lord." Do you see it? "But now in us all is reflected the glory of the Lord." The idea in our English version and this idea in the German are both correct. We see in the face of Christ the glory and are changed into the same image from glory to glory and then there is also reflected in us the glory of the Lord.

Now I will read the rest of the verse of the German. "But now is reflected in us all the glory of the Lord with uncovered face and we are glorified in the same image from one glory to another as from the Lord, who the Spirit is." The Lord who is the Spirit; the previous verse said the Lord is that Spirit.

So you see that the whole sense is that God shall be glorified in us, that we shall be glorified by that glory, and that this may be reflected to all men everywhere in order that they may believe and glorify God.

Look now again at the seventeenth of John. He tells the same story there, in John 17:22. I will read again the fourth and fifth verses:

> I have glorified thee on the earth; I have finished the work which thou gavest me to do. And now, O Father, glorify thou me with thine own self with the glory which I had with thee before the world was.

Now the twenty-second verse: "And the glory which thou gavest me I have given them." He has given it to us. Therefore, it belongs to us. This glory belongs to the believer in Jesus. And when we yield ourselves to Him, He gives us that divine mind that empties ourselves and then God in Jesus Christ shines into our hearts from which is reflected His own glory, His own divine image. And this will be so perfectly accomplished that when He comes in every believer upon whom He looks He will see Himself. "He shall sit as a refiner and purifier of silver." He sees Himself reflected in His people, so that all reflect the image and glory of God.

Let us use natural things that we may, if possible, see this a little clearer. There is the sun shining in the heavens. You and I would like to look upon the sun and see Him as

He is. But even a glance so dazzles our eyes that it takes a moment for them to recover their natural strength. Thus we cannot look upon the sun to behold the glories that are there. The sun has glories and beauties as He shines forth in the heavens. Now if you take a prism – a three-sided, three edged piece of glass – and hold it to the sun that the rays of the sun may shine through it, you see reflected on the wall, upon the ground, or wherever it may be that the reflection falls – in such reflection you see the sun as he is in himself. But what do you see? What is it called? A rainbow. And what is more beautiful than a rainbow? You cannot have a more wonderful blending of colors than are in the rainbow. But that rainbow is simply the sun, with his glory so distributed that we can look upon it and see how beautiful he is. We look yonder. All this glory is there, but we cannot see it there. We cannot see it in the face of the sun. The sun is too bright. Our eyes are not accustomed to the light. We cannot take it in. Therefore, the prism takes that glory and causes it to shine forth in such rays that we can look upon it. And this enables us to see the sun as we could not otherwise. Yet when we look upon the rainbow, we are only looking at the sun. Looking at the rainbow, we see simply the glory that there is in the sun as he shines in the heavens. Looking though into the open face of the sun we cannot see him as he is. But looking at the reflection we see the glory of the sun in a way that it delights us to look upon it.

Now God is ever so much brighter than the sun. If the sun dazzles our eyes by a mere glance, what would the transcendent glory of the Lord do upon our mortal, sinful eyes? It would consume us. Therefore, we cannot look upon Him as He is in His unveiled, unmodified glory. Our nature is not such as to bear it. But He wants us to see His glory. He wants the whole universe to see His glory. Therefore, Jesus Christ puts Himself here between the Father and us and the Father causes all His glory to be manifest in Him, and as it shines forth from His face, the glory is so distributed, so modified, that we can look upon it, and it is made so beautiful that we delight in it. Thus we are enabled to see God as He is. In Jesus Christ we see nothing that is not of God in the full brightness of His unveiled glory.

Now the sun shines in the natural heavens day by day and all these glories He makes known to the sons of men and places before the children of men. All that the sun needs in order to keep his glories ever before us in that beautiful way is a prism – a medium through which to shine for the refraction of His glory and something for these rays to fall upon for reflection, after they have passed through the prism. You could have a rainbow every day in the year, if you had a prism and something for the refracted rays to fall upon.

So also you can have the glory of God manifest every day of the year, if you will only hold Jesus Christ before your eyes as a blessed prism for refracting the bright beams of God's glory and your own self presented to God just as God would have you, for these refracted rays to fall upon for reflection.

Then not only you but other people will constantly see the glory of God. All that God wants, all that He needs, in order that man shall see and know His glory is a prism through which to shine. In Jesus Christ that is furnished in completeness. Next He wants something upon which these refracted rays may fall and be reflected, that people can see it. Will you let yourself stand there, open to the refracted rays of the glory of God, as they shine through that blessed prism which is Christ Jesus? Let those rays of the glory of God fall upon you, that men looking there may see reflected the glory of God. That is what is wanted.

Another thought: Take your prism and hold it up to the sun. The refracted rays of light fall on the wall of the house and behold in the reflection the beautiful rainbow! But that plastered wall is only mud. Can that mud manifest the glory of the sun? Can the sun be glorified by that mud? Yes. Certainly. Can that mud reflect the bright rays of the sun so that it will be beautiful? How can mud do that? O, it is not in the mud. It is in the glory. You can hold the prism up to the sun and let the refracted rays fall upon the earth. You can hold it there and that earth can manifest the glory of the sun, not because the earth has any glory in itself, but because of the glory of the sun.

Is it too much, then, for us to think that sinful flesh, such as we, worthless dust and ashes, as are we – is it too much for us to think that such as we can manifest the glory of the Lord, which is refracted through Jesus Christ – the glory of the Lord shining from the face of Jesus Christ? It may be that you are clay; it may be that you are the lowest of the earth; it may be that you are sinful as any man is, but simply put yourself there and let that glory shine upon you as God would have it and then you will glorify God. O, how often the discouraged question is asked, "How can such a person as I am, glorify God?" Why, dear brother or sister, it is not in you. It is in the glory. The virtue is not in you to make it shine any more than it is in the mud to make the rainbow shine. It is our art to furnish a place for the glory to fall, that it may shine in the beautiful reflected rays of the glory of God. The virtue is not in us; it is in the glory. That is what it is to glorify God.

It requires the emptying of self that God in Christ may be glorified. The mind of Christ does that, and then God is glorified. Though we have been sinful all our lives and our flesh is sinful flesh, God is glorified, not by merit that is in us but by the merit that is in the glory. And that is the purpose for which God has created every being in the universe. It is that every being shall be a means of reflecting and making known the brightness of the glory of the character of God as revealed in Jesus Christ.

Away back yonder there was one who was so bright and glorious by the glory of the Lord that he began to give himself credit for that and he proposed to shine of himself. He proposed to glorify himself. He proposed to reflect light from himself. But he has not shined any since with any real light. All has been darkness since. That is the origin of darkness in the universe. And the results that have come from that, from the beginning until the last result that shall ever come from it, are simply the results of that one effort to manifest self, to let self shine, to glorify self. And the end of that is that it all perishes and comes to naught.

To glorify self is to come to naught, is to cease to be. To glorify God is to continue eternally.

What He makes people for is to glorify Him. The one who glorifies Him cannot help but exist to all eternity. God wants such beings as that in the universe. The question for every man is indeed, "To be, or not to be; that is the question." Shall we choose to be and to be a means of glorifying God to all eternity? or shall we choose to glorify self for a little season and that only in darkness and then go out in everlasting darkness? O, in view of what God has done, it is not hard to decide which way to choose, is it? It is not hard to decide. Then shall it not be our choice now and forever to choose only God's way? To choose to glorify Him and Him alone?

Now another word as to what that takes. Here is a passage in John 12:23:

> Jesus answered them, saying, The hour is come, that the Son of man should be glorified.

Then, again, twenty-seventh verse:

> Now is my soul troubled; and what shall I say? Father, save me from this hour? but for this cause came I unto this hour.

What then did He say? "Father, glorify thy name." There He was, standing in the shadow of Gethsemane. He knew the hour was coming and He knew what it meant. Here was this trouble pressing upon His divine soul and drawing from Him, "What shall I say? Father, save me from this hour? but for this cause came I unto this hour." The only thing, then, there was to say, as He came to that hour for that purpose, the only thing He could say was, "Father, glorify thy name." After that came Gethsemane and the cross and death. But in this surrender, "Father, glorify thy name," there was taken the step that gave Him victory in Gethsemane and on the cross and over death.

There was His victory and you and I shall come to that place many a time. We have been in that place already – where there comes a time when upon me there may be this demand made. That experience has to be passed through and looking at it as it stands and as we see it, we shall be tempted to say, "Oh, is it necessary that that shall be borne? Is it not more than even God requires of man to bear?" "Now is my soul troubled; and what shall I say? Father, save me from this hour?" Who brought you to that hour? Who brought you face to face with that difficulty? How did you get there? The Father is dealing with us; He brought us there. Then when under His hand, we are brought to the point at which it seems as though it would take the very soul out of a man to bear it, what shall we say? Father save me from this hour? Why, for this cause I am come to this hour.

He brought me there for a purpose. I may not know what the experience is that He has for me beyond that; I may not know what is the divine purpose in that trial, but one thing I know. I have chosen to glorify God. I have chosen that God, instead of myself, shall be glorified in me, that His way shall be found in me instead of my way. Therefore, we cannot say, Father, save me from this hour. The only thing to do is to bow in submission; the only word to say is Father, glorify thy name. Gethsemane may follow immediately. The cross will certainly follow, but it is victory in that Gethsemane. It is victory upon that cross and over all that may come.

This is certainly true, for God does not leave us without the word.

Read right on now.

> What shall I say? Father, save me from this hour? but for this cause came I unto this hour. Father, glorify thy name. Then came there a voice from heaven, saying, I have both glorified it and will glorify it again.

That word is for you and for me in every trial, because "the glory which thou gavest me, I have given them." It belongs to us. He will see that it is reflected upon us and through us that men shall know that God is still manifest in the flesh. What, then, shall be our choice? Let it be settled once and forever. It is, To be, or not to be? Which shall we choose? To be? But to be, means to glorify God. The sole purpose of existence in the universe is to glorify God. Therefore, the choice to be is the choice to glorify God and the choice to glorify God is the choice that self shall be emptied and lost and God alone shall appear and be seen.

Then when all is done the fifteenth chapter of 1 Corinthians gives the grand consummation. Twenty-fourth to the twenty-eighth verses:

> Then cometh the end, when he shall have delivered up the kingdom to God, even the Father; when he shall have put down all rule, and all authority and power. For he must reign till he hath put all enemies under his feet. The last enemy that shall be destroyed is death. For he hath put all things under his feet. But when he saith, All things are put under him, it is manifest that he is excepted which did put all things under him. And when all things shall be subdued unto him, then shall the Son also himself be subject unto him that put all things under him, that God may be all in all.

All in how many? He will be all in me; He will be all in you; He will be all in everybody through Jesus Christ. There we see the plan completed. It is that the whole universe and everything in it shall reflect God.

That is the privilege that God has set before every human being. It is the privilege which He has set before every creature in the universe. Lucifer and multitudes of them who went with him, refused it. Men refused it. What shall you and I do? Shall we accept the privilege?

Let us see if we can get some idea of the measure of that privilege. What did it cost to bring that privilege to you and me? What did it cost? It cost the infinite price of the Son of God.

Now a question: Was this gift a gift of only thirty-three years? In other words, having consisted in eternity until He came to this world, did Jesus then come to this world as He did for only thirty-three years and then go back as He was before, to consist in all respects as He was before throughout eternity to come? And thus His sacrifice be practically for only thirty-three years? Was this sacrifice a sacrifice of only thirty-three years? or was it an eternal sacrifice? When Jesus Christ left heaven, He emptied Himself and sank Himself in us – for how long a time was it? That is the question. And the answer is that it was for all eternity. The Father gave up His Son to us, and Christ gave up Himself to us for all eternity. Never again will He be in all respects as He was before. He gave His life to us.

Now I do not undertake to define this. I shall simply read a word on this from the Spirit of Prophecy, that you may know that it is a fact, and that you will know that we are on safe ground, and then take it as the blessed truth and leave the explanation of it to God and eternity.

Here is the word:

> God so loved the world that he gave his only begotten Son." He gave him not only to live among men, to bear their sins and die their sacrifice; he *gave* him to the fallen race. Christ was to identify himself with the interests and needs of humanity. He who is one with God has linked himself with the children of men by ties that are never to be broken.

Wherein did He link Himself with us? In our flesh, in our nature. To what extent did He link Himself with us? "By ties that are never to be broken." Thank the Lord! Then He sank the nature of God, which He had with God before the world was, and took our nature, and He bears our nature forevermore. That is the sacrifice that wins the hearts of men. Were it looked upon, as many do look upon it, that the sacrifice of Christ was for only thirty-three years and then He died the death on the cross and went back into eternity in all respects as He was before, men might argue that in view of eternity before and eternity after, thirty-three years is not such an infinite sacrifice after all. But when we consider that He sank His nature in our human nature to all eternity, *that is a sacrifice*. That is the love of God. And no heart can reason against it. There is no heart in this world that can reason against that fact. Whether the heart accepts it or not, whether the man believes it or not, there is a subduing power in it, and the heart must stand in silence in the presence of that awful fact.

That is the sacrifice which He made.

And I read on:

> He who is one with God has linked himself with the children of men by ties that are never to be broken. Jesus is "not ashamed to call them brethren"; our Sacrifice, our Advocate, our Brother, *bearing our human form* before the Father's throne and *through eternal ages;* one with the race he has redeemed – the Son of man.

That is what it cost: The eternal sacrifice of one who was one with God. This is what it cost to bring to men the privilege to glorify God.

Now another question: Was the privilege there worth the sacrifice? or was the price paid to create the privilege? Please think carefully. What is the privilege? We have found that the privilege brought to every soul is to glorify God. What did it cost to bring that privilege to us? It cost the infinite sacrifice of the Son of God. Now did He make the sacrifice to create the privilege, or was the privilege there and worth the sacrifice.

I see that this is a new thought to many of you, but do not be afraid of it. It is all right. Please look at it carefully and think. That is all that is needed. I will say it over, even two or three times if necessary, for it is fully worth it. Ever since that blessed fact came to me that the sacrifice of the Son of God is an eternal sacrifice and *all for me,* the word has been upon my mind almost hourly, "I will go softly before the Lord all my days."

The question is, Did He create the privilege by making the sacrifice? or was the privilege there already and we had lost it and it was worth the sacrifice that He made to bring it to us again?

Then who can estimate the privilege that God gives us in the blessed privilege of glorifying Him? No mind can comprehend it. To be worth the sacrifice that was paid for it – an eternal sacrifice – O, did not David do well when he said, looking at these things, "O Lord . . . such knowledge is too wonderful for me; it is high, I cannot attain unto it"? and, "In the multitude of my thoughts within me thy comforts delight my soul"?

"Great is the mystery of godliness; for God was manifest in the flesh." The Son of man received up into glory, that means ourselves. And in that He brought to us the infinite privilege of glorifying God. That was worth the price that He paid. We never could have dreamed that the privilege was so great. But God looked upon the privilege, Jesus Christ looked upon the privilege, of what it is to glorify God.

And looking upon that and seeing where we had gone, it was said, It is worth the price. Christ said, "I will give the price." And "God so loved the world that he gave his only begotten Son," and thus brought to us the privilege of glorifying God.

Sermon 21

February 28, 1895

We are still studying what we have in Christ. We must [not] forget that the Lord has raised us up and set us in Christ at His own right in the heavenly existence. And thank the Lord that that is where we abide, in His glorious kingdom. We are still studying what we have in Him where He is and what the privileges and the riches are that belong to us in Him.

We will begin this lesson this evening with Eph. 2:11, 12, 19:

> Wherefore remember, that ye being in time past Gentiles in the flesh, who are called uncircumcision by that which is called the circumcision in the flesh made by hands; that at that time ye were without Christ, being aliens from the commonwealth of Israel, and strangers from the covenants of promise, having no hope, and without God in the world.
>
> Now therefore ye are no more strangers and foreigners, but fellow citizens with the saints and of the household of God.

Well, I am glad of that. Our place is altogether changed, our condition is changed. And all this is accomplished in Christ; this change is wrought in us in Him, for "he is our peace."

> But now, in Christ Jesus, ye who sometime were far off are made nigh by the blood of Christ. For he is our peace, who hath made both one [God and us, one], and hath broken down the middle wall of partition between us; having abolished in his flesh the enmity… for to make in himself of twain one new man, so making peace… For through him we both [those that are far off and those that are nigh] have access by one Spirit unto the Father. Now therefore [for this reason, because we have access unto the Father in him – for this reason] we are no more strangers and foreigners, but fellow citizens with the saints.

The German gives another turn to the words in the nineteenth verse, thus, "So are ye now no more guests and strangers, but citizens." The force of that will be seen more clearly when I mention that in Leviticus where our Bible reads "strangers and sojourners with thee," the German gives it, "The guest and the stranger that is with thee." So in Christ we are no more strangers and foreigners; we are not even guests. We are closer than that.

Ephesians 2:19 again:

> Ye are no more guests and strangers but fellow-citizens *and of the household of God*.

A guest is not one of the household; he is one who is welcome but he merely comes and goes. But the one who belongs to the household comes and stays. The German word where our word "household" is used will help us to see the real relationship signified. The word is *Hausgenossen* and is a derivation of *essen,* which means, "to eat." *Hausgenossen* is one that eats in the house and lives there. He is at home, and when he comes in, he does not come in as a guest. He comes in because he belongs there.

That text shows the contrast thus far between what we were and what we are, but there are other texts that bring us still nearer than that. Turn to the fourth chapter of Galatians, beginning with the first verse and get the full contrast:

> Now I say, That the heir [one who is in prospect of the inheritance], as long as he is a child, differeth nothing from a servant, though he be lord of all; but is under tutors and governors until the time appointed of the father. Even so we, when we were children, were in bondage under the elements of the world; but when the fullness of the time was come, God sent forth his Son, made of a woman, made under the law, to redeem them that were under the law, that we might receive the adoption of sons. And because ye are sons, God hath sent forth the Spirit of his son into your hearts, crying Abba, Father. Wherefore thou art no more a servant.

We are not in the house as a servant – no more a servant. We are servants of the Lord, that is true, and our service is due to the Lord, but what we are studying now is our relationship to the Lord and the place He gives us in the family.

This shows that the Lord gives us a closer relationship to Himself than that of a servant in the household. We are not in that heavenly family as servants but as children.

> Wherefore thou art no more servant but a son; and if a son, then an heir of God through Christ.

The view given us here is of the child, who may be the only child; all the property of the parents will fall to him in the regular course of heirship, but he is a child yet, and he is under tutors and governors and is trained and guided in the way that the father wishes until he becomes of such an age that the father will call him into closer relationship to himself in the family affairs and in the business and all the affairs of the estate. While the boy is a child, he does not know anything about the business affairs of the estate. He has something else to learn before he is taken into that closer relationship, even to his father, but when he has received the training that his father intended him to have and has reached the proper age, then the father takes him into a closer relationship with himself. He will tell him all about his business affairs. He may give him a partnership in the business and let him have an oversight of it equally with himself.

Now turn to John 15:13-15. It is Christ who is speaking. "Greater love hath no man than this, that a man lay down his life for his friends. Ye are my friends, if ye do whatsoever I command you. Henceforth I call you not servants." "The servant abideth not in the house forever: but the Son abideth ever." There is a good reason why Jesus does not call us servants any more. We are to abide in the house forever. We belong there; our home is there. "I call you not servants," I call you sons, because the son abideth in the house forever. We were strangers and foreigners before; He brought us closer than even a guest, much less a stranger. And He brought us closer than even a servant who would think of living in the house as long as he lives. He brought us closer than the child who has not yet reached the state of manhood. He brings us beyond all that, into the estate of friends and sons in possession, to be taken into the councils of Him who is head and owner of all the property.

Read the rest of this verse. "Henceforth I call you not servants; for the servant knoweth not what his lord doeth: but I have called you friends." He does not call us servants, because the servant does not know what his lord does. He calls us friends, because He is not going to keep anything back from us. Jesus says, "I call you not servants; for the servant does not know what his lord is doing." I take you closer than that. I call you friends. Why? "I have called you friends, for all things that I have heard of my Father I have made known unto you."

You see, then, that He proposes to take us right into His home councils. He has no secrets to keep back from us. He does not propose to keep anything back. This is not to say that He is going to tell it all in a day. He cannot do that, because we are not large enough to grasp it all, if He were to try, but the fact is He says to us, All things I have heard of my Father I make known to you. You are welcome to a knowledge of it. But He gives us time so that we can get His truth. How much time does He give us? Eternal life, eternity. So we say, "Lord, go ahead; take your time. Tell it. Tell us your own will. We will wait to learn."

Now look at Ephesians again. There is a word which, taken with the German, illustrates this yet more fully.

Eph. 1:3-7:

> Blessed be the God and Father of our Lord Jesus Christ, who hath blessed us with all spiritual blessings in heavenly places in Christ. [The German reads, "Heavenly possession," heavenly goods.]: According as he hath chosen us in him before the foundation of the world, that we should be holy without blame before him in love: having predestinated us into the adoption of children [we are coming to the same point we had a moment ago] by Jesus Christ to himself, according to the good pleasure of his will, to the praise of his glory of his grace, wherein he hath made us accepted in the beloved: in whom we have redemption through his blood, the forgiveness of sins, according to the riches of his grace, wherein he hath abounded toward us in all wisdom and prudence; having made known unto us the mystery of his will, according to his good pleasure which he hath purposed in himself.

"Made known unto us the mystery of his will"; the German word for "mystery" here is *geheimnis*. *Geheimnis*, in German, is, of course, the same as our word here "mystery." It is secret. But we want to go back to the root of that word and then we will see the secret that we are after here. Now it is true that *geheimnis* is a secret thing or something that is mysterious, concealed, or covered. Now secretly, in the German is *heimlich*. Joseph of Arimathaea was a disciple of the Lord, but *heimlich* – for fear of the Jews; that is, secretly for fear of the Jews. But what does that *heimlich* signify? *Heim* is home. *Geheimnis* is the private home affairs, or more literally, home secrets. In every family there are what are known as family secrets. They belong of right only to the family. A stranger cannot come into these. A guest may come and go, but he has no right ever to become acquainted with any of these family secrets. They are not made known to him. Now that word "secrecy," – the sacred secrecy of the family affairs, between husband and wife and children – those things that pertain particularly to the family, to the home interests, and the secret counsels of the family – that is the idea of the German word for "secret" or "mystery." So now Jesus has taken us into his home and makes known to us the *geheimnis* of his will – the home secrets of the heavenly family. The Lord takes us into such intimate relationship to Himself that the secret things of the family – even the very home family secrets – are not kept from us. He says so.

There is another verse that we can read. Now note: there are affairs of this divine family, there are secrets of this family, that date from away back yonder, long before the time when we ever entered the family. We were strangers to the family. We had no connection with the family at all. But the Lord called and we came, and now He has adopted us into the family and brings us into that close relationship to Himself in which He proposes to make known to us all the family secrets. In order to do that, as we found awhile ago, we need a long time in which to be there, and He needs a long time to do it, any way, because our capacity is so small in comparison with the great wealth of this, that it will take a great while for Him to do it.

More than that: we need one to tell us this who is thoroughly acquainted with all the family affairs from the beginning. Is there any one in the family that is acquainted with all the family affairs from the beginning and who will undertake to show us around and tell to us what we are to know? Turn to Proverbs 8, beginning with verse 22:

> The Lord possessed me in the beginning of his way, before his works of old. I was set up from everlasting, from the beginning, or ever the earth was. When there were no depths, I was brought forth; when there were no fountains abounding with water. Before the mountains were settled, before the hills was I brought forth; while as yet he had not made the earth, nor the fields, nor the highest part of the dust of the world. When he had prepared the heavens, I was there: when he set a compass upon the face of the depth: when he established the clouds above: when he strengthened the fountains of the deep: when he gave to the sea his decree, that the waters should not pass his commandment: when he appointed the foundations of the earth: then I was by him, as one brought up with him.

Now He is the one who has said to you and me, I call you not servants, but friends, for the servant does not know what the Lord doeth, but all things that the Father has made known to me, I make known to you. And He is there as one brought up with Him from the days of eternity He was there. Now He says, I call you friends, because all that the Father hath told me, I tell you. He not only gives us time in which to have Him tell it, but He is one who is qualified to tell it, because He has been there from the beginning. He knows all these affairs and He says that nothing does He propose to keep back from you. Well, brethren, that shows that He has a great deal of confidence in us. I will read a word that came in the last mail from Australia and you will recognize the voice:

> Not only is man forgiven through the atoning sacrifice, but through faith he is accepted through the Beloved. Returning to his loyalty to God, whose law he has transgressed, he is not merely tolerated but he is honored as a son of God, a member of the heavenly family. He is an heir of God and a joint heir with Jesus Christ.

But it is so natural to think of ourselves that He does only tolerate us when we believe in Jesus; to think that by forcing Himself to do so He can bear our ways a little longer, if by any means we can make ourselves good enough so that He can like us well enough to have confidence in us. I say, It is so natural to put ourselves in that position. And Satan is so ready to talk to us like that and to get us to put ourselves in that position.

But the Lord does not want us to stand hesitating and doubting as to our standing before Him. No, sir. He says, "When you have believed in me, when you have accepted me, you are accepted in me, and I do not propose to tolerate you merely to try to get along with you. I propose to put confidence in you as in a friend and take you into the councils of my will and give you a part in all the affairs of the inheritance. There is nothing that I propose to keep back from you. That is confidence.

I have heard people say that they were thankful for the confidence they had in the Lord. I have no objection to that, but I do not think it is a very great accomplishment or a thing worthy of any very great commendation that I should have confidence in such a being as the Lord, considering who I am and who He is. I do not think it a very great draft upon me to have confidence in the Lord. But it is an astonishment that He should have confidence in me. That is where the wonder comes. Seeing who He is and what I was, then that He should take me up and tell me in plain words what He proposes to do with me and how close He takes me to Himself and what confidence He puts in me – that is wonderful. Looking at it in any way whatever, I say, it is an astonishing thing to me all the time and something that draws upon my thanksgiving that God has confidence in me. That He should have any confidence at all in us, that is a great thing, but the truth is that there is no limit to His confidence in us.

From the texts that we have read, you can see that there is no limit to His confidence in us. Is there any limit to a man's confidence in a friend whom he takes into his household, makes one of the family, and takes right into his own family and home secrets? You know that it is the very last point that a human being can reach in confidence and friendship among human beings, that the family secrets should be laid open to him and he should be welcomed to them. When a man takes another into his own home affairs and his own family secrets, that demonstrates that that man has no limit at all to his confidence in the other man. Yet that is precisely the way the Lord treats the believer in Jesus.

That other man may betray the sacred confidences that this man has placed in him, but that does not alter the fact that this confidence was put upon him. So we may fail in our appreciation of the confidence which God has put in us and men may indeed betray the sacred trust, but the point is that God does not ask whether we are going to do that or not. He does not take us upon suspicion nor does He merely tolerate us. He says, "Come unto me." You are accepted in the Beloved. I put confidence in you. Come, let us be friends. Come into the house, you belong here. Sit down at the table and eat there. You are henceforth one of the family, equally with those who have always been here. He is not going to treat you as a servant, but He will treat you as a king and make known to you all there is to know.

Brethren, shall not that draw on our gratitude and friendliness to the Lord? Shall we not treat Him more as He treats us? Shall we not let that confidence draw upon us and cause us to yield to Him and prove ourselves worthy of that confidence? As a matter of fact, there is nothing which so draws upon a man's manliness anyway, as to show confidence in Him. Suspicion never helps Him.

> Ye are my friends, if ye do whatsoever I command you. Henceforth I call you not servants; for the servant knoweth not what his lord doeth: but I have called you friends; for all things that I have heard of my Father I have made known unto you.

Now the sixteenth chapter and the twelfth verse:

"I have yet many things to say unto you." To whom? Let us not put this away back there to those disciples. It is to you and me, here and now. Has He not raised us up from the dead? Has He not given us life with Jesus Christ? And "along with him" has He not raised us up and seated us "along with him" at His own right hand in heaven? "I have yet many things to say unto you." Who has? Jesus. "But ye cannot bear them now."

Very good. Eternity will give me room to grow in knowledge and understanding, so that I can bear them. We need not be in a hurry.

"Howbeit when he, the Spirit of truth, is come, he will guide you into all truth: for [that is, because] he shall not speak of himself." That is, He shall not speak from Himself. It is not that He shall not talk about Himself; that is not the thought. It is true He will not talk about Himself; but the thought here is that He will not speak as from Himself.

He does not set Himself forth and propose to tell something as from Himself, just as He, when He came to the world, did not speak from Himself. For He said, "The words that I speak unto you I speak not of myself." "The Father which sent me, he gave me a commandment what I should say and what I should speak." John 12:49. And just as Jesus set not Himself forth to tell something as from Himself, but what He heard from the Father, that He spoke; so the Holy Spirit speaks not from Himself; but what the Spirit of God hears, that He speaks.

> He shall not speak of himself: but whatsoever he shall hear, that shall he speak; and he will show you things to come.

Very good. Here we are of the heavenly family. Jesus is the one who has been in the family from the beginning and to Him is given charge of us and He is the one who is to tell us all these things. And it is written, you know, that "they follow the Lamb whithersoever he goeth." Good! He has something to tell us, He has something to show us and He gives the Holy Spirit as His personal representative, bringing His personal presence to us, that by this means He can reveal these things to us, that by Him He can speak to us what He has to tell.

> He will show you things to come. He shall glorify me; for he shall receive of mine, and shall show it unto you.

What, then, is the office of the Holy Spirit? To receive those things of the heavenly family, and show them to us.

Now the next verse:

> All things that the Father hath are mine: therefore said I, that he shall take of mine, and shall show it unto you.

Now why did Jesus say that the Holy Spirit shall take of mine and show it unto you? Because "all things that the Father hath are mine: therefore, said I, that he shall take of mine and shall show it unto you." How many things are there that the Holy Spirit is to show to us? All things. All things of whom? All things that the Father hath. There is nothing to be kept back.

Now turn to 1 Corinthians 2:9-12:

> As it is written, Eye hath not seen, nor ear heard, neither have entered into the heart of man, the things which God hath prepared for them that love him.

We are heirs of God and joint heirs with Jesus Christ, and God has appointed Him "Heir of all thing." "All things," then, that the universe contains He has prepared for them that love Him. All things that the Father hath, He has prepared for them that love Him. That, of itself, should draw us to love Him. But as eye has not seen nor ear heard, nor have ever entered into the heart of man, these great things, how, then, can we know them? Ah! "God hath revealed them unto us by his Spirit: for the Spirit searcheth all things, yea, the deep things of God."

Why does He search the deep things of God? to bring them forth to us. They are too deep for us. If the Lord should open them up to us and say, Enter there and find out all you can, we could not find them out. They are too deep, but He does not leave us thus. He proposes to reveal them to us, therefore, He puts all into the hands of Jesus, who has been brought up with Him and who is one of us and Jesus Christ reveals them unto us by His Spirit.

> For what man knoweth the things of a man, save the spirit of man which is in him? Even so the things of God knoweth no man but the Spirit of God.
> Now we have received, not the spirit of the world, but the Spirit which is of God.

What does He say? We *have* received it. Let us thank Him that we have received it. Why, I saw the other day a line from the Testimony of Jesus, that some are looking for the time *to come* when the Holy Spirit is to be poured out. It says that the time is "*now,*" and that we are to ask and receive now.

> The descent of the Holy Spirit upon the church is looked forward to as being in the future; but it is the privilege of the church to have it now. Seek for it, pray for it, believe for it.

He says, "Receive ye the Holy Ghost." "As my Father hath sent me, even so send I you." "Now we have received . . . the spirit which is of God." Have we not surrendered to Him? Have we not given ourselves completely to Him? Have we not opened our hearts to receive the mind of Jesus Christ, that we may know Him that is true and be in Him that which is true, even in His Son Jesus Christ? And this is the true God and eternal life. That being so, then "because ye are sons, God hath sent forth the Spirit of His Son into your hearts." He hath sent it forth; He says so. Therefore, thank Him that He has and "receive ye the Holy Ghost." Receive Him with thanksgiving and let the Spirit use us, instead of waiting and longing to receive some wonderful outward demonstration that will give us such a feeling that we think, Now I have the Spirit of God. O, now *I* can do great things. It will never come to you in that way. If the Holy Spirit were to be poured out upon us tonight as it was on Pentecost, the man that had that idea of it would not receive any of it.

But I say, We must revolutionize our thoughts concerning this and get them off from any outward demonstration that we can see with our eyes or that will give us a tangible feeling by which we shall know that we have the Spirit of God and that *we* shall be able to do great things. God has spoken the word; He has made the promise. He has raised us up and seated us at His own right hand in Jesus Christ and now He says, Everything is open to you and the Spirit is there to show you everything and tell you everything that there is to know. What more can we ask then? What more can we ask of Him, to show His mind and His willingness that we shall have the Spirit of God now?

Heaven is waiting to bestow it; what is required to receive it? Seek for it, pray for it, believe for it. When that is done there is nothing that keeps Him back; when that is done, then all that He asks us to do is to "receive the Holy Spirit." He tells us how to receive it; it is to seek for it, pray for it, believe for it. And he that believeth has received. If we ask according to His will, He hears us, and if we know He hears us, we know *we have* the petition that we desired of Him.

The Spirit of God is leading us. The Lord has led us into His truth thus. He has raised us up unto heights by His truth that we have never known before. What has He raised us up there for? He has shown us what is essential. It is to give up the world and everything but God only, to all eternity. Surrender all plans, all prospects, everything you ever had your mind upon. Drop out self and the world and everything and receive God and be bound to nothing but God. Then we are in Jesus Christ at the right hand of God and all the universe to all eternity is open to us and the Spirit of God is given to us to teach us all these things and to make known the mysteries of God to all who believe.

> Now we have received, not the spirit of the world but the Spirit which is of God; that we might know the things that are freely given to us of God.

Therefore, let us all now take this text as our text of thanksgiving, our prayer, to which we shall say, Amen. Eph. 3:14-21.

> For this cause I bow my knees unto the Father of our Lord Jesus Christ [What do you say?], of whom the whole family in heaven and earth is named… That Christ may dwell in our hearts by faith; that ye, being rooted and grounded in love, may be able to comprehend with all saints what is the breadth and length and depth and height.

What is all this for? So that we may know what that is which He has given us, that we may comprehend and hold and grasp and enjoy forever all that He has so freely given us in Christ.

> And to know the love of Christ, which passeth knowledge, that ye might be filled with all the fullness of God. Now unto him that is able to do exceeding abundantly above all that we ask or think, according to the power that worketh in us, unto him be glory in the church by Christ Jesus throughout all ages, world without end. Amen.

And let all the people, forever, say, Amen and Amen.

Sermon 22

March 3, 1895

Our lesson tonight will begin with Ephesians 1, verses 19-21. The lesson is still the study of what we have in Christ where He is. This is the part of that prayer that "ye may know . . . what is the exceeding greatness of his power to usward who believe, according to the working of his mighty power, which he wrought in Christ, when he raised him from the dead and set him at his own right hand in the heavenly places," or heavenly existence, as we have had in the second chapter and sixth verse. And that same thought is given in Phil. 3:8-10:

> I count all things but loss for the excellency of the knowledge of Christ Jesus my Lord: for whom I have suffered the loss of all things, and do count them but dung, that I may win Christ, and be found in him, not having mine own righteousness, which is of the law, but that which is through the faith of Christ, the righteousness which is of God by faith: that I may know him, and the power of his resurrection.

That is the same thing that the Lord desires that we shall know, as recorded in the text, "That ye may know . . . what is the exceeding greatness of his power to usward who believe, according to the working of his mighty power, which he wrought in Christ, when he raised him from the dead." Now says Paul, "That I may know him, and the power of his resurrection." That is, not His power alone in raising Paul from the dead after he had died and gone into the grave. That is not it. But it is to know the power of His resurrection now while we live; that is, the power which is brought to us by Him, by which we are crucified with Him, and are dead with Him and buried with Him, and then made alive with Him and then raised with Him and seated with Him at the right hand of God in heaven. That is the power which He referred to.

Read on, and you will see that is it so:

> That I may know him, and the power of his resurrection, and the fellowship of his sufferings, being made conformable unto his death; if by any means I might attain unto the resurrection of the dead [or out from among the dead].

He wants to know the power of Christ's resurrection in order to attain for Himself unto the resurrection out from among the dead. The man who in this life never knows the power of Christ's resurrection will never know it in the other life. True, He will be raised from the dead, but He will not know *the power* that raised from the dead, so that whoever does not get acquainted with the power of Christ's resurrection before He dies will never know the power of Christ's resurrection from that death.

There is the Lord's prayer, that I might know what is the exceeding greatness of His power toward the man that believes, according to the working of His mighty power which He wrought in Christ when He raised Him from the dead and seated Him there. In Him we know the power that raises us from deadness in trespasses and sins along with Him, and seats us with Him in the heavenly existence. Now Eph. 1:20, 21:

> And set him at his own right hand in the heavenly places, far above all principality and power and might and dominion and every name that is named, not only in this world but also in that which is to come.

This power of God which raised us in Christ above all the principalities and powers and might and dominion that are in this world, is what we are studying tonight. Therefore we must study first what is the nature of these principalities and powers which are in this world. Before this, however, let us notice once more that there stands the fact that in Christ we have and are to know what is the power which raises us in Him and with Him, above all principalities and power and might and dominion that are in this world. There is a separation of church and state; there is a separation from the world, that puts us in the place where we have better protection than from the powers of this world. There stands this fact of faith.

Now as to the nature of these powers, read right on into the second chapter for further connection:

> And you hath he quickened, who were dead in trespasses and sins; wherein in time past ye walked according to the course of this world, according to the prince of the power of the air, the spirit that now worketh in the children of disobedience.

There is a spirit that works in this world in the children of disobedience and that spirit is the spirit of this prince of the power of the air. The German says, "after the prince that in the air rules; namely, after the spirit that to this time has worked in the children of unbelief."

Formerly, when we were dead in sins, we "walked according to the course of this world, according to the prince of the power of the" world.

Now from that word "prince" comes the idea of principality. In monarchical forms of government there are principalities, dukedoms, kingdoms, and empires. A principality is the jurisdiction, the territory, or dominion, of a prince; a dukedom is the dominion of a duke; a kingdom, the dominion of a king; an empire, the dominion of an emperor.

In the text Christ has raised us above all principality and power and so on, that is in this world and that is of this world. He has raised us above the rule of the spirit that rules in the children of disobedience.

We can be glad, therefore, and thank the Lord that in Christ we are raised above this prince and all his jurisdiction and all his power. That is the thought, for in Christ He has raised us far above all principality and power and might and dominion that are in this world.

Now the sixth chapter of Ephesians, beginning with the tenth verse:

> Finally, my brethren, be strong in the Lord and in the power of his might. Put on the whole armor of God, that ye may be able to stand against the wiles of the devil.

Now who is it against whom the Christian is to contend in this world? As relates to the principalities and power and empires of this world, who is it with whom the Christian is to contend? The devil, "That ye may be able to stand against the wiles of the devil."

Then when any government is set against any Christian and interferes with him and persecutes him, is the Christian wrestling with that government? Is he contending with it? No. He is wrestling with the devil. That is what we want to get our minds upon. We are to understand that when governments, kingdoms, emperors, and rulers persecute the Christian, persecute us, we have nothing to do with *them* as such. We are not warring against them. We are not wrestling with them. We are wrestling against the devil and warring against *him*.

And this suggests a testimony that came last spring in which it was stated that the ministers should never forget to hold before the people everywhere and all the time that the strifes and commotions and contentions and conflicts that are presented outwardly in this world do not come simply from this world and from the things that we see but they are only the result, the outward workings of the spiritual powers that are out of sight, that all these elements of evil that are working up and that we see coming so fast are simply the outworkings of that power, of that spirit, that is back of them. And the instrumentalities that we see spreading abroad the Lord's message and carrying forward His work, demonstrate on this side that these are simply the outward workings of the Spirit and power of God that is back of these. And the word is given that we ministers see to it that we call the attention of the people to the fact that all these commotions and conflicts and contentions between right and wrong are simply the contentions between Jesus Christ and Satan – that it is the great controversy of all the ages.

It is so easy for us to get our mind upon men and governments and powers and think we are contending with them. No. We have no contention with governments. We are not to do anything against governments, because it is written, "Let every soul be subject unto the higher powers." We are not to contend against the government.

Every Christian will always be in harmony with any right law that any government can make. So he never raises any question with himself as to what law is going to be made, this way or the other, in this respect, so far as the government legislates within its own jurisdiction. He does not care what laws are made there, because his life as a Christian, in the fear of God, will never come into conflict with any right law that is made – with any law that Caesar may make within his own jurisdiction, which God has set to him.

When Caesar gets out of that place and gets beyond his jurisdiction into the kingdom of God, then of course every law he makes the Christian will be in conflict with, because *he* is right and the other thing is *wrong*. The Christian has not changed his attitude, but the other power has. Therefore, we are not to have our minds upon whether we are contending against the government or not. We have nothing to do with that. We are to have our minds upon the fact that if the government gets out of harmony with right and takes such a course that it conflicts with us, we are not then contending with it – we are always contending against the devil. We wrestle not with flesh and blood. Governments are flesh and blood. Men, courts, judges, legislators – they are flesh and blood.

> We wrestle not against flesh and blood, but against principalities, against powers, against the rulers of the darkness of this world, against wicked spirits in high places (Marginal reading).

The margin is, "In heavenly places," which would refer to this heavenly jurisdiction in which Jesus Christ rules. The verbal translation of this sixth chapter and twelfth verse runs thus, "We wrestle not against flesh and blood, but against principalities, against authorities, against the rulers of the darkness of this age, against the spiritual power of wickedness in the heavenlies." It is the same heavenlies in which God has raised us up with Him, and set us with Him in the heavenlies far above all principalities and power and might and dominion that are upon the earth. So that the marginal reading of that verse is the correct one. "Wicked spirits in heavenly places." Ours reads wicked spirits in high places.

The German reads fully as forcibly as the Greek there. Thus: "For we have not with flesh and blood to contend, but with prince and power; namely, with the lord of the world." That is the God of this world – Satan. So then we have not to wrestle with flesh and blood but with the lord of the world: "Namely, with the lord of the world that in the darkness of this world rules, with the base spirits under heaven."

That is strong. That is forcible. We see who it is – it is the lord of this world; it is he against whom we wrestle – the one who rules in the darkness of this world – the prince of this world, that in the darkness of this world rules.

Now we know, or at least ought to know, that it is not going to be very long until every dominion of this earth is going to be under the rule of the lord of this world, who rules in the darkness and all are going to be bound in one and aimed at the truth of God and those in whom it is represented in this world. Now I wish all knew that we are going to be there soon. I wish that every Seventh-day Adventist knew that which is the fact, that we are at the point now where all the kingdoms and dominions of the earth are, as such, set against the truth of God. But if there be those (I do not say there are) who now do not know this, it will be but a very short time, in the way in which things have been going lately and are going *now,* before they will be forced to recognize it.

As I mentioned here once before, the United States has been held before the world and has always stood, as the very citadel of liberty of rights and of freedom of conscience and Switzerland was the one little country, the one little republic, in Europe where freedom was likewise most full. Yet Switzerland and the United States are the two countries now on earth that are doing most against the remnant and the seed of the church who keep the commandments of God and have the testimony of Jesus Christ. And England has now actively joined these. Now, when these countries which have been the exemplars of the world, of the rights of men and the freedom of conscience, set themselves up against God and against His truth – then isn't it time that we learned that all the world is now under the rule of Satan, ready to be swung against the truth of God and the power of Jesus Christ?

Yet in the face of it all, I say that in Christ we are all right, for in Him there works that power that raises us, with Him, from the dead, and that has seated us at the right hand of God in the heavenly existence, far above all the power and might and dominion and principalities that are upon earth and in the hand of Satan. And just now, as we are to be forced into that conflict, isn't it good that the Lord Jesus comes with His blessed truth to shine forth before us and to raise us to where He sits, so that we shall know that we are above all these things all the time and triumph over them?

Now we will study these things a little further; this is so much for the principality. But He says He has raised us far above all principality and power.

That word "power" you can look at the Greek word whenever you choose, yourself and you will see that the absolute meaning of the word is the power of authority that is exercised as of "might as against right." That is what the word means.

The literal translation is authority. There are accommodated uses of the word, that is true, aside from the absolute meaning. In accommodated uses, the character of the power is proved by the relationship in which it stands. For instance, if that word should be used of the power of Christ and the authority of the Lord, it would be proper and legitimate authority, of course, because it is the authority of the Lord. But when it is used of the powers of this world, in every instance it takes its associations from the nature of this world and the spirit that rules here and then it runs clear back to the absolute meaning, which is the authority and power of "might as against right."

Where did there start in this universe the assumption of any authority or power of might, as against right? It originated with the rebellion of Lucifer in that assumption of self, away back there. He brought that power into this world and fastened it upon this world by deception when he got possession of this world. Therefore, that word is properly used to show that when God in Christ has lifted us above all the principality and power of this world, it is above this power of might as against right, which is the power of Satan, as he has brought it into this world and as he uses it in this world.

This simply emphasizes the thought we mentioned a moment ago, that our contest is simply the contest that has been waged from the beginning between the two spiritual powers, between the legal and the illegal powers, between the power of right as against might, and the power of might as against right. The contest is between these two spiritual powers. We have been under the power of might as against right – the power of force. Jesus Christ brought to us the knowledge of right as against might – the power of love. We forsook the dominion and power of might as against right – the power of force, and have joined our allegiance to the power of right as against might – the power of love. And now the contest is between these two powers and concerning us. The contest is always between these spiritual powers. Whatever instruments may be employed in this world as the outward manifestation of that power, the contest is always between the two spiritual powers, Jesus Christ and the fallen prince.

Let us follow this, then, a little further, and see wherein we have the victory and wherein He has brought to us the victory over these illegal powers, this power of might as against right. Read in Colossians 2, beginning with the ninth verse.

> In him dwelleth all the fullness of the Godhead bodily. And ye are complete in him, which is the head of all principality and power: in whom also ye are circumcised with the circumcision made without hands, in putting off the body of the sins of the flesh by the circumcision of Christ: buried with him in baptism, wherein also ye are risen with him through the faith of the operation of God, who hath raised him from the dead. and you, being dead in your sins and the uncircumcision of your flesh, hath he quickened together with him [Christ], having forgiven you all trespasses.

Made you alive together with Him. You see it is the same story we read in the second of Ephesians the other night – that He has made us alive and has raised us up with Him from the dead and made us sit with Him where He sits. But now here comes in the key of how this victory came to us in Him. "And having spoiled principalities and powers, he made a show of them openly, triumphing over them in it" or, as the margin and the German read, "triumphing over them *in himself*." Col. 2:15. The word "power" here is the same word in the Greek that expresses this power of might as against right. I need not turn to the parable Jesus spake: "When a strong man armed keepeth his palace, his goods are in peace: but when a stronger than he shall come upon him, and overcome him, he taketh from him all his armor wherein he trusted, and divideth the spoil."

Satan was the one who originated the authority of might as against right. By deception he became the head of this world by becoming the controlling power or the head of him who was the head of the world. And having taken Adam and his dominion under his control, he became the head of this dominion, the head of this world, and the head of all principality and power in the world and of it.

But a stronger than he came into the world. We know He is stronger, because the battle has been fought and won. A second Adam came, not as the first Adam was but as the first Adam had caused his descendants to be at the time at which He came. The second Adam came at the point in the degeneracy of the race to which the race had come from the first Adam. That second Adam came thus and disputed the dominion of this one who had taken possession. The contest was between these two upon the earth. It was a contest as to whether the spoil should be divided or whether it should be kept intact in the hands of him who had taken it by might as against right. He who came into this rebellious dominion, proved to be stronger than he who had possession and He defeated him at every step while He lived. Then in order to show to the universe how completely more powerful He is than the other, Jesus not only defeated Satan at every step while He was alive, but after that He gave Himself over, dead, into the hands, into the power, of this other one, who was in possession. And this one who was in possession shut Him up in his stronghold, dead, and even then He broke the power of Satan. Thus Christ has demonstrated that He is not only stronger than Satan when He is alive but that *when dead* He is stronger than Satan. When dead He was stronger than Satan, and therefore He came forth from the tomb and exclaimed before the universe, "I am he that liveth, and was dead; and, behold, I am alive forevermore, Amen; and have the keys of hell and of death." Very good! He is alive now, thank the Lord!

Well, then when a dead Christ is stronger than all the power of the devil, what can a living Christ not do, who sits at the right hand of God today? Is there any room for our being discouraged? Is there any room for fear, even in the presence of all the principalities and powers and mights and dominions that the devil can muster on the earth? No. For He who is with us now alive, when dead was stronger than Satan with all his power. Now Jesus is alive forevermore; we are alive in Him; and His power is enlisted in our behalf – His *living* power. His dead power would be enough, wouldn't it? But He does not stop at that. It is living power. Be glad and rejoice and conquer in it.

Jesus came unto the dominion and at last entered into the very citadel of the stronghold and the stronghold of the citadel of this illegal power, of this one who held the power of this world of might as against right. This One that is stronger than he, entered in, and took possession and came forth, carrying the key, and He holds them still. Thank the Lord! Then if this illegal power should even get some of us into the same place, into the prisonhouse, it is all right. He cannot keep us there, for our Friend has the keys. When He wants us to come forth, the key is turned, the door is wide open, and out we come. And to show how completely He did have the keys, when He came forth He brought the keys and holds them yet and forever. For that reason it is written (Eph. 4:7, 8):

Unto every one of us is given grace according to the measure of the gift of Christ. Wherefore He saith, When He ascended up on high, He led captivity captive, and gave gifts unto men.

He spoiled principalities and powers; He led a multitude of captives from this dominion of Satan and of death when He came forth.

It is written in the twenty-seventh chapter of Matthew, verses 51-53, speaking of the time of the crucifixion of Christ:

> And the earth did quake and the rocks rent; and the graves were opened; and many bodies of the saints which slept arose, and came out of the graves after his resurrection.

The graves were opened at His crucifixion. When did they come out? After His resurrection. Assuredly. When He came forth, it is written, He divided the spoil. When He came forth, He led a multitude of captives, and when He ascended up on high, He led them on high in His train of captives recovered from the land of the enemy. That is the figure that is referred to here, in this having spoiled principalities and powers and made a *show* in a grand parade of them openly, triumphing over them in it. The word "triumph" here refers to the Roman triumph. The Roman triumph was granted to the Roman general who had gone into an enemy's country, fought the enemy, taken spoil and captives from there, and brought them home to his own city. If any of the Roman citizens were captives in that land, he brought them home. And when his victory was complete and he had returned, the Senate granted him a triumph. In his triumph he was seated in a great and grand chariot, having six or more of the finest horses, of one color, and he, drawn by these, with all the spoil and the captives in his train, would parade up and down the streets of Rome, around about, everywhere – all the people out in the great gala-day, doing honor to him in his triumph.

Jesus Christ, our Conqueror, the conqueror in our behalf, came into *this* land of the enemy, fought our battles – we were prisoners, taken under the power of this illegal one; our Friend came here, our General fought our battles clear through; he went into the stronghold of the enemy and burst his bond and broke open the citadel. He brought the keys. He took the spoil. He brings forth the captives and leads them in triumph upon high to his own glorious city. Now "thanks be unto God which always causeth us to triumph" in Christ. In Him we triumph over this illegal power, this one whose is the power of might as against right. And in this triumph over Satan, there is displayed before the assembled universe the power of right as against might.

Now note:

The power of right as against might can never use any might. Do you see that? Do you not see that in that lies the very spirit that is called of Christians, that is, the very Spirit of Jesus Christ, which is nonresistance? Could Christ use might in demonstrating the power of right as against might? No.

To maintain the power of might as against right, might is to be used at every opportunity, because that is the only thing that can be used to win. In that cause *the right* has only a secondary consideration, if it has any consideration at all.

But on the other hand, the power of right as against might, *is in the right,* not in the might. The might is in the right itself. And he who is pledged to the principle of right as against might and in whom that is to be demonstrated can never appeal to any kind of might. He can never use any might whatever in defense of the power of right. He depends upon the power of *the right itself* to win, and to conquer all the power of might that may be brought against it. That is the secret.

Then don't you see that that explains in a word why it is that Christ was like a lamb in the presence of these powers and this might that was brought against Him? He had nothing to do with using any might in opposing them. When Peter drew the sword and would defend Him, He said, Put up your sword: he that taketh the sword shall perish by the sword.

When we get hold of that, all things will be explained as to what we shall do here, there, or the other place. We are pledged to allegiance to the power of right as against might – the power of love. And Jesus Christ died as a malefactor, abused, tossed about, mobbed, scoffed, spit upon, crowned with thorns, every conceivable contemptible thing put upon Him, and He *died under it,* in His appeal to the power of right as against might. And that power of right which He died in allegiance to has moved the world ever since, and it is to move the world in our day as it never has been moved before. Just as soon as God can get the people who are professedly pledged to the principle, to be pledged in heart to the principle and put the thought upon nothing at all and never expect to appeal to anything at all other than the absolute principle of the right and the power of it to which we are allied and to which we are pledged, then we shall see and the world shall see this power working as never before.

Sermon 23

March 4, 1895

I referred last night also to a Testimony on the thought as to this contest between the spiritual powers.

I will read that at this point, because it touches not only that, but this thing that we have studied right here, as to our being absolutely dependent upon the power of right, itself, to win. We need not get stirred up, nor be abusive, nor anything of the kind, but just state the principle, and let it stand, trusting to itself to win.

> In these times of special interest, the guardians of the flock of God should teach the people that the spiritual powers are in controversy; it is not human beings that are creating such intensity of feeling as now exists in the religious world. A power from Satan's spiritual synagogue is infusing the religious elements of the world, arousing men to decided action to press the advantages Satan has gained, by leading the religious world in determined warfare against those who make the word of God their guide and the sole foundation of doctrine. Satan's masterly efforts are now put forth to gather in every principle and every power that he can employ to controvert the binding claims of the law of Jehovah, especially the fourth commandment, that defines who is the Creator of the heavens and the earth.
>
> The man of sin has thought to change times and laws; but has he done it? This is the great issue. Rome and all the churches that have drunk of her cup of iniquity, in thinking to change times and laws have exalted themselves above God, and torn down God's great memorial, the seventh-day Sabbath. The Sabbath was to stand representing God's power in his creation of the world in six days, and his resting upon the seventh day. "Wherefore" He "blessed the Sabbath day and hallowed it," because that in it he had rested from all his works which God created and made. The object of the masterly working of the great deceiver has been to supersede God. In his efforts to change times and laws, he has been working to maintain a power in opposition to God, and above him.
>
> Here is the great issue. Here are the two great powers confronting each other – the Prince of God, Jesus Christ, and the prince of darkness, Satan. Here comes the open conflict. There are but two classes in the world, and every human being will range under one of these two banners – the banner of the prince of darkness or the banner of Jesus Christ.

But to appeal to any kind of might in favor of the right, is to step on which side of the contest? It is instantly to put ourselves on the side of might as against right. And that is the wrong side and that puts us on the wrong side, whatever our profession may be.

But to hold steadfastly to the principle of right as against might, right with the might within itself, to win – that is the side of divinity.

> God will inspire his loyal and true children with his Spirit. The Holy Spirit is the representative of God and will be the mighty working agent in our world to bind the loyal and true into bundles for the Lord's garner. Satan is also with intense activity gathering together in bundles his tares from among the wheat.
>
> The teaching of every true ambassador for Christ is a most solemn, serious matter now. We are engaged in a warfare which will never close until the final decision is made for all eternity. Let every disciple of Jesus be reminded that we "wrestle not against flesh and blood, but against principalities, against powers, against the rulers of the darkness of this world, against spiritual wickedness in high places." O, there are eternal interests involved in this conflict, and there must be no surface work, no cheap experience, to meet this issue. "The Lord knoweth how to deliver the godly out of temptation, and to reserve the unjust unto the day of judgment to be punished… Whereas angels, which are greater in power and might, bring not railing accusation against them before the Lord."

Here is the principle, you see, that we have no reproach, no railing accusation, to bring against anybody, or against any opposition anybody may make. We trust the truth which we preach. The power is in the thing, not in us. It is not only its own defense but it is our defense too. And we do not have to defend it by condemning others.

The Lord would have every human intelligence in His service withhold all severe accusations and railings. We are instructed to walk with wisdom toward them that are without. Leave with God the work of condemning and judging.

It is all the same story: the truth itself is to be its own defense; the right itself is to be its own support, *and ours too.*

> Christ invites us, "Come unto me, all ye that labor and are heavy laden, and I will give you rest. Take my yoke upon you, and learn of me; for I am meek and lowly in heart: and ye shall find rest unto your souls." Every one who heeds this invitation will yoke up with Christ. We are to manifest at all times and in all places the meekness and lowliness of Christ. Then the Lord will stand by his messengers, and will make them his mouthpieces, and he who is mouthpiece for God will never put into the lips of human beings words which the Majesty of heaven would not utter when contending with the devil. Our only safety is in receiving divine inspiration from heaven. This alone can qualify men to be co-laborers with Christ.

Now we will study a little further along that line, in our study of the principle. The power of might as against right, we found in the previous lesson, had taken possession of this world by deceiving and bringing under his power the one into whose possession this world and the dominion of it had been put. Now the Lord, the God of heaven, did not propose to use any of the power of might, any kind of force, to take that dominion out of Satan's hands, even though it be true that he unjustly held it. There would have been no injustice in so taking it back. But that is not God's way of working; that is what we are studying.

I will say this here and can think upon it to all eternity: The universe of God rests upon the principle of self-sacrifice. The support, the stay of the very universe itself, is the principle of sacrificing self to win; that is, to win by nonresistance – to win by the sheer principle of the power of right *in itself*. That is what holds the universe up. In that it consists. That is simply the gospel. It would be plain enough to say the gospel is that that holds up the universe, but the principle of the gospel is the principle of the sacrifice of Jesus Christ and of God denying Himself and giving Himself in Him.

So the Lord, in recovering this lost dominion, would not use any might that is not right in itself. Therefore, when He wanted to recover this whole dominion and all of mankind, He went at it in such a way that Satan himself and all of his partisans can never say that it was not fairly done.

Now it was lost by man and it is regained by Man. That is what we had in the second of Hebrews when we began this study:

> For unto the angels hath he not put in subjection the world to come, whereof we speak. But one in a certain place testified, saying, What is man, that thou art mindful of him? or the son of man, that thou visitest him? Thou madest him a little lower than the angels; thou crownest him with glory and honor, and didst set him over the works of thy hands: thou hast put all things in subjection under his feet. For in that he put all in subjection under him, he left nothing that is not put under him. But now we see not yet all things put under him. *But we see Jesus.*

We see Jesus in the place of the man and as the man. God has not put in subjection to the angels the world to come whereof we speak, but He has put it in subjection to man, and Jesus Christ is that Man.

There is the second Adam. So that I say, by man it was lost, and by Man it is regained. By Adam it was lost, and by Adam it is regained. The Adam who regains it does so, *not* from the place at which the first Adam stood when he lost it but from the place which the first Adam's descendants had reached in degeneracy under the influence and power of sin at the time when He entered upon the field to contest the right of Satan.

I mean, when He entered upon the field in the open, bodily contest. Practically, He entered upon the field before the universe was made, and since man's sin He entered upon it also, but He had not taken flesh and entered upon the actual contest until He came into the world in human flesh. The Lord Jesus entered upon the open field in contest with Satan, in human flesh, at the point which human flesh had reached in degeneracy at the moment when He was born into the world. There, in the weakness of human nature as it was in the world when He came into the flesh, He fought the battle.

Human nature will never be any weaker, the world will never be any worse in itself, human nature will never reach any lower condition in itself, than it had reached when Jesus Christ came into the world. The only means by which human nature will be any worse is that the same stage of iniquity will be professing Christianity. Now a man may be just nothing but wickedness, as the world was when Christ was born into the world, yet if he makes no profession of Christianity, if he does not make any profession of the principles of the gospel, God can reach that man in his lost condition by the gospel and save him through it.

But let that man profess the gospel in his wickedness and use the profession of the gospel only as a form, as a cloak to cover his wickedness, then he takes out of the hand of God the only means the Lord has of saving man and perverts it to the support of his own iniquity. And that makes him worse in this respect in that he has cut himself off from salvation by taking God's means of salvation and making it a cloak for his iniquities and the support of his wickedness. In himself, in the flesh, his own practical fleshly wickedness is not any greater: only now he is a hypocrite as well as wicked. The world in the last days will not be any worse *in itself* than it was when Christ was born into the world. The only way in which it will be worse is that in having a form of godliness, but denying the power thereof it uses the profession of Christianity to cover its ungodliness and so perverts God's only means of salvation as to destroy itself against all remedy.

Jesus Christ came into the world in that weakest stage of human flesh and in that flesh as a man He fought the battle with Satan.

Thus Satan himself can never find any fault with the way of salvation as being in any sense unfair. Satan deceived and overcame man, as the man stood in the glory and image of God with all the blessing and the power and the goodness of God on his side.

Now when this second Adam comes into human flesh right at the point to which Satan had brought the whole race by sin and there in all this weakness enters upon the contest, Satan can never say that that is not fair. He can never say, "You have taken an unfair advantage. You have come here with too strong a panoply about you, with too many safeguards, for it to be a fair contest." He cannot do it, for there stood Christ in the very weakness of the flesh to which Satan himself had brought man. Christ came in the very weakness which Satan had brought upon the race; and in that weakness says, "Here we are for the conflict." And our Brother won it! He won it! Thank the Lord!, and glory to His name!

Now another view or another phase of the same view: You remember in the Week of Prayer readings one of them was on the subject of loyalty to God and the passage in Job was considered relative to the sons of God which came before the Lord, and Satan came also among them.

The thought was presented that these sons of God were those from the other worlds – the different parts of the universe – corresponding to what Adam was as he stood at the head of this world when the world was made and put under his power and given to him as his dominion. The Scripture says Adam was the son of God. Now when Satan came into this world and took the dominion by taking under his power the head of this dominion, he then stood in the place in this world where Adam should have stood. Therefore, when the sons of God from the other worlds came to present themselves before the Lord, Satan came also among them and presented himself before the Lord, as the representative of this world, which is under his dominion. I simply present this to call your attention to the thought for further study.

Now from Satan's dominion here, ever since he obtained it, God has been calling from this world people to Himself. Ever since the day that Satan obtained control of this world and God said, "I will put enmity between thee and the woman and between thy seed and her seed," God has been calling people from the ranks of Satan unto Himself and into His dominion. And many had been coming all the time. But all the time Satan had been making the charge that that was not fair. He was arguing, "These are *my* rightful conquest and you are leading them off to you. What have you done that, by right, you can do that, when I gained it here?" Thus he was always contesting the right of God to do this and was also accusing all those whom God called out of this world unto Himself. He was accusing them before God day and night. He declared, "These are my property. They are my rightful subjects. They are laden with sin and are altogether wicked. Yet you call them out and justify them and hold them before the universe, and propose to hold them up before the universe as though they had been good all the time. That is not fair. They are sinners; they are wicked. They are just like the rest of us over here." Thus he is the accuser of the brethren, accusing before God day and night every one who had turned from his authority unto God's.

Now Jesus came into the world to demonstrate that He had the right to do all this and that it was fair. And He came at the point of weakness which we considered awhile ago and entered upon the contest with Satan to recover, by right, the headship of this lost dominion. Now notice: Satan had gained, *not by right,* but by *might* as against right, the headship of this dominion from the first Adam to whom it was rightfully given. The second Adam comes, *not* by might as against right, but by *right* against might and regains the headship of this world and all the dominion of it. Therefore, when He was raised from the dead, He was raised up to the headship of all principality and power and might and dominion, not only of this world but also of that which is to come.

Now turn to the twelfth chapter of Revelation. There is the passage from which is derived all this that I have been saying. When Christ was born into the world, the vision opens and there stood Satan ready to devour Christ as soon as He should be born. Seventh verse:

> There was war in heaven: Michael and his angels fought against the dragon; and the dragon fought and his angels.

Now the ninth verse:

> And the great dragon was cast out, that old serpent, called the devil and Satan, which deceiveth the whole world: he was cast out into the earth, and his angels were cast out with him. And I heard a loud voice saying in heaven, Now is come salvation, and strength, and the kingdom of our God, and the power of his Christ: for the accuser of our brethren is cast down, which accused them before our God day and night.

Now the word "accuser" there signifies in the Greek, "he who accuses another in a court" – that would correspond in our country to a prosecuting attorney. The German translation gives the same idea exactly. Our word "accuser" does not give it so clearly, because one man may accuse another falsely and tell lies about him and backbite as thousands of people do. That is following the same principle of Satan, of course, but that is not the thought here. Here this accuser is one who comes as a prosecuting attorney into a court. You see the situation: Here was Satan, who had this dominion, and God was calling and receiving those who would turn to Him from the power of Satan, but Satan claimed the right to all these subject. Now he would enter into the court of God and there as a prosecuting attorney he would prosecute all these, his subjects, as slave-holders used to do under the Fugitive Slave Law in the United States. He would prosecute all these in that court and demand that they should be given up once more to his authority and that it was not in justice or out of right that they should be taken thus away.

And, too, there was room for him to present that argument with an apparent shadow of right to it, because the contest had not yet been carried on, the battle had not been fought and the victory won so completely that his argument and his right as a prosecuting attorney should be annihilated. Now it is true that the promise was certain and the victory was certain and the promise of God secure but still it was yet to be tested in an open conflict in the flesh. So that when Christ came in the flesh there was just as much temptation upon Him through the power of Satan as though there never had been any promise of redemption. Or shall we say that much? Shall we say that when Christ did come in the flesh, there was as much temptation for Him to meet and it was as real a temptation as though no promise had ever been made of redemption? Assuredly. If not, then He was guarded against temptation and the conflict was not real but more imaginary than real.

He came into the world to demonstrate the unrighteousness of that argument that Satan was presenting in the courts of God, as the prosecuting attorney from this country. That is the thought; it is legal all the way through. Jesus came here into Satan's territory and took human nature at the point to which Satan himself had brought it. In this human nature He met Satan on his own ground and against all his own power defeated him merely by the power of trusting in right itself as against might. He exercised no shadow of right [sic] Himself to do anything of Himself, to protect or help Himself. He trusted completely and fully in that divine power of right as against might and all that it can bring. And He conquered and thus became by right the head of this dominion again and of all who will be redeemed from it and of the redemption of the dominion itself.

And now that word also in the Greek which says that the accuser of our brethren "is cast down," conveys the idea of a prosecuting attorney who comes into court but he has no case any more. He is repudiated. He has no place for argument. Why? Because now we have an Advocate in the court, Jesus Christ the righteous. Yes. Thank the Lord!

In the court, before Jesus Christ came in the flesh, there was the accuser of the brethren a prosecuting attorney, pleading his legal rights to the subjects of his dominion, as they were leaving his dominion, and going over to the other. He could present that argument with the appearance of a shadow of right, because his dominion, his authority, had not yet been positively contested. But Christ came and did contest it righteously and fairly at every step of the way and so fairly that Satan himself cannot bring any charge of unfairness against it. And having won it, now Christ takes the place in court, not as a prosecuting attorney, but as an Advocate. And when He comes into court as Advocate by right, the other one, the accuser, the prosecuting attorney, is repudiated; he is shut out; he has no case at all against those whom he would accuse. That is good; that is good.

"These things write I unto you, that ye sin not. and if any man sin," there may be the accuser still. He may enter his plea as a prosecuting attorney, but now "we have an advocate with the Father, Jesus Christ the righteous" and by His standing in court, that prosecuting attorney is repudiated, put out, and cast down. That is the story, and I am glad of it. That is the value of our Advocate in the court. He shuts out the prosecuting attorney and takes away his case so that he has no place in court at all. Thank the Lord!

Now we come to another point. It is in answer to a query that has arisen in the minds of some upon the point that was made the other night, that the Lord Jesus in heaven will never be *in all respects* as He was before. The query is this: There stands the scripture – we read it that night – we took the text upon that, "Father, glorify thou me with thine own self with the glory which I had with thee before the world was." That will be done. That glory which He had before the world was, is His now, and will be His to all eternity. And so you look in the Bulletin, pages 331, 332, and you will see the Testimony which I read upon the humiliation of Christ. He who was born in the form of God took the form of man. "In the flesh he was all the while as God, but he did not appear as God." "He divested himself of the form of God, and in its stead took the form and fashion of man." "The glories of the form of God, He for awhile relinquished."

Note the difference: The *glories* of the form of God He *for awhile* relinquished. But the *form* of God itself, He to all eternity relinquished. That is the contrast that is in the

Scriptures and in that contrast that is here. Being in the form of God, He took the form of man. Then, on page 382 of the Bulletin we read again from the Testimony this word: "Bearing *our human form* before the Father's throne and *through eternal ages.*" Do you see? The difference is not in the *glory*. It is in the *form* upon which the glory rests and through which it is manifested and through which it is reflected.

Now there is something else in that that comes right along with the thought. He was in the form of God – He left that, He emptied Himself and the French version is translated "He annihilated himself," and it is none too strong for as to *the form* which He bore, He annihilated Himself and in that form He will never again appear. "Our *human* form" He bears "before the Father's throne and through eternal ages." And the glory of the form of God which He had when He was in the form of God – that glory He brings to our human form. "The glory which thou gavest me, I have given thee." He has given the glory of God everlastingly to us, to the human form, to human flesh.

Instead of Christ's being lowered, we are exalted. Instead of divinity's being lowered or lessened, humanity is exalted and glorified. Instead of bringing Him down to all eternity *to where we are,* it lifts us to all eternity to where He is. Instead of robbing Him of His glory and putting Him where we are, who have none, He laid aside this glory for a season and became ourselves and took our form forever in order that He in this form and we in Him shall be exalted to the glory which He had before the world was.

Now there is a little more in that yet. In what form was the contest carried on with Satan? In our human form, in my form, in my nature, in your nature. For how much of God's universe was that contest carried on? How much was involved in it? The whole of it. Then in this world and in our flesh and form there was carried on the contest, there was fought the battle and there was gained the victory that involves the whole universe. In this contest the whole universe was involved, one way or the other, whichever way it should have turned.

Therefore, to carry out God's eternal purpose, He had to come into this world and to take our form and nature, because in this world and in our form and nature is where that purpose was contested and where it all centered. He who was one with God emptied Himself and took our form and nature and fought the battle in this form and nature and the battle was won in this form and nature. To what form and nature belongs the victory? To our form and nature belongs the victory. In the nature of things, it is to our form and nature in Jesus Christ and joined with Jesus Christ that the victory belongs. So you see that this contest, this victory, not only carries us in the universe to where Adam was, nor only to where He would have been, but to where Jesus Christ, by divine right, is. O, it is wonderful. That is so. and the best of all is that *it is true.*

We too often lose sight of the glory of this in looking only at the misfortune of the entrance of sin. It was a misfortune, it is true, that sin should enter the universe at all.

And in that sense it was a misfortune that sin struck this world so that the battle had to be fought in this world for the universe. But having struck this world and involved this world, it involved you and me, so that here, in our nature, had to be fought the contest for the universe, and we can thank God that the victory is won and that we have a share in this victory for the universe. Therefore, it is not altogether a misfortune, you see, because God is able to turn our greatest misfortunes into the grandest victories. It would have been the greatest misfortune for us *if there were no redemption*. But when God puts His hand to a thing, He turns our greatest misfortunes into the grandest victories. And this greatest misfortune to the universe, God turns to the grandest victory for the universe. O, He makes it turn to the absolute and eternal triumph of the universe!

Christ did empty Himself of the form of God and take our human form. He did empty Himself of the nature of God and take our human nature. And in so doing He brought divinity to humanity. In so doing He caused humanity to conquer Satan and sin. Against all Satan's power, Christ won the victory in our human nature, and therefore He says not only, "Father, glorify thou *me* with thine own self with the glory which I had with thee before the world was," but He says, further, "The glory which thou gavest me *I have given them.*" Instead of bringing Him to all eternity to where we were, it takes us to all eternity to where He is.

"Thanks be unto God for His unspeakable gift." We have an Advocate in the heavenly court, who, by every conceivable right, stands there as our Advocate and shuts out the prosecuting attorney that would accuse us before God day and night. He wins our cases, because He *has* won them. And now being in the form of God, He emptied Himself and took the form of a servant. "And being found in fashion as a man, he humbled himself and became obedient unto death, even the death of the cross. Wherefore God also hath highly exalted Him [and He has exalted *us* in Him], and given Him a name which is above every name: that at the name of Jesus every knee should bow, of things in heaven, and things in earth, and things under the earth; and that every tongue should confess that Jesus Christ is Lord, to the glory of God the Father."

We delight to bow our knees to Him now, in that day we shall rejoice to do it also, in His glory. But whether one does it now or not, in that day when Jesus Christ is crowned with His triumphal crown before the universe and for the universe, then every knee, from Lucifer unto the last man that has rejected Him, will also bow and will confess that Jesus Christ is Lord, and they will do it to the glory of God the Father. And in that day every tongue in the universe will confess the divinity of the truth and the everlasting righteousness of the principle of right as against *might*.

Sermon 24

March 5, 1895

THE text for tonight is in Acts 10:28: "And he said unto them, Ye know how that it is an unlawful thing for a man that is a Jew to keep company or come unto one of another nation."

The Interlinear Greek that I have here, shows that this was spoken really stronger than our translation gives it. "He said to them, Ye know how unlawful it is for a man, a Jew, to unite himself, or come near, to one of another race." Not simply, Ye know that it is an unlawful thing; but, 'Ye know *how* unlawful it is" to do so.

Now was it unlawful? Was it unlawful for a Jew to keep company or associate with one of another race? The Jews regarded it as being unlawful, but was it unlawful? The Jews were God's people. They had professed to be His people for ages. By this time they should have learned that whatever God said and *that alone* was lawful, and that nothing that anybody else should say had any force of law, and therefore could never properly be spoken of as lawful and consequently any violation of it could never be spoken of as unlawful. They should have learned that, but instead of learning it they learned the opposite of it, and so entirely opposite was it that what men said was counted really as more binding than what God Himself said. Men's commandments, men's customs, and men's ways made void the word of God itself, even as Jesus said. "Ye have made the commandment of God of none effect by your tradition."

Now Christ in His work which He did in the world and which He has done in Himself for all who are in Him, was just the reverse of that whole order of things. He turned the matter so as to bring men to see that what man or any collection of men may say cannot be spoken of as lawful and has no place in the Christian category as lawful or the disregard of it as unlawful. But what God alone says, that alone is lawful, and not to do what He says, that alone is unlawful.

Now this is the principle that we are going to examine in a study or two – maybe more – and this is the principle we need to examine now, because we have come to the borders of the time and shall soon be fully into the time when the world will be bound as entirely under men's commandments and men's traditions and men's prejudices which make void the law of God, as those people were when Christ came into the world. And therefore as certainly as our allegiance shall be to Him, as it must be, so certainly we will be drawn so close to what God says that that alone will be our whole rule and definition of conduct. That alone will be our guide, and that in Christ, as it is lived in Christ and wrought out in Him.

And when that shall be so with the world wedded to forms and ceremonies and traditions by which they make void the law of God, they will deal with those who do concerning their traditions as Christ did concerning the others, as they did in that day with Him. Therefore, it was never God's purpose that it should be counted unlawful to associate with people of other nations, and if the Jews had remained faithful to God, it would never have been counted by anyone of them unlawful to associate or have anything to do with one of another nation. They had come to this position by a direct shutting of their eyes and a turning of their backs upon the Lord's dealings and God's teaching from the beginning and all the way down.

Just look a moment at the position of the Jews as set forth by Peter in the text which was the expression of the whole idea of the Jewish nation. In their estimation all the nations were shut away from God and had no place at all with Him. Yet all the way along, the Lord had been constantly showing them that this was not so at all.

In the days of Jonah and the glory of the kingdom of Assyria, before the kingdom of Babylon had come into history at all – away back there God called one of His people – Jonah – to go to that heathen nation and tell them of the doom that was hanging over them and the destruction that was to come, if by means of the warning they might repent and escape the ruin. He said to the Lord, There is no use for me to do that, because thou art a gracious God and repenteth thee of the evil, and if I go over there and tell them what you have told me to tell them and if they repent of the evil and turn from their wickedness, you will not destroy the city. What then is the use of my going on that journey to tell them that the city will be destroyed? You will not do it if they turn from their evil ways.

But the Lord insisted that he should go to Nineveh. But he, still holding to his views, started off to Joppa to go to Tarshish. The Lord brought him back, and by that time he was convinced that he would better go to Nineveh. He went to Nineveh and entered the city – three days' journey – preaching, "Yet forty days and Nineveh shall be overthrown." Word came to the king of Nineveh and he sent word to all the people to turn from their evil ways, put on sackcloth and ashes, and cause even the animals to fast, and to have the people cry mightily unto God. The Lord heard their cry, accepted their repentance, and saved the city. Jonah went out and sat on a height before the city to see whether God was going to destroy it, and He did not destroy it, and then Jonah didn't like it at all. He said, Now that is just what I told you before I started. I told you that if I came here and told them what you told me to tell them, they would repent of the evil and you would forgive them and not destroy their city and it came out that way, and I would better have stayed at home.

> And God saw their works, that they turned from their evil ways; and God repented of the evil that he said that he would do unto them, and he did it not. But it displeased Jonah exceedingly, and he was very angry. And he prayed unto the Lord, and said, I pray thee, O Lord, was not this my saying, when I was yet in my country? Therefore, I fled before unto Tarshish.
>
> For I knew that thou art a gracious God, and merciful, slow to anger, and of great kindness, and repentest thee of the evil. Therefore, now, O Lord, take, I beseech thee, my life from me; for it is better for me to die than to live. Then said the Lord, Doest thou well to be angry? Jonah 3:10; 4:1-4.

Then it tells how Jonah went out and sat on the east side of the city and there made a booth and sat under it until he might see what would become of the city. And the Lord prepared a gourd, and it withered and Jonah got very angry about that and prayed again that he might die.

> And God said to Jonah, Doest thou well to be angry for the gourd? And he said, I do well to be angry, even unto death. Then said the Lord, Thou hast had pity on the gourd, for the which thou hast not labored, neither madest it grow; which came up in a night, and perished in a night: and should not I spare Nineveh, that great city, wherein are more than six score thousand persons that cannot discern between their right hand and their left hand; and also much cattle?

Well, it is supposed that Jonah himself learned this lesson finally. and further, this was recorded and it was kept as one of the holy books in the hands of the people from which they were taught. And they should have learned the lesson which it taught, that the Lord had a care for other nations and that He wanted His people to care for other nations.

Jonah knew and said that he knew that "thou art a gracious God and merciful, slow to anger, and of great kindness and repentest thee of the evil." Knowing that, he should have been that much more ready to go to those people and preach to them the Lord's message that they might repent and be delivered. But in spite of that book which they had, in spite of that lesson which it positively taught, from that day forward they went directly opposite to it. They thought that God cared not for the heathen except as they became as the Jews, and the Saviour told those who thought that way that the proselyte they had compassed "sea and land to make" was "twofold more the child of hell" than themselves. It was so.

After that they went on in their crooked course, away from the true idea of God respecting them and the nations around and became so self-inclusive, so shut up within themselves and so evil as to be worse than the heathen around them. Then the Lord scattered them among all the nations around them and they were obliged to associate with other people; they had to do it. And yet Peter says: "Ye know how unlawful it is for a man, a Jew, to unite himself or come near to one of another race" – with men that were uncircumcised. In the eleventh chapter, the brethren at Jerusalem charged him, "Thou wentest in to men uncircumcised and didst eat with them."

Daniel and his three brethren had eaten at a heathen king's table and with heathen day in and day out for years, and God was with them all the time and made Daniel one of the great prophets, and He delivered the three from the fiery furnace. Now what was that recorded for and put in their hands for as one of the books which they were constantly to study? You can see that it was simply to teach them directly the opposite of what they were saying and doing.

More than this: Turn to the book of Daniel, fourth chapter:

> Nebuchadnezzar the king, unto all people, nations, and languages, that dwell in all the earth. Peace be multiplied unto you. I thought it good to show the signs and wonders that the high God hath wrought toward me. How great are his signs! And how mighty are his wonders! His kingdom is an everlasting kingdom, and his dominion is from generation to generation.

That is Nebuchadnezzar preaching to all nations, kindreds, and languages the truth as to the true God and how good He is and how great His wonders are. They had this in their hands. They had this in their own records, that God had given Nebuchadnezzar a dream and had given Daniel the interpretation of the dream for the king and that by this means God had brought Nebuchadnezzar to this place where he sends forth a proclamation to all nations and languages telling how good the true God is, how great He is, and how good it is to trust Him. Look at the last verses of that chapter. Nebuchadnezzar has told his experience; how he had offended against God and was driven out and the Lord brought him back in His own good time:

> At the same time my reason returned unto me; and for the glory of my kingdom, mine honor and brightness returned unto me; and my counselors and my lords sought unto me; and I was established in my kingdom, and excellent majesty was added unto me. Now I Nebuchadnezzar praise and extol and honor the King of heaven, all whose works are truth, and his ways judgment: and those that walk in pride he is able to abase.

There was a lesson, then, constantly before them, by which the Lord was trying to teach them that all these notions of theirs were directly the opposite of the truth. He was teaching them that He was ready to reach the heathen and wanted to reach them, and that He had separated Israel from among the nations that they might know more of Him and tell it to all nations. And if they had stood in the place where God wanted them to stand from the beginning, no such task as this would ever have fallen to a heathen king, for the people of God themselves would have proclaimed His glory to all the nations. But when they shut themselves away from God and in that shut themselves away from the nations, then God had to use the heads of these heathen nations to bring the knowledge of Himself to all the nations.

Look at the sixth chapter also. There is the instance of Darius and the persecution of Daniel and his deliverance.

Let us read the decree of Darius in the twenty-fifth verse:

> Then King Darius wrote unto all people, nations, and languages, that dwell in all the earth; Peace be multiplied unto you. I make a decree, That in every dominion of my kingdom men tremble and fear before the God of Daniel; for he is the living God, and steadfast forever, and his kingdom that which shall not be destroyed, and his dominion shall be even unto the end. He delivereth and rescueth, and he worketh signs and wonders in heaven and in earth, who hath delivered Daniel from the power of the lion.

There again the knowledge of the true God is made known to all peoples, nations, and languages by the word of one who to the Jews was an outcast, utterly forsaken, and repudiated of God. But there it stood in their own language, in their own hands, year after year, and it was ever teaching them the opposite of the things that they were teaching and doing.

One more instance, related in the first chapter of Ezra, we will read in connection with the last two verses of the last chapter of 2 Chronicles:

> Now in the first year of Cyrus king of Persia, that the word of the Lord spoken by the mouth of Jeremiah might be accomplished, the Lord stirred up the spirit of Cyrus king of Persia, that he made a proclamation through all his kingdom, and put it also in writing, saying, Thus saith Cyrus king of Persia, All the kingdoms of the earth hath the Lord God of heaven given me; and he hath charged me to build him a house in Jerusalem, which is in Judah. who is there among you of all his people? The Lord his God be with him, and let him go up.

Now we need the first three verses of Ezra 1:

> Now in the first year of Cyrus king of Persia, that the word of the Lord by the mouth of Jeremiah might be fulfilled, the Lord stirred up the spirit of Cyrus king of Persia, that he made a proclamation throughout all his kingdom, and put it also in writing, saying, Thus saith Cyrus king of Persia, the Lord God of heaven hath given me all the kingdoms of the earth; and he hath charged me to build him a house at Jerusalem, which is in Judah. Who is there among you of all his people? His God be with him, and let him go up to Jerusalem, which is in Judah, and build the house of the Lord God of Israel (he is the God), which is in Jerusalem." Ezra 1:1-3.

That is enough. There are plenty more instances in the Scriptures to show how entirely the Jews had shut their eyes and turned their backs upon the Lord in order to reach the point where they stood when Christ came into the world and where He found them.

Now it is true that in the books of Moses, when the Lord brought the children of Israel out of Egypt and in other Scriptures, it was told them that they were to be separate from all the nations. That is so. It also told them how that separation was to be accomplished.

In the thirty-third chapter of Exodus, in verses 14-16, this is told:

> My presence shall go with thee, and I will give thee rest. And he said unto him, If thy presence go not with me, carry us not up hence. For wherein shall it be known here that I and thy people have found grace in thy sight? Is it not in that thou goest with us? So shall we be separated, I and thy people, from all the people that are upon the face of the earth.

So shall we be separated. How is that "so"? *Thou goest with us.*

Thus they were taught the means by which they should be separated from all the people.

Now, if they had courted His presence and also had His presence with them, they would have been separated from all the people indeed, in heart and in life. Yet they would have associated with all people upon the earth. They would have gone to all people and nations and languages and tongues, telling them of the glories of God and His goodness and power, just as Nebuchadnezzar and Darius and Cyrus did.

But, instead, they did not court His presence and have Him ever with them to sanctify them – for to be separated from the world unto the Lord is to be sanctified. If they had had the Lord's presence to sanctify them, they could have gone anywhere on the earth and still they would have been separate from all the people.

But not having that which would separate them and which alone could separate them, then if they were to be separated from the world, how was it to be done? How alone could it be done? We know they did not have Him whose presence alone could do it. The only way, then, by which it could be done at all was for them to do it themselves according to their own ideas of what God meant when He said they should be separated. But a man's ideas of what God means – we know how near the truth they are, for He says, "My thoughts are not your thoughts, neither are your ways my ways, saith the Lord. For as the heavens are higher than the earth, so are my ways higher than your ways, and my thoughts than your thoughts." Isa. 55:8,9. So it is as far away from the truth as a man can get.

Having not the presence of God to do it for them and in them, they took it upon themselves and they had to take it upon themselves to do it if they were to be separated at all.

But when they did not have the presence of God, which alone could do it, then their attempting to separate themselves, what alone could it do? Think, now, what alone could that end in? It could not possibly end in anything else than the building up, the enlarging, the great, overtopping growth, of *self*. Self-confidence, self-pride, self-exaltation, self-righteousness – every kind of selfishness – more and more increasing itself upon itself, and all in the vain effort of themselves to fulfill the Scriptures by which the Lord had said they should be separated from all the nations.

And when by this means they had reached the point at which they were worse than the heathen around about, the Lord had to take them out of the land and scatter them abroad among all the nations. And when they were so scattered, they were more separated from the nations than they had ever been at any time from the day that they came into the land. Because when they were scattered among the nations, they sought the Lord as they had not in their own land, they trusted Him as they had not in their own land; they found Him as they had not appreciated Him there, and His presence with them separated them from the heathen when they were scattered *among* the heathen.

In all these ways the Lord was trying to teach them that they were not going the right way, to teach them the true way in which it alone could be done. Yet in spite of it all they took the wrong way to do it. Yet more than this: Not having the presence of God, which would give meaning to all that He had said and all that He had appointed for them to observe in their services and worship, this self-seeking way led them to pervert the Lord's appointed forms of worship. It led them to make these a means of salvation. And when they had practiced these, they held that that made them righteous, and the other nations not having the, therefore they could not be righteous. They held that God had given these forms for this purpose and had not prescribed them to other nations and therefore God thought more of them than He did of anybody else.

Thus they not only put themselves in the place of God but all the services which He had appointed for another purpose they perverted and turned altogether to the service of self-righteousness and self-exaltation and self-exclusion.

If they had had His presence as He appointed for them, all these appointed forms would have had to them a divine meaning and a divine life in every phase of service which God had appointed. Then they would have found Jesus Christ Himself and His living presence and converting power and that would have given living energy to every form that was appointed and to all these symbols that were before them. Then all these things would have had to them a living interest, for they would have represented only a present Christ – Christ present with them.

Thus the lack of the presence of Christ in the life by a converted heart led altogether to the enlarging of themselves in the place of God and to making all the divine forms which God had appointed, *only* forms and outward ceremonies, by which they expected to obtain life. It lead to the putting of these things in the place of Christ as the way of salvation.

Now I think we have just about time enough in the present hour to read some passages respecting what they had made of all this in the time of Christ. I ask you to think carefully on this.

I have here some of the advance chapters of the new "Life of Christ," by Mrs. E. G. White, and a great deal is said upon this subject which we have studied so far tonight, and I thought it would be valuable to all our ministers and workers especially and to all people also, if we could bring these statements together here, where we can have them in the Bulletin before our eyes to use in the time to which we are coming.

I have therefore brought this down and will now read passages without making any particular comment upon them tonight, but the next lesson will follow the consequence of this and all these points are necessary to our further study.

As the "Life of Christ" is not yet printed but still in manuscript, I cannot, of course, give references.

> The Jewish leaders refrained from associating with any class but their own. They held themselves aloof, not only from the Gentiles but from the majority of their own people, seeking neither to benefit them nor to win their friendship. Their teachings led the Jews of all classes to separate themselves from the rest of the world in manner which tended to make them self-righteous, egotistical and intolerant. This rigorous seclusion and bigotry of the Pharisees had narrowed their influence and created a prejudice which the Saviour desired to remove, that the influence of his mission might be felt upon all. This was the purpose of Jesus in attending this marriage feast, *to begin the work of breaking down* the exclusiveness which existed with the Jewish leaders and to open the way for their freer mingling with the common people.
>
> The Jews had so far fallen from the ancient teachings of Jehovah as to hold that they would be righteous in the sight of God, and receive the fulfillment of his promises, if they strictly kept the letter of the law given them by Moses. The zeal with which they followed the teachings of the elders gave them an air of great piety. Not content with performing those services which God had specified to them through Moses, they were continually reaching for rigid and difficult duties. They measured their holiness by the number and multitude of their ceremonies, while their hearts were filled with hypocrisy, pride, and avarice. While they professed to be the only righteous nation on the earth, the curse of God was upon them for their iniquities.
>
> They had received unsanctified and confused interpretations of the law given them by Moses; they had added tradition to tradition; they had restricted freedom of thought and action, until the commandments, ordinances, and services of God were lost in a ceaseless round of meaningless rites and ceremonies. Their religion was *a yoke of bondage.* They were in continual dread lest they should become defiled. Dwelling constantly upon these matters had dwarfed their minds and narrowed the orbit of their lives.

Now a question:

What was the root of that whole thing? Self, self, self-ishness all the time!

> Jesus began the work of reformation by bringing himself into close sympathy with humanity. He was a Jew and he designed to leave a perfect pattern of one who was a Jew inwardly. While he showed the greatest reverence for the law of God and taught obedience to its precepts, he rebuked the Pharisees for their pretentious piety and endeavored to free the people from the senseless exactions that bound them.
>
> Jesus rebuked intemperance, self-indulgence, and folly; yet he was social in his nature. He accepted invitations to dine with the learned and noble, as well as with the poor and afflicted. On these occasions his conversation was elevating and instructive.

> He gave no license to scenes of dissipation and revelry, but innocent happiness was pleasing to him. A Jewish marriage was a solemn and impressive occasion, the joy of which was not displeasing to the Son of man. The miracle at the feast pointed directly toward *the breaking down* of the prejudices of the Jews. The disciples of Jesus learned a lesson of sympathy and humility from it.

In another chapter, on Nicodemus and his visit to Christ, we have this:

> At that time the Israelites had come to regard the sacrificial service as having in itself virtue to atone for sin and thus had lost sight of Christ to whom it pointed. God would teach them that all their services were as valueless, in themselves, as that serpent of brass, but were, like that, to lead their minds to Christ, the great sin-offering.

Of the woman of Samaria at the well:

> Sinful though she was, this woman was in a more favorable condition to become an heir of Christ's kingdom than were those of the Jews who made exalted professions of piety, yet trusted for their salvation to the observance of outward forms and ceremonies. They felt that they needed no Saviour and no teacher; but this poor woman longed to be released from the burden of sin...
>
> Jesus was a Jew, yet he mingled freely with the Samaritans, setting at naught the customs and bigotry of his nation. He had already begun to break down the partition wall between Jew and Gentile, and to preach salvation to the world. At the very beginning of his ministry, he openly rebuked the superficial morality and ostentatious piety of the Jews...
>
> In the temple at Jerusalem there was a partition wall, separating the outer court from the apartment of the temple itself. Gentiles were permitted to enter the outer court, but it was lawful only for the Jews to penetrate to the inner enclosure. Had a Samaritan passed this boundary, the temple would have been desecrated, and his life would have paid the penalty of its pollution. But Jesus, who was virtually the originator and foundation of the temple, drew the Gentiles to him by the ties of human sympathy and association, while his divine grace and power brought to them the salvation which the Jews refused to accept.
>
> The stay of Jesus at Samaria was not alone to bring light to the souls that listened so eagerly to his words. It was also for the instruction of his disciples. Sincere as they were in their attachment to Christ, they were still under the influence of their earlier teachings – of Jewish bigotry and narrowness. They had felt that in order to prove themselves loyal to their nationality, it was incumbent upon them to cherish enmity toward the Samaritans.

Do you see the connection between that and the previous quotation? Talking with the woman of Samaria, Jesus had begun to break down the partition wall between the Jews and other nations; and the disciples thought it was incumbent upon them to cherish "enmity." Do you see that when Jesus wanted to break down that partition wall, He did it by abolishing the enmity?

They were filled with wonder at the conduct of Jesus, who was breaking down the wall of separation between the Jews and the Samaritans and openly setting aside the teachings of the scribes and Pharisees. The disciples could not refuse to follow the example of their Master, yet their feelings protested at every step. The impulsive Peter and even the loving John could hardly submit to this new order of things. They scarcely endure the thought that they were to labor for such a class as those Samaritans.

During the two days while they shared the Lord's ministry in Samaria, fidelity to Christ kept their prejudices under control. They would not have failed to show reverence to him; but in heart they were unreconciled; yet it was a lesson essential for them to learn. As disciples and ambassadors of Christ, their old feelings of pride, contempt, and hatred must give place to love, pity, and sympathy. Their hearts must be thrown open to all, who, like themselves, were in need of love and kindly, patient teaching…

Jesus did not come into the world to lessen the dignity of the law, but to exalt it. The Jews had perverted it by their prejudices and misconceptions. Their meaningless exactions and requirements had become a by-word among the people of other nations. Especially was the Sabbath hedged in by all manner of senseless restrictions. It could not then be called a delight, the holy of the Lord, honorable; for the scribes and the Pharisees had made its observance a galling yoke. A Jew was not allowed to light a fire upon the Sabbath nor even to light a candle upon that day. The views of the people were so narrow that they had become *slaves to their own useless* regulations. As a consequence, they were dependent upon the Gentiles for many services which their rules forbade them to do for themselves.

They did not reflect that if these necessary duties of life were sinful, those who employed others to do them were fully as guilty as if they had done the act themselves. They thought that salvation was restricted to the Jews, and that the condition of all others being entirely hopeless, could neither be improved nor made worse. But God has given no commandment which cannot be consistently kept by all. His laws sanction no unreasonable usage nor selfish restrictions…

The simplicity of his teachings attracted the multitudes who were not interested in the lifeless harangues of the rabbis. Skeptical and world-loving themselves, these teachers spoke with hesitancy when they attempted to explain the word of God, as if its teaching might be interpreted to mean one thing or exactly the opposite… Both by his words and by his works of mercy and benevolence, he was breaking the oppressive power of the old traditions and man-made commandments, and in their stead presenting the love of God in its exhaustless fullness…

The Sabbath, instead of being the blessing it was designed to be, had become a curse through the added requirements of the Jews. Jesus wished to rid it of these encumbrances…

The Old Testament Scriptures, which they professed to believe, stated plainly every detail of Christ's ministry… But the minds of the Jews had become dwarfed and narrowed by their unjust prejudices and unreasoning bigotry… The Jewish leaders were filled with spiritual pride. Their desire for the glorification of self manifested itself even in the service of the sanctuary. They loved the highest greeting in the marketplaces and were gratified with the sound of their titles on the lips of men. As real piety declined, they became more jealous for their traditions and ceremonies.

We will have one more quotation:

> These admonitions had effect, and as repeated calamities and persecutions came upon them from their heathen enemies, the Jews returned to the strict observance of all the outward forms enjoined by the sacred law. Not satisfied with this, they made burdensome additions to these ceremonies. Their pride and bigotry led to the narrowed interpretation of the requirements of God. As time passed, they gradually hedged themselves in with the traditions and customs of their ancestors, till they regarded the requirements originating from them as possessing all the sanctity of the original law. This confidence in themselves and their own regulations, with its attendant prejudices against all other nations, caused them to resist the Spirit of God, which would have corrected their errors, and thus it separated them still farther from them.
>
> In the days of Christ these exactions and restrictions had become so wearisome that Jesus declared: "They bind heavy burdens and grievous to be borne, and lay them on men's shoulders." Their false standard of duty, their superficial tests of piety and holiness, obscured the real and positive requirements of God. In the rigid performance of outward ceremonies, heart-service was neglected.

Sermon 25

March 5, 1895

THAT we may have the subject, or rather the particular point of it, clearly before us, I will repeat a few expressions in the passages with which we closed last night's lesson:

> At the marriage of Cana, Jesus began the work of breaking down the exclusiveness which existed among the Jews.

> Their religion was a yoke of bondage.

> The miracle at the feast pointed directly toward the breaking down of the prejudices of the Jews.

> Jesus was a Jew, yet he mingled freely with the Samaritans, setting at naught the customs and bigotry of his nation. He had already begun to break down the partition wall between Jew and Gentile and to preach salvation to the world.

Of the disciples at Samaria it says:

> They had felt that in order to prove themselves loyal to their nationality, it was incumbent upon them to cherish enmity toward the Samaritans. They were filled with wonder at the conduct of Jesus, who was breaking down the wall of separation between the Jew and Samaritans and openly setting aside the teachings of the scribes and Pharisees. . . During the two days while they shared the Lord's ministry in Samaria, fidelity to Christ kept their prejudices under control. They would not fail to show reverence to him; but in heart they were unreconciled. Yet it was a lesson essential for them to learn.
>
> Jesus did not come into the world to lessen the dignity of the law but to exalt it. The Jews had perverted it by their prejudices and misconceptions. Their meaningless exactions and requirements had become a by-word among the people of other nations. Especially was the Sabbath hedged in by all manner of senseless restrictions. It could not then be called a delight, the holy of the Lord, and honorable, for the scribes and Pharisees had made its observance a galling yoke. A Jew was not allowed to light a fire upon the Sabbath, or even to light a candle on that day. The views of the people were so narrow that they had become slaves to their own useless regulations.
>
> The Sabbath, instead of being the blessing it was designed to be, had become a curse through the added requirements of the Jews.

> The Jewish leaders were filled with spiritual pride. Their desire for the glorification of self manifested itself even in the service of the sanctuary.
>
> As repeated calamities and persecutions came upon them from their heathen enemies, the Jews returned to the strict observance of all the *outward forms* enjoined by the sacred law. Not satisfied with this, they made burdensome additions to these ceremonies. Their pride and bigotry led them to the narrowest interpretation of the requirements of God. As time passed, they gradually hedged themselves in with the traditions and customs of their ancestors, till they regarded the requirements originating from men as possessing all the sanctity of the original law. This confidence in themselves and their own regulations, with its attendant prejudices against all other nations, caused them to resist the Spirit of God.

Now a few more short quotations:

> In all His lessons, Jesus presented to men the worthlessness of merely ceremonial obedience… The Jews had become earthly and they did not discern spiritual things. And so when Christ set before them the very truths that were the soul of all their service, they, looking only at the external, accused him of seeking to overthrow it… He knew that they would use these works of mercy as strong arguments to affect the minds of the masses, who had all their lives been bound by the Jewish restrictions and exactions. Nevertheless, He was not prevented by this knowledge from breaking down the senseless wall of superstition that barricaded the Sabbath.
>
> His act of mercy did honor to the day, while those who complained of Him were by their many useless rites and ceremonies themselves dishonoring the Sabbath.
>
> The Jews accused Christ of trampling upon the Sabbath, when He was only seeking to restore it to its original character. The interpretations given to the law by the rabbis, all their minute and burdensome exactions, were turning away the Sabbath from its true object, and giving to the world a false conception of the divine law and of the character of God. Their teachings virtually represented God as giving laws which it was impossible for the Jews, much less for any other people, to obey. Thus in their earthliness, separated from God in spirit while professedly serving him, they were doing just the work that Satan desired them to do – taking a course to impeach the character of God and cause the people to view him as a tyrant; to think that the observance of the Sabbath, as God required it, made man hard-hearted, unsympathetic and cruel.
>
> Christ did not come to set aside what the patriarchs and prophets had spoken; for He Himself had spoken through these representative men. He Himself was the originator of all truth. Every jewel of truth came from Christ. But those priceless gems had been placed in false settings. Their precious light had been made to minister to error. Men had taken them to adorn tradition and superstition. Jesus came to take them out of the false settings of error and to put them into the framework of truth.

What could more fully express the thought of the "form of godliness without the power," than do those people and their services in that day? Can you imagine? Every one of these statements is simply another way of stating the truth that they had a "form of godliness without the power." Now we are in a time in the world's history when that same thing – "the form of godliness without the power" – is cursing the world. And the same truths that were written in the Scriptures against that thing *in that day*, are the light and truth of Jesus Christ against that thing *in this day*. The same thing that saved the people from the form of godliness without the power in that day – the same thing that saved the people from the senseless round of forms and ceremonies, of ceremonialism and the ceremonial law, which is simply ceremonialism – the same thing that saved the people from that in that day is to save the people from that in this day.

What saved the people from this thing in that day? "He is our peace, who hath made both one, and hath broken down the middle wall of partition between us; having abolished in his flesh the enmity, even the law of commandments contained in ordinances [contained in ceremonies, contained in forms without the power]; for to make in himself of twain one new man, so making peace." It was an absolute surrender to Jesus Christ of every interest in the universe and thus finding in Him the destruction of the enmity in that day that saved people from ceremonialism, and nothing short of that will save people from ceremonialism in this day. Nothing short of that will save Seventh-day Adventists from ceremonialism and from following the same track of the old ceremonial law.

[*Professor Prescott:* I would like to know if we get the thought clearly, because it all seems to center right there. Are we to understand that thought, that Jesus Christ did at that time really abolish not simply that ceremonial law, but that He did a great deal more than that; that He abolished ceremonial law everywhere and always, no matter how expressed.]

Yes, sir; that is the point exactly.

We will come at that in another way. What was the cause of all this? What was the cause of that separation between Jews and Gentiles? What was the cause of their having a form of godliness without the power? What was the matter with the disciples with Jesus at Samaria? Enmity. Enmity, sin, self. But enmity, sin, self, *is all self*. It was the putting of self in the place of God that not only perverted God's appointed services and forms of service, but added to these a whole mountain of ceremonies and additions of their own, as we have read. What was the object of it all? What were they doing all this for? To be saved; to be righteous. But there is no form or ceremony that even God Himself appointed that can save a man. That is where they missed it. That is where thousands of people still miss it. And that is the "form of godliness without the power" and that is ceremonialism, and if you will receive it, that is the ceremonial law, that was abolished by the abolishing in His flesh of the enmity and so breaking down the middle wall of partition.

It was the lack of the presence of Jesus Christ in the heart by living faith that caused them to put their trust in these other things for salvation. Not having Christ for salvation, they did these other things, that by these they might be righteous. And thus they took the means which God had appointed for other purposes – they took the ten commandments, they took circumcision, they took sacrifices and offerings, and burnt offerings, and offerings for sin. They took all these, which God had given for another purpose and used them to obtain salvation by them, used them to obtain righteousness by the performance of them.

But they could not find righteousness by the doing of these things. They could not find peace. They could not find satisfaction of heart, because it is not there. It was all of themselves. Therefore, in order to be certain of it, they had to draw out these things which God had appointed and the things which He had said into ten thousand hair-splitting and casuistic distinctions so that they could be so certain to come directly to the exact line that they could be sure that they had the righteousness they were after. Yet all these things did not satisfy. They did not find peace of heart yet, and consequently they had to add a great many things of their own invention and all these were their own invention anyhow. It was all ceremonialism from beginning to end, and it was all done that by these they might become righteous.

But nothing but faith in Jesus Christ can make a man righteous, and nothing but that can keep him righteous. But they did not have that. They did not have Him abiding in the heart by living faith so that His virtue itself would shine out in the life through these things that God had appointed, which Christ Himself appointed for that purpose. And therefore when they attempted by these things – simply the expression of their own selves working out thus – to obtain righteousness they missed real righteousness, and thus that *self* in them built up this that the testimony calls so often "middle wall," "a wall of partition," "senseless exactions," "hedging about" – using the expressions over and over again in almost every conceivable way.

What caused that wall to be built up? Did God build it up? No. Who did build it up? They themselves. And what was it in them that was the foundation of the whole thing? Self. And that self, as we have studied so often, is enmity against God. It is not subject to the law of God, neither indeed can be. And we read that the disciples "felt that in order to prove themselves loyal to their nationality, it was incumbent upon them to cherish enmity toward the Samaritans." To acquire it? O, no, but to cherish it, to hold fast to it.

Then as that enmity, which is simply the expression of self, is that which caused all this wall to be built up, when Jesus Christ wanted to break down the wall and destroy it, annihilate it, what was the only way effectually to do it? Is it the way to break down a wall, a building, to begin at the top, and take off a layer of stone here and another there or to begin in the middle and take out a stone here and another there? No.

If you want to break down the whole thing, you take away the foundation and the thing is done. The wall is destroyed; the building is torn down.

Jesus Christ wanted to abolish that whole thing. He wanted to break down that wall absolutely and leave it in ruins. Therefore, He struck at the foundation of the thing. And as the spring, the foundation, of the whole senseless wall was this enmity, Jesus broke down the wall by "having abolished in Himself in his flesh *the enmity*" and along with that "even the law of commandments contained in ordinances."

[*Mr. Gilbert:* That word "righteousness" itself has become perverted, so that now the meaning of the word "righteousness" is a man that gives alms; that is, a man that gives a certain amount of alms has obtained righteousness.]

Brother Gilbert, who is a born Hebrew, and a Jew indeed now, says that that same idea still prevails among the Jews. That the word "righteousness" and the idea of righteousness itself, has been perverted and that now it means simply that which they receive as the consequence of that which they have done, in giving alms, or whatsoever it may be, in the way of right doing. It is all righteousness by works, righteousness by deeds, *without Jesus Christ*. It is all ceremonialism. and it is just as bad for Seventh-day Adventists today as for any Pharisee in Judea eighteen hundred years ago. All have it who have the profession of Christianity without Christ, who have the form of godliness without the power. It is only the fruit of the enmity, that is all.

Whenever, wherever, you have the enmity, you will have ceremonialism. You cannot get rid of the thing without getting rid of the enmity, and as certainly as that enmity is there, it will show itself. In some places it shows itself in what is called a color line. In other places it shows itself in national lines – a German line, a Scandinavian line, etc., etc. – so that when fully developed, there would be as many lines in the Third Angel's Message as there are nationalities and colors on the earth. but in Jesus Christ no such thing can ever be. And if we are not in Jesus Christ, we are not in the Third Angel's Message.

In Jesus Christ the enmity is abolished and consequently in Him there is no color line. There is no Scandinavian line. There is no German line, nor any other kind of line. There is neither white nor black, neither Germans, nor French nor Scandinavians nor English nor anything else but just Jesus Christ manifest upon all and through all and in you all. But we will never find that out – even Seventh-day Adventists will not certainly find it out – until that enmity is abolished by a living faith in Jesus Christ that surrenders the will to Him, to receive that living, divine image of which we heard in Brother Prescott's lesson tonight. That is where we are, and this is present truth today and for Seventh-day Adventists as well as for other people.

O, it is still the same cry, "Come out of her, my people, that ye be not partakers of her sins and that ye receive not of her plagues, for her sins have reached unto heaven, and God hath remembered her iniquities."

Here is another word right upon that. It tells the whole story on both sides:

> At that time the Israelites had come to regard the sacrificial service as having in itself virtue to atone for sin, and thus had lost sight of Christ, to whom it pointed. God would teach them that all their services were as valueless in themselves as that serpent of brass, but were, like that, to lead their minds to Christ, the great sin-offering. Whether for the healing of their wounds or the pardon of sin, they could do nothing for themselves but to manifest their faith in the remedy which God had provided. They were to look and live.

Now see the *present* truth:

> There are thousands in the Christian age who have fallen into an error similar to that of the Jewish people. They feel that they must depend on their obedience to the law of God to recommend them to his favor.

Who have fallen into that similar error with the Jews? Those who feel that they must depend upon their obedience to the law of God to recommend them to His favor. Is that you? Have you ever seen anybody like that any time in your life? Thank God that He has broken down the middle wall of partition.

> The nature and importance of faith have been lost sight of, and this is why it is so hard for many to believe in Christ as their personal Saviour.

It is that same determined drawing of that enmity that will not let go until it is crucified, dead, and buried with Jesus Christ – it is that that draws and draws. "O, I must do something. I am not good enough for God to like me. He is not good enough to care for one as bad as I. I must do something to pave the way. I must do something to break down the barriers that are between Him and me and make myself good enough so that He can take favorable notice of me. And therefore I must and I will keep the ten commandments. I will sign a contract and enter into a bargain to do it." And then you try to do it as hard as you can.

Here is a passage from Farrar's *Life of Paul*, page 40, that I will read:

> The Jewish priests had imagined and had directed that if a man did not feel inclined to do this or that, he should force himself to do it by a direct vow.

Precisely. And so if you do not have it in your heart to do it, why, you must do it anyhow, because it is right and you want to do right, and so we will sign the covenant, take a vow, "O, well, now I have signed the covenant, of course I must do it. I have no pleasure in it. It is a galling yoke. But I have signed the covenant and I must keep the pledge of course." That is ceremonialism. And it springs from the enmity which is self.

> There are thousands in the Christian age who have fallen into an error similar to that of the Jewish people. They feel that they must depend on their obedience to the law of God to recommend them to his favor. The nature and importance of faith have been lost sight of and this is why it is so hard for many to believe in Christ as their personal Saviour.

And when Christ is believed in as your personal Saviour, when true faith lives and reigns in your heart, you need no vows to force yourself to do this or that. No, but the heart will always gladly exclaim, "I delight to do thy will, O my God, yea thy law is within my heart."

But Jesus Christ has broken down that middle wall of partition. He has abolished in His flesh that enmity that would fight against faith and keep man away from God. He has abolished that enmity that would keep man away from Christ, that would put something else, everything else, in place of Christ and that causes men to depend upon anything and everything under the sun for salvation – everything but Jesus Christ – whereas, nothing, nothing under the sun, in heaven or earth, nor anywhere else, can save, but simply Jesus Christ and faith in Him. That is the only thing that saves. And if any one expects to be saved by what he calls faith in Christ *and something else,* it is still the same old ceremonialism. It is still the working of the enmity. Men are not saved by faith in Christ *and something else.*

Some may think that is too strong and perhaps I would better read the rest of that sentence:

> When they are bidden to look to Jesus by faith and believe that without any good works of their own He saves them, solely through the merits of his atoning sacrifice, many are ready to doubt the question. They exclaim with Nicodemus, "How can these things be?"
>
> Yet nothing is more plainly taught in the Scriptures. Than Christ "there is none other name under heaven given among men, whereby we must be saved." Acts 4:12. Man has nothing to present as an atonement, nothing to render to divine justice, on which the law has not a claim. If he were able to obey the law perfectly from this time forward, this could not atone for past transgression.
>
> The law claims from man entire obedience through the whole period of his life. Hence it is impossible for him by future obedience to atone for even one sin. And without the grace of Christ to renew the heart, we cannot render obedience to the law of God. Our hearts are by nature evil and how, then, can they bring forth that which is good? "Who can bring a clean thing out of an unclean? Not one." Job 14:4. All that man can do without Christ is polluted with selfishness and sin. Therefore, he who is trying to reach heaven by his own works in keeping the law, is attempting an impossibility. True, man cannot be saved in disobedience, but his works should not be of himself. Christ must work in him to will and to do of His own good pleasure. If man could save himself by his own works, he might have something in himself in which to rejoice. But it is only through the grace of Christ that we can receive power to perform a righteous act.
>
> Many err in thinking that repentance is of such value as to atone for sin, but this cannot be. Repentance can in no sense be accepted as atonement. And, furthermore, even repentance cannot possibly be exercised without the influence of the Spirit of God. Grace must be imparted, the atoning sacrifice must avail for man, before he can repent.
>
> The apostle Peter declared concerning Christ, "Him hath God exalted with his right hand to be a Prince and a Saviour, for to give repentance to Israel, and forgiveness of sins."

> Acts 5:31. Repentance comes from Christ just as truly as does pardon. The sinner cannot take the first step in repentance without the help of Christ. Those whom God pardons, He first makes penitent.

Nothing, nothing, nothing but faith in Jesus Christ and in Him alone – nothing but *that* saves the soul and nothing but that keeps the soul saved.

The great trouble with the Jews from the beginning unto the end was in having the Lord so far away that even the things which God had given to signify His perfect *nearness* were taken and used as the tokens of His being *far away*. Sacrifices, offerings, the tabernacle, the temple, its services, all those things were used by the Jewish teachers and the great mass of the people in such a way that all that these services meant to them was that they pointed to Christ away off yonder somewhere. It was understood that these things meant the Messiah, but it was the Messiah afar off. And they must make themselves good so as to bring Him near, and these things were looked to as having virtue in themselves and so as able to give righteousness.

I am not certain whether Seventh-day Adventists have got beyond the idea of those things back there, that they signified Christ afar off. I am not saying now that Seventh-day Adventists think that Christ is now away off. But I am afraid that they have not gotten away from the idea, when they look at the sanctuary and its services, the sacrifices and offerings, that that was intended to teach them of Christ away off yonder somewhere. So it is said that these things all pointed to Christ. These things did all point to Christ, that is the truth. But it was Christ near and not far off. God intended that all these things should point to Christ living in their hearts, not 1800 years away, not as far off as heaven is from the earth, but pointing to Christ in their living experience from day to day. When we get fast hold of that idea and then study the sanctuary, the sacrifices, the offerings, in short, the gospel as it is in Leviticus – then we shall see that that meant Christ a living, present Saviour to them day by day and we shall also see that He is that to us today also.

There is gospel, there is Christian experience, for us today in Leviticus, in Deuteronomy, in Genesis, in Exodus, and in the whole Bible. But when we read those passages and say that those sacrifices and offerings all pointed to Christ afar off from the Jews and expect that the Jews were to look through these services away off yonder to Christ to come sometime – when we read those scriptures and look at them that way, then we are reading those scriptures precisely as the Jews did and we are standing precisely where they did at that time in those scriptures.

That will never do. No. We are not to look at the sanctuary with its furniture and paraphernalia standing as God placed it, with God's presence therein, and think that signified to them that they were to learn by it that God dwelt only in the sanctuary in heaven. When we look at it that way, then we are ready to think that that is about as near as He is to us, because that is as near as we have had Him come to them. For if we look at it for them in that way, then if we had been there in their places, how would we have looked at it for ourselves? In the same way, and this shows that had we been there we would have been precisely as they were.

The tendency is, even with us, to read of the sanctuary and its services and God dwelling in the sanctuary and the text, "Make me a sanctuary that I may dwell among them," and say, Yes, God dwelt among them in the sanctuary and that pointed to the sanctuary that is in heaven and the time is coming when God will dwell with His people again, for He says of the new earth, "Behold the tabernacle of God is with men, and God will dwell with them and be their God and they shall be his people." So when the new earth comes God is going to dwell with His people again. *But where is God now?* That is what we want to know. What matters it to me that He is going to dwell with His people on the new earth? What matters all this, if He does not dwell with me now? For if He cannot dwell with me now, it is certain that He never can dwell with me on the new earth nor anywhere else, for He has no chance. What I want to know and what every soul needs to know is, Does He dwell with me *now?* If we put Him away back yonder in the days of the Jews and then put Him away off on the new earth, what does that do for us now? How does that give Him to men now? In that way, how is He with us now? That is what we need constantly to study.

Now, you can see that there is a great deal more in that system of ceremonialism than simply a little passing thing that disturbed the Jews a little while and then vanished. For human nature is still and ever bothered with it as certainly as the devil lives, as certainly as the enmity is in the human heart. That mind which is not subject to the law of God, neither indeed can be – just as certainly as that is in the world and as long as it is in the world, just so long the world will be cursed with ceremonialism. And as long as there is any of that in my heart, I shall be in danger of being cursed with ceremonialism.

What we are to do is to find such deliverance in Jesus Christ, such absolute victory and exaltation at the right hand of God in heaven, *in Him,* that that enmity should be completely annihilated in us in Him. Then we shall be free from ceremonialism; then we shall be free from traditions and men's commandments, and men making themselves a conscience for us. Men say, "You must do this or you cannot be saved. You have got to do that or you cannot be saved." No, no. Believe in Jesus Christ or you cannot be saved. Have true faith in Jesus Christ and you are saved.

It is the same battle that was fought out in Paul's day and work. He was preaching Jesus Christ alone for salvation. But certain Pharisees "who believed" followed him around, saying "O, yes, it's all well enough to believe in Jesus Christ, but there is something else. You have got to be circumcised and keep the law of Moses or you cannot be saved." That contest lasted for years and against it all Paul fought all the way. He would not compromise a hair's breadth at any point. "If ye be circumcised, Christ shall profit you nothing." "Whosoever of you are justified by the law, ye are fallen from grace." Nothing, nothing but Christ and faith in Him! Well, they took it to the council at last, and there the Spirit of God decided that Christ and not ceremonialism is the way of salvation. That is the whole story. One was an attempt to fasten ceremonialism upon Christianity or rather in the place of Christianity; the other was the living principle of Jesus Christ by living faith, actuating the life and the heart of those who believe in Him.

There is a vast difference between ceremonialism and principle. Jesus Christ wants us to find Him so fully and so personally that the living principles of the truth of God, as they are in Jesus Christ, shall be our guide and that those living principles shining in the life of the man by the glory of Jesus Christ shall be our guide at every point, and we shall know what to do at the time. Then we do not need any resolutions or vows to force ourselves to do this, that, or the other. That is the difference between ceremonialism and the principle of the living presence of Christ in the heart. One is all formalism and outward service, without Christ; and the other is all in Christ and Christ all and in all.

Let us look again at the things the Jews were doing back there at the temple services, the sacrifices and the offerings that you may see this a little more fully yet. I know and so do you that the sanctuary, the temple, was a representation of the sanctuary which is in heaven, that the sacrifices were representations of the sacrifice of Jesus Christ and the priesthood and its service were representations of the priesthood of Christ. In all these things God would teach them and us too of Himself as He is revealed in Christ. There was a sanctuary first and there was the temple built in place of the sanctuary. There was the temple standing on Mount Zion in Jerusalem. And from that, God taught them that yonder is the true temple on Mount Zion in the heavenly Jerusalem. God dwelt in this temple on Mount Zion in Jerusalem, in Palestine, and by that He showed them that He dwelt yonder in the heavenly temple in Mount Zion, in the heavenly Jerusalem.

And He said also – and this was true in both places and from both sides –:

"Thus saith the high and lofty One that inhabiteth eternity, whose name is Holy; I dwell in the high and holy place." Anywhere else? "With him also that is of a contrite and humble spirit." When? We are reading away back yonder. When did He dwell "with him also that is of a contrite and humble spirit," as well as "in the high and holy place?" Did He do this seven hundred years before Christ, when Isaiah spoke? Yes. But did the Lord begin only *then* to dwell with him that is of a humble and contrite spirit, as well as in the high and holy place on Mount Zion? No.

A thousand years before Christ, when David spoke, did He do it then? Yes. But had He only begun it then? No. He always, eternally, dwells in both places – with the humble and contrite as well as on high.

Well, then, did not God, in that temple on the earth, teach them not only how He dwelt in that heavenly country, but how He dwelt in the temple of the heart also? Most assuredly.

There was the earthly Mount Zion right before their eyes, representative of the heavenly Zion, which God would have right before their eyes of faith. There upon Mt. Zion, the high and lofty place in the earthly Jerusalem, was the temple and God dwelling in the temple. And in this God would show that He dwelt not only there but also in the temple of the heart, the sanctuary of the soul, of Him that is of a contrite and humble spirit. And in putting His temple among sinful men and dwelling therein Himself, He was showing also how He would Himself dwell in the temple of Christ's body, among sinful men and in sinful flesh.

There too was a priesthood of the earthly temple on Mount Zion in Jerusalem. There was a priesthood of the sanctuary at Shiloh in the wilderness. That, it is true, represented the priesthood of Christ, but did that represent any priesthood of Christ before A. D. 1? Shall we say that that represented a priesthood of Christ that was afar off? No. That priesthood in Jerusalem, in the sanctuary in the wilderness, represented a priesthood that was already in existence after the order of Melchisedek? Thou *shalt* be a priest forever after the order of Melchisedek? No, No. "Thou *art* a priest forever after the order of Melchisedek." Was not Melchisedek a priest in the days of Abraham? and is not the priesthood of Christ forever after the order of Melchisedek?

Do you not see, then, that this whole system of services given to Israel was to teach them the presence of the Christ then and there for the present salvation of their souls and not for the salvation of their souls eighteen hundred years or two thousand years or four thousand years away? Surely, surely, it is so.

O, it has always been Satan's deception and has always been the working of his power to get men, all men, to think that Christ is as far away as it is possible to put Him. The farther away men put Christ, even those who profess to believe in Him, the better the devil is satisfied. And then He will stir up the enmity that is in the natural heart and set it to work in building up ceremonialism and putting this in the place of Christ.

There was also circumcision.

Was that a sign of something that was coming away off yonder? No. It was a sign of the righteousness of God which they obtained by faith and which was there present in them who believed and when they believed. It was that to Abraham, and God intended it to be that to every man. But instead of this they had taken it and made it a sign of righteousness by circumcision itself, by works itself. Thus they left Christ all out and put circumcision in His place. It was a sign of righteousness of faith.

They did not have faith and therefore they undertook to make it a sign of righteousness by some other means and thus it became only a sign of selfishness.

God gave them His law – the ten commandments. Was it that they might obtain righteousness by that? No, but that it might witness to the righteousness which they obtained by faith in Jesus Christ abiding in the heart. That is what the ten commandments were for, just as they are today.

So were not the sacrifices offered typical of Christ? Yes. But it was typical of Christ present by faith. Was not Christ right there? Was not Christ the Lamb slain from the foundation of the world? Was not Christ a gift of God there before the world was? Then when He called on men from Adam unto all – as long as the sacrifices were offered in that way – when He taught them to offer those sacrifices, what was that but teaching them that that was a token of their appreciation of the great sacrifice that God had already made for them, and of which they were enjoying the benefit by having that gift in the heart which was Jesus Christ?

Well, we need not go any farther. That is enough to illustrate it.

Is it not plain, then, that everything that God gave to them in that day was intended to teach them concerning the personal, living Saviour, personally present with them, if they had only received Him? And all they needed to do to receive Him was to believe in Him. The gospel was preached unto them. Heb. 4:2: "But the word preached did not profit them, not being mixed with faith in them that heard it." "Let us therefore fear, lest, a promise being left us of entering into his rest any of you should seem to come short of it." How did they come short of it? How? By not seeing Christ crucified present with themselves in the thing which they were doing.

Now when we read over those things and study them, the sanctuary, for instance, and see only so many boards, and so many sockets and so many curtains and all these in type of something up yonder in heaven and that all there is to it, and not see or know Christ in that in our own personal experience, wherein are we different from them? I do not say that is the way that it is done, but I say that if a person looks at it now in that way, then where is the difference between Him and the Jews of old? – There is none. Is Christ away off still? No. He is "not far from every one of us." What is "not far"? It does not say, He is not *very* far. No. It says, "He is *not far*." And as certainly as you get a definition of "not far," you have the word "near." He is near to everybody, to us, and He always has been. He was also near to them and He always was near. But by unbelief they could not see Him near.

And now, in all those services which He gave them, as well as those which He has given us, He wants us all to see the nearness of the living Christ dwelling in the heart and shining in the daily life. That is what He wants us all to see. And He wants us all to see it all. That is the way He wants us to look at it.

Now another thing:

What was it that caused all that? What was it that caused them to put Christ afar off and changed the sacred, living services of God into ceremonialism? It was the "enmity."

It was self, the enmity of self, that caused it all. And that self expressed itself in unbelief, because it is not subject to the law of God, neither indeed can be. That put a veil over their faces so that they could not see to the end of that which was before their eyes.

They could not "look to the end of that which is abolished." 2 Cor. 3:13. Not that this end was so far off that they could not see from where they were, clear down to the end of it; that is not the thought at all. But they could not see the object of it. They could not see what was the intent of it, with themselves, at that time. We are too ready to give to that expression the thought that here was something which pointed to something else away down yonder, and they could not see from there clear down to the end of it. But that is all wrong. No, those things which were before their eyes were intended to point to something right close to them, and that was Christ Himself personally present with them and within their hearts at that time. That was the end of it. That was the object, the aim, the purpose of it.

Therefore, through the enmity, this unbelief which produced formality blinded their eyes and put a veil over their faces so they could not see the meaning, the object, of that which was abolished. Of course not, and as long as that enmity is in the heart of a man even today, it produces unbelief there and it puts a veil over *his* face so that he cannot see to the end of these things that were abolished. He cannot see that the object of these things was the living presence of Christ in the temple of the heart day by day, as the service was going on. It all means Christ and He is not far, the object, the end, of all these things is right near, but they cannot see it. Why? Let us read now that passage in the third chapter of second Corinthians, beginning with the first verse:

> Do we begin again to commend ourselves? or need we, as some others, epistles of commendation to you or letters of commendation from you? Ye are our epistle written in our hearts, known and read of all men: forasmuch as ye are manifestly declared to be the epistle of Christ ministered by us, written not with ink, but with the Spirit of the living God; not in tables of the stone, but in fleshly tables of the heart. And such trust have we through Christ to God-ward: not that we are sufficient of ourselves to think anything as of ourselves; but our sufficiency is of God; who also hath made us able ministers of the new testament, not of the letter. . .

Letter of what? Of "the new testament." They had the letter of it, did they not? They had the letter of the new and the old both, but all they had was the letter, and was in the letter.

> Who also hath made us able ministers . . . not of the letter, but of the spirit: for the letter killeth.

What letter kills? Letter of what kills? Letter of the New Testament, as well as any other letter. Here is a book: There are some letters in it. Those are simply the forms which express ideas. Those letters are not the ideas, they are the forms that contain the ideas and convey those ideas to us. Those things back there were the letter, the forms, that contained the ideas, the spirit, and the grace of God. That is true, but in it all they saw only the letter. Did they get the idea, the grace, the spirit? No, they had only the form, the letter, even as we read in Romans 2:20: "Which hast the form of knowledge and of the truth." There is the law of God. Take it there as a man sees it in letters, that is the form – the perfect form, too – of knowledge and truth. Take it as it is in Jesus Christ, and we have the thing itself, the complete idea of it, and all the grace and the spirit of it.

That you may see this, I will read one of the finest expressions I have seen upon that subject: "The righteousness of the law was presented to the world in the character of Christ." In the letter of the law we have the form of it. As man looks at it and sees it as it is in tables of stone or on a leaf, he sees the form of knowledge and truth, but in Christ we have the perfect substance and idea itself. In the letter we have the perfect pattern, the perfect form, of knowledge and truth; yet it is only the form. In Christ we get the very substance and idea of knowledge and of truth expressed in the words, the letters, which are the form containing the truth. So then, while the letter killeth, "the spirit giveth life." Thank the Lord!

> But if the ministration of death, written and engraven in stones, was glorious, so that the children of Israel could not steadfastly behold the face of Moses for the glory of his countenance, which glory was to be done away, how shall not the ministration of the Spirit be rather glorious? And not as Moses, which put a veil over his face.

Why was it necessary that he should put a veil over his face? Was it to keep them from seeing it? Was it to prevent their looking to the end of it? No. It was because "their minds were blinded." Moses came down from the mount with his face radiant with the glory of God. But their sinfulness which was the consequence of their unbelief, which was the consequence of the enmity, caused them to be afraid of the bright, shining glory of God and they ran away. When Moses discovered why they did not come near, he put a veil over his face. And this veil was upon his face simply *because of the veil that was upon their hearts* through unbelief. Do you see?

They could not see the object of that glory upon Moses's face. Why? Because their minds were blinded. But were their minds blinded only then and at that time? No. "Until this day remaineth the same veil untaken away." Where? When? "In the reading of the Old Testament," the veil is still there.

But O when the heart "shall turn to the Lord, then the veil shall be taken away," because in Christ is abolished the enmity that created the unbelief.

> Their minds were blinded: for until this day remaineth the same veil untaken away in the reading of the Old Testament; which veil is done away in Christ. But even unto this day, when Moses is read, the veil is upon their heart. Nevertheless, when it shall turn to the Lord, the veil shall be taken away.

Upon how many hearts is the veil then? Upon every natural heart; for the mind of the natural heart is enmity against God, for it is not subject to the law of God, neither indeed can be. "Now the Lord is that Spirit, and where the Spirit of the Lord is, there is liberty." Where? O, in Him in whom we find the abolition of this enmity, in whom we find the breaking down of all this formalism, in whom we find the annihilation of all ceremonialism in whom we find life, the light, the bright, shining glory of Jesus Christ – in Him there is liberty. Now, in the Old Testament, in the services which He had appointed, in the rites and forms which He there gave, we shall see Christ; and in the performance of all that is appointed we shall see only the expression of the love of Christ that is in the heart already by faith.

2 Corinthians 3:18:

> We all, with open face beholding as in a glass the glory of the Lord, are changed into the same image from glory to glory, even as by the Spirit of the Lord.

I am glad that Jesus Christ has abolished the formality. He has cleared away, broken down, and left in ruins, that middle wall of partition that was between men and taken it out of the way, nailing it to His cross. When we in Him and with Him are nailed to the cross, then we find the enmity abolished, the wall broken down, and we are all one in Jesus Christ; Christ is all in all, and all this, in order that God may be all in all.

Sermon 26

April, 1895

We will begin the present lesson where we closed the former one – 2 Cor. 2. To begin with, I desire to refer to the special point I made upon the statement that "they could not look to *the end* of that which was abolished, and the idea of the end there not being the end of it but the object – the aim of it.

The Greek word *telos* signifies "*the fulfillment* or *completion of anything; i.e., its consummation, issue, result*, NOT its cessation or *termination* or *extremity*. The strict sense *telos* is not as *the ending of a past state* but *the arrival of a complete and perfect one.*"

Thus you see that the very idea in the text is that the *object* – the aim – of these types and ceremonies and ordinances that God gave, was hidden from their eyes so they could not see it. And the reason that it was hidden was because of the unbelief and hardness of their own hearts.

By unbelief the veil was upon their hearts so Moses put a veil over his face, hiding the glory of his face and thus representing the veil that was upon their hearts that caused them not to be able to look upon the brightness of the glory for fear.

Turn to 2 Corinthians 3. I will read in the German beginning with the third verse:

> That ye a letter of Christ are through our service prepared and written, not with ink, but with the Spirit of the living God; not in stony tables, but in fleshy tables of the hearts; but such confidence have we through Christ to God. Not that we capable are from ourselves (or of ourselves) somewhat to think as from ourselves, but that we capable are, is from God (that is, it is from God our capability comes) who also us capable has made, that ministry to carry – the New Testament – not the letter, but the Spirit; for the letter kills, but the Spirit makes alive.

Now the 7th verse:

> But as that ministry that through the letter killed, and in the stone is (literally built) inscribed, imaged glory had, so that the children of Israel could not look upon the face of Moses on account of the glory of his face, which there ceased; how shall not much more that ministry with the Spirit have glory.

If that that ceased had glory, how much more does that which remaineth have glory. If that had glory which through the letter killed, how much more will that have glory which through the Spirit gives life.

> For as that ministry that the condemnation preached had glory, much more has the ministry which the righteousness preached overflowing glory; for even that former part that was glorious is not to be estimated (or counted) glorious in comparison with the overflowing glory; for as that had glory that there ceased, much more will that have glory that abides.

Now we want to study for a moment what that ministration of death was.

The English reads, "The ministration of death written and graven in stones was glorious." The German, the ministration that through the letter killed – the ministration of the letter which was death, would be, literally, in harmony with ours. The ministration of the letter, which was death, was glorious. Now if we know what that ministration of death was, then we can go on with the rest of the text and read the whole story. That we may the better understand what is the ministration of death.

I will read again a few lines from the Testimony of Jesus.

> The Jewish leaders were filled with spiritual pride. Their desires for the glorification of self manifested itself even in the service of the sanctuary.

Then according to this what was their service of the sanctuary? What kind of ministration was it? It was a ministration of self, was it not? But what is self? It is of the enmity; it is sin. What is the end of it? Death. Then what was the ministration of death? What was the ministration of the letter of that thing without seeing what it meant? It was only death, there was no salvation in it. We will see that more fully as we go on.

> Thus in their earthliness, separated from God in spirit, while professedly serving him, they were doing just the work that Satan desired them to do.

In the sanctuary, in their offering the sacrifices whom were they serving? Satan. What was the ministration then? It could be nothing else than a ministration of death.

> They were doing just the work that Satan desired them to do, taking a course to impeach the character of God and cause the people to view him as a tyrant.

In their ministration, in their performance of the services, they were taking such a course and giving to the people the impression that God is a tyrant. And such ministry as that could be only a ministry of death – condemnation, the ministry of condemnation.

Here is an awful sentence:

> In presenting their sacrificial offerings in the temple, they were as actors in a play.

This is all from the Spirit of Prophecy. What was the worship then? What was the ministry?

> The rabbis, the priests, and rulers had ceased to look beyond that (the symbol) for the truth that was signified by their outward ceremonies.

They ministered only the outward ceremony, and they did that as actors in a play. They did that in such a way that it caused the people to view God as a tyrant. Then all that was a ministry – the condemnation of death.

> The gospel of Christ was prefigured in the sacrificial offerings and Levitical types.

Therefore, it was glorious; don't you see? In itself that thing was glorious, but they hid from themselves the glory by the veil that was upon their hearts. They did not see it or allow it to appear. Even that ministration of death was glorious, because in all that which they were doing there was signified the glory of the gospel of Christ – if only they had allowed the veil to be taken away from their eyes so they could see it and so that there could have been manifest the ministration of the Spirit and therefore of life. The ministration of death was glorious by virtue of the truth that was hidden in it – not glorious by virtue of their ministering it in that way. Their missing the Christ that was signified in it all, caused it to be to them a ministration of death. But yet, in itself, it was glorious in the truth that was hidden there, which they would not allow to appear.

> The gospel of Christ was prefigured in the sacrificial offerings and Levitical types. The prophets had high, holy, and lofty conceptions, and had hoped that they would see the spirituality of the doctrines among the people of their day; but one century after another had passed by and the prophets had died without seeing their expectations realized. The moral truth which they presented and which was so significant to the Jewish nation, to a large degree lost its sacredness in their eyes. As they lost sight of spiritual doctrine, they multiplied ceremonies. They did not reveal spiritual worship in purity, in goodness, in love for God and love for their fellow-men. They kept not the first four or the last six commandments, yet they increased their external requirements.

As Brother Gilbert said today, there were "four hundred and one requirements added to the fourth commandment alone."

> They knew not that One was among them who was prefigured in the temple service. They could not discern the Way, the Truth, and the Life.

They could not look to the end – they could not see the aim and object – of that which was abolished.

> They had gone into idolatry and worshiped external forms. They continually added to the tedious system of works in which they trusted for salvation.

Now I was glad that Brother Gilbert could give that talk here today, because I could see all the way through that that was the best possible preparation there could be for the lesson tonight. Those who were here saw from the few illustrations which he gave that there is even to this day a deep spiritual truth underneath these forms that the Jews are using at this time. The very truth and righteousness and life of Jesus Christ is beneath these forms yet, at the core of it, but all this is completely lost sight of and nothing is seen but the mere outward form and in this they trust for salvation.

The enmity that is in the natural heart causes their minds to be blinded to the end of that which has been abolished and which, if their hearts would turn to the Lord, they would clearly see was abolished. But we whose hearts have turned to the Lord must see these things now, else we shall fall into the like system of forms and ceremonies, even in observing the things that Christ has appointed.

When Brother Gilbert was telling of these things today, it seemed to me that it was a perfect preparation for this study, that we might see the reality of the truth in this third chapter of 2 Corinthians in regard to the thought of the ministration of death. That ministration was glorious on account of the truths therein contained, even though they were hidden, yet it had no glory in comparison with the glory that comes through living faith in Christ, who has broken down the wall, abolished the enmity, and set his people free with open face to behold as in a mirror the glory of the Lord to be changed into the same image from glory to glory even as by the Spirit of the Lord. The enmity of the carnal mind is the foundation of the whole wall, the middle wall of partition, of ceremonialism, that was built up and which was indeed the ceremonial law as it was in the day that Christ came. And in abolishing the enmity He broke down, annihilated, and keeps annihilated forever that wall for all who are in Him, because in Him alone it is done.

Now a word further. There was always a *true ceremonial law* apart from the law of God, and apart from the ceremonialism of the blind-hearted people of Israel. God appointed these very services, which they perverted into mere forms in order that the people through them might see Christ more fully revealed, that they might see God's personal presence day by day, and that thus they might appreciate the glorious salvation from sin – the transgression of the law of God. But not only did they pervert all these points of ceremonies which God had given for this blessed purpose, but they perverted the whole law of God itself into the same system of ceremonialism, so that it all suggested righteousness and salvation by *law* – all by *deeds,* by works, by ceremonies. Yet as all these things which the Lord appointed, when they had perverted them, could not satisfy the heart, they had to heap upon them mountains of their own inventions in order if possible to supply the lack and so be sure of salvation, but it was all only death. Thus in this, too, it was true that "the commandment which was ordained to life" they "found to be unto death."

So I say there was all the time a true ceremonial law and they would have had all the time a true ceremonial law if they had been faithful to God. And if they had been faithful, that true ceremonial law would have caused them to see Christ so everywhere present and so perfectly allied to them and living in them that when He came, the whole nation would have received Him gladly, because He would have seen Himself reflected in them as He is to do when He comes the second time. So there was the true ceremonial law which God appointed for that purpose in order that through these they might be brought to see the spirituality of the law of God, which is the character of Christ and His righteousness reflected and which is found in Him alone. These things were to help them to understand Christ, that they might see Him as the fulfillment and the glory and the actual expression of the ten commandments themselves and might find Him to be indeed the end, the object, and the aim of the whole of it – the ten commandments with the rest. But when their hearts turned away and their minds were blinded to these things, this caused them to turn everything into a form as will always be done where the enmity is.

The same evil thing runs through all. But, thank the Lord, there stands the blessed word that *when the heart shall turn to the Lord,* the veil shall be taken away and then they with open face will see the glory of the Lord. Isn't that then a direct commission from God to us to go to the Jewish people with blessed truth and the power of Christ? To show them that salvation in Christ is the end, object, and aim of all these things. O, let this be preached to all people, that if by any possible means the heart may turn to the Lord, the veil may be taken away, that all with open face may see the glory of the Lord.

But we can never go with that commission until that veil is taken away from our own hearts – until that ceremonialism is taken away from our lives. What would be the use of one who is steeped in ceremonialism going to those who are in it to get them saved from it? Therefore, God hath brought us this word at this time; He has "abolished in his flesh the enmity, even the law of commandments contained in ordinances," contained in ceremonies, in order to make in Himself of two one new man, so making peace. Then both Jews and ourselves have access through one Spirit unto the Father.

I do not know that we need to look at that side of the question any further, because we can illustrate the subject on this side of the cross. It is almost perfected right in the mystery of iniquity today, against which our work from this time forward is to be pitted as never before.

Now note:

When Christ had taken away all those forms and ceremonies, even those which He Himself had appointed, when He had met them in Himself – He was the end, the object, the aim of them – He left others on this side of the cross. He appointed the Lord's supper; He appointed baptism and the whole of the law of God still abides *as it is in Himself,* not as it is in the letter, because the enmity that is in a man's heart will turn that into the ministration of death today as well as it ever did. And man who is trying to seek life in keeping the ten commandments and teaching others to expect life by keeping the ten commandments that is even yet the ministration of death. It is a universal truth that Paul expressed when he was a Pharisee, a ceremonialist: "The commandment which was ordained to life, I found to be unto death."

On this side of the cross, Jesus appointed the Lord's supper, baptism, other things, the Sabbath with the rest. And *in Him* they all have deep and divine meaning. But what was it that caused the people away back yonder not to see Christ in those things and so to use them for the purposes of self-exaltation and self-glorification? That enmity that is not subject to the law of God, neither indeed can be; that desire of self to be glorified and magnified. Was there prophesied an exaltation of self, a magnifying, a glorification of self this side of the cross? Assuredly there was. There was to come "the man of sin, the son of perdition, who opposeth and *exalteth himself*." We know that self – the enmity – on the other side of the cross perverted God's ordinances into ceremonialism. What would self – the enmity – do on this side of the cross? It would do the same thing. It will always and everywhere do the same thing.

That enmity on this side of the cross manifested itself thus in those whose hearts were not turned to the Lord, in those who were not converted. And the idea in this word, "When it shall turn to the Lord," is that of conversion. It is not simply to turn around, but the idea, both in the German and in the Greek, is to turn to the Lord *in conversion*. Those whose hearts are not converted and who yet profess to be Christians have the form of godliness without the power; they have the profession without the thing. On this side of the cross there came in men who had a form of Christianity without the power; a profession, a name, without having the thing. And here were the ordinances which the Lord had appointed and which are to be used in Him. But these formalists, not having the salvation of Jesus Christ in themselves by living faith, not being in Him, expect salvation *in the forms* which they observe. Therefore, with the papacy, regeneration is *by baptism*. And regeneration being by baptism instead of by Christ, baptism becomes the essential of salvation. It is put in the place of Christ by the papacy, as really as ever circumcision was by the Jews. That is why it is that the priests must always be so prompt to reach the bedside even of a dying infant in order to make the sign of the cross and sprinkle the water so that the child may be regenerated and saved.

To make regeneration salvation by baptism, whether it be in one form or another, that is the enmity, it is ceremonialism. Indeed, on this side of the cross, it is the mystery of iniquity.

Of the Lord's supper Jesus said, "Ye do show the Lord's death till he come." "Do this in remembrance of me." But the papacy makes it the very Christ Himself. They make it the very Christ Himself, and in taking it expect to take *Him,* not "take *it* in remembrance" of Him. And thus in taking it they expect to be saved.

Christ taught that His presence should go with His people still. "I am with you alway, even unto the end of the world." This is by the Holy Ghost and *by faith* the Holy Ghost is received. But the papacy, not having faith, and so not having the Holy Ghost and therefore not having the presence of Christ to go with them, turns the Lord's supper from a memorial of Him to the Lord Himself and when the water is taken and swallowed, then the Lord is in them.

That is the papal system concerning these ordinances. And as for commandments, why, not having the life of the Lord Jesus, which is in itself an expression of all the commandments, they must heap upon themselves a multitude of rules and hair-splitting distinctions of their own of every sort and every kind. Just as it was with Phariseeism before Christ – precisely so.

Here is an expression written by Farrar in his *Life of Paul*, page 26, concerning the system of Phariseeism when Paul was there and Christ came into the world. It is word for word descriptive of the papacy in every phase of it as it is:

> When we speak of Phariseeism, we mean obedience petrified into formalism, religion degraded into ritual, morals cankered by casuistry; we mean the triumph and perpetuity of all the worst and weakest elements in religious party spirit.

In the system of "morals" is the very citadel of casuistry. Here, too, genuine morals are cankered into the very elements of death by casuistry.

That tells the story of the working of the enmity – the story of formalism and ceremonialism – on both sides of the cross of Christ. Why, then, was not that on the other side of the cross the papacy as well as that on this? This is why: On the other side of the cross Christ had not appeared in His fullness as He is and as He did appear in the world. There were ceremonies – forms – given that were intended to teach the people of Him, and they perverted these forms. Then in the fullness of time, Christ Himself came and the papacy perverts Christ Himself into formalism.

I will repeat it. Before Christ came, Phariseeism, this enmity, this self-exaltation, perverted *the forms* by which God would teach them of Christ until He should come in His fullness. But the papacy takes Christ after He has come in His fullness and perverts *Him,* as well as all the forms which He has appointed; perverts the truth that is manifested in Him in His fullness and turns the whole of it into ceremonialism and formalism still.

But Christ, as He was manifested in the world, is the Mystery of God. God was manifest in the flesh, and Christ was the ministration of the mystery of God in its fullness. He is the ministration of righteousness which is overwhelmingly glorious. Now, when all this was wholly perverted by this enmity which came from Satan and which is sin itself enmity against God and is not subject to the law of God neither indeed can be –

when that mystery of God is thus perverted, that is also a mystery, but what mystery alone can it be? Only the mystery of iniquity. That is why it is the mystery of iniquity this side of the cross and not so great the other side. It is the same spirit working all the time, but not developed to the same degree. It is ever and always the ministration of death.

Now let us spend the few minutes we have remaining on Christianity, genuine *Christianity*.

Gal. 5:6. I will read, beginning with the first verse, and come up to the sixth. "Stand fast therefore in the liberty wherewith Christ hath made us free, and be not entangled again with the yoke of bondage." We have read what that yoke of bondage was – all this whole mass of slavery to which they had bound themselves, these forms and ceremonies were a yoke of bondage. Christ has set us free from all that in the second of Colossians, the second of Ephesians and in the third chapter of 2 Corinthians. Christ has set us free from formalism and ceremonialism, from going by rules and resolutions and all these things but ever to be guided, actuated, and inspired by the living principle of the life of Jesus Christ itself. The difference between a principle and a rule is that the principle has in it the very life of Christ itself, while a rule is *a form* that a man makes in which he will express *his idea* of the principle and which he would fasten not only upon himself but upon everybody and make them do just like himself. That is the difference between Christianity and ceremonialism. That is the difference between principle and rule. The one is life and freedom; the other is bondage and death.

Here is a passage in Gospel Workers, page 319, which I will read. It is concerning Christ. "There is not a monastic order upon the earth from which He [Christ] would not have been excluded for overstepping the prescribed rules." Exactly. You cannot bind the *life of God* by rules and of all things you cannot bind it by man-made rules. He wants us therefore to be so imbued with the life of Jesus Christ *itself* and the life of Christ *Himself* that the living life of Jesus Christ and the principles of the truth of God shall shine and work in the life in order that the life of Christ shall still be manifest in human flesh. That is where God has brought us in Him. And we are brought to this place in Him by being by faith ourselves crucified with Him and dead with Him and buried with Him and made alive with Him and waked up with Him and raised up with Him and seated with Him in the heavenly existence where He sits at the right hand of God in glory.

The Bible is not a book of rules; it is a book of *principles*. The statements in the Bible are not rules at all. They are the principles of the life of Jesus Christ, the principles of the life of God. They are Jesus Christ in that shape. The work of Christianity is to take Christ from that shape and by the overshadowing of the Spirit of God transform Jesus Christ from that shape once more into this human shape. When Christ was in the world, He was the Bible, the Word of God, in human shape. The Word of God before He came into the world was in that Bible shape. Now He has gone back to God in heaven, and He says, "Christ in you, the hope of glory." Christ fully formed in you; Christ all in all of you; all there is of you shall be Christ within.

Now, then, when Christ is full-formed in you and me, the Word of God, Jesus Christ, will once more be transformed from that Bible shape into human shape. Then God will put His seal upon it and glorify it as He has glorified that human shape already, which was the transformation, or the *transfiguration,* of the word of God. That is the point to which Christ has raised us in this series of studies. O, shall we sit together with Him in the heavenly existence to which He has raised us?

> Stand fast therefore in the liberty wherewith Christ hath made us free, and be not entangled again with the yoke of bondage. Behold, I Paul say unto you, that if ye be circumcised, Christ shall profit you nothing. For I testify again to every man that is circumcised, that he is a debtor to do the whole law.

And what were those people preaching circumcision for? For salvation. Then he is a debtor to do everything that was ever spoken by God for salvation.

> Christ is become of no effect unto you, whosoever of you are justified by the law; ye are fallen from grace.

That is true today, isn't it? Don't you see that these very Scriptures that were aimed at ceremonialism in that day are the living power of God against ceremonialism and the papacy and the form of godliness without the power that curse the world in the last days even to the day of the coming of Jesus Christ?

> Christ is become of no effect unto you, whosoever of you are justified by law; ye are fallen from grace. For we through the Spirit wait for the hope of righteousness by faith.

Now, the verse, "For in Jesus Christ." Where? Looking *at* Jesus Christ from the outside? going to Him as to a reservoir or a fountain and taking something out and taking it off with me outside? No. "*In* Jesus Christ," in Him, in Him, "neither circumcision availeth anything, nor uncircumcision, but faith which worketh by love." That is Christianity. Anything less than that is ceremonialism in this day as well as in that day. Everything less than that is the mystery – of iniquity. Everything else than that is the mark of the beast. And whosoever has not that living principle of the living power in his life will worship the beast and his image and thus all the world will worship him, whose names are not written in the book of life of the Lamb slain from the foundation of the world." Thank God for His unspeakable Gift.

What was circumcision to them? It was everything, actually, for circumcision itself was the seal of the perfection of righteousness by works. It actually stood in the place of Jesus Christ. Ah, but in Jesus Christ that avails nothing at all. Circumcision meant works, all-absorbing works for righteousness and salvation. Paul was a "Tell-me-any-thing-more-to-do-and-I-will-do-it Pharisee." That is the kind of Pharisee he was. That is what circumcision meant. It was the one word that meant the whole system of works for salvation. But in Jesus Christ what avails for salvation? Circumcision avails nothing, neither works avail anything for salvation, nor any works at all, but *faith which works.* Faith finds the salvation of Jesus Christ a living power in the life and working there the righteousness of God by the love of God and this is the love of God that we keep His commandments. O let Christianity prevail. Let Christianity be spread abroad! "Go ye into all the world and preach the gospel to every creature."

For the last part of our study we will read a few verses in Colossians. Turn to the second chapter of Colossians. We will read, beginning with the first chapter and 25th verse, of the mystery of the gospel:

> Whereof I am made a minister, according to the dispensation of God to fulfill the word of God [margin, fully to preach the word of God]: even the mystery which hath been hid from ages and from generations, but now is made manifest to his saints. To whom God would make known what is the riches of the glory of this mystery among the Gentiles [among the heathen]; which is Christ in you, the hope of glory; whom we preach.

Who preach? Where preach? *You* preach as you go. Whom we preach, "warning every man, and teaching every man in all wisdom; that we may present every man perfect." *In Him,* always *in Him,* "present every man perfect *in* Christ Jesus." We are to bring them unto Jesus, so that they shall abide in Christ, live in Him, walk in Him.

> Whereunto I also labor, striving according to his working, which worketh in me mightily. For I would have ye know what great conflict I have for you, and for them at Laodicea, and for as many as have not seen my face in the flesh.

Who are they who have not seen his face in the flesh? That takes in *us* who are here. That is for us. What now? "That their hearts might be comforted." Good. "Being knit together in love." All joined together, or woven together? No, that is not enough, but "*knit* together," in and in, each stitch held on to the other and only one thread – Christ and His love – in it all.

> Being knit together in love and unto all riches of the full assurance of understanding, to the acknowledgement of the mystery of God, and of the Father, and of Christ.

What is that mystery? Christ in you. The annihilation of ceremonialism, the abolition of the enmity, the breaking down of every wall that separates the hearts of men.

"In whom are hid all the treasures of wisdom and knowledge. And this I say." Why did He say this for you and me, who have not seen His face in the flesh? "This I say *lest any man should beguile you* with enticing words," into ceremonialism, into formalism, into false dogmas and doctrines. "This I say, lest any man should beguile you with enticing words." "As ye have therefore received Christ Jesus the Lord, so walk ye in him." In Him, in Him, ever in Him. It seems to me that that expression has come into our studies enough for us to count it our motto for all this Institute. We may have "In Him" our watchword. I do not know what it would be too much to go away with that ringing in our ears and fastened upon our minds – in Him, in Him; preaching in Him, praying in Him, working in Him, teaching in Him; turning men to Him, that they may be found in Him, so that we shall all always walk in Him, rooted and built up in Him.

> Rooted and built up in him, and established in the faith, as ye have been taught, abounding therein with thanksgiving. Beware lest any man spoil you through philosophy and vain deceit, after the tradition of men, after the rudiments of the world, and not after Christ. Col. 2:7.

Beware of that. We are coming face to face with the mystery of iniquity. Beware of false philosophy, vain deceit, traditions, and the elements of the world – of the natural mind and the carnal heart. Beware of it. Christ, Christ, in Him; in Him alone, in Jesus Christ. Nothing avails but faith that works by love, and that love the love of God which keeps the commandments of God.

> For in him dwelleth all the fullness of the Godhead bodily. And ye are complete in him, which is the head of all principality and power; in whom also ye are circumcised with the circumcision made without hands, in putting off the body of the sins of the flesh by the circumcision of Christ.

He put off the body of flesh by destroying the enmity in sinful flesh; by conquering all the tendencies of the sinful flesh and bringing the whole man in subjection to the law of God. This is the circumcision of Christ and it is accomplished by the Spirit of God Itself. And the same blessed work still goes on in all who are in Him.

> The Holy Ghost shall come upon thee, and the power of the Highest shall overshadow thee; therefore, also that holy thing which shall be born of thee shall be called the Son of God.
>   Behold what manner of love the Father hath bestowed upon us, that we should be called the sons of God; therefore, the world knoweth us not, because it knew him not.
>   Buried with him in baptism, wherein also ye are risen with him through the faith of the operation of God, who hath raised him from the dead.

"And ye being dead." Are you dead? Are you dead with Him? IN HIM? and out of deadness in sins and the circumcision of your flesh hath He quickened you together with Him?

"Having forgiven you all trespasses." Thank the Lord. The record is clean; God has cleared away the trespasses against us, blotting out the handwriting of ordinances that was against us and imputing to us His own righteousness. What turned these ordinances against us? That enmity that turns into self-service everything that God has given. Blotting out that which was against us, which was contrary to us, taking it out of the way, nailing it to His cross. And having spoiled principalities and powers, He made a show of them openly, triumphing over them in it. Let no man therefore make a conscience for you. Let no man judge you or decide for you. Let the love of Jesus Christ in the heart decide and do the thing that is right. Let no man therefore make a conscience for you in meat or in drink or in respect of a holy day or of the new moon or of the sabbath days: which are a shadow of things to come; but the body is of Christ.

Let no man beguile you of your reward! Let no one turn aside your aim, as we had it in the study on pages 166 and 167 of the Bulletin. "Let no man beguile you of your reward in a voluntary humility." What is a voluntary humility but following self-made rules and the perversion of God's ordinances for the cultivation of our own ways? "Vainly puffed up by his fleshly mind." What is the mind of the flesh? What is the minding of the flesh? It "is enmity against God; for it is not subject to the law of God neither indeed can be." But Jesus Christ has abolished in His flesh the enmity, and in Him the enmity is abolished in our flesh, and we have the victory.

> Vainly puffed up by his fleshly mind, and not holding the Head, from which all the body by joints and bands having nourishment ministered, and knit together, increaseth with the increase of God. Wherefore if ye be dead with Christ from the rudiments of the world, why as though living in the world, are ye subject to ordinances (touch not; taste not; handle not; which all are to perish with the using), after the commandment and doctrines of men? Which things have indeed a show of wisdom in will worship, and humility, and neglecting of the body; not in any honor to the satisfying of the flesh. If ye then be risen with Christ, seek those things which are above.

Are you risen with Him? Has He raised us up? Are you there with Him?

> Seek those things which are above, where Christ sitteth on the right hand of God. Set your affection on things above, not on things on the earth. For ye are dead, and your life is hid with Christ in God. When Christ, who is our life, shall appear, then shall ye also appear with him in glory.
>
> Behold what manner of love the Father hath bestowed upon us, that we should be called the sons of God; therefore, the world knoweth us not, because it knew him not. Beloved, now are we the sons of God, and it doth not yet appear what we shall be: but we know that, when he shall appear, we shall be like him; for we shall see him as he is.

And the day is near and He is bringing it closer and closer. Thank God for His unspeakable gift, "and thanks be unto God, which always causeth us to triumph in Christ; and maketh manifest the savor of his knowledge by us in every place." Amen.